DETERMINISM

DETERMINISM

BY BERNARD BEROFSKY

PRINCETON UNIVERSITY PRESS   1971

Copyright © 1971, by Princeton University Press

ALL RIGHTS RESERVED

Library of Congress Catalogue Card Number: 70-112994

ISBN: 0-691-07169-1

Printed in the United States of America
by The Maple Press, York, Pennsylvania

TO THE MEMORY OF MY FATHER

ACKNOWLEDGMENTS

THIS BOOK IS an extensively revised version of my Ph.D. thesis, which was written on a Samuel S. Fels Fellowship and submitted to Columbia University in 1963. Initial revisions were made on a Horace H. Rackham Fellowship at the University of Michigan in the summer of 1966. I am also grateful to the American Philosophical Society and Vassar College for grants that defrayed typing expenses.

My indebtedness to my teacher, Ernest Nagel, is evident in this book. The benefits to me of his intellectual guidance and the inspiration of his person have been enormous.

I owe a special debt of gratitude to Arthur Danto for his very helpful comments and suggestions, and for the faith in my work he has sustained over the years.

I am also especially grateful to Sidney Morgenbesser from whom I have learned (and continue to learn) what philosophy is all about. This book displays the results, good or bad, of the hard work required to approach the standards he has, in conversation and through his own work, taught me to attempt to meet.

I wish to thank the following people for their comments and suggestions: William P. Alston, Charles Evans, Sidney Hook, Norbert Lipper, Jack Meiland, John O'Connor, Richard Shope, Michael Slote, Richard Taylor, Frank Tillman, James F. Urmson, Gary Vanderveer, and James J. Walsh.

My thanks are due also to my mother, whose clerical skills proved invaluable.

To my wife, Barbara, I find it impossible to express in words my debt for her encouragement and the spiritual enrichment that helped me so much.

ACKNOWLEDGMENTS

I WISH TO THANK the editors of the following journals for allowing me to reprint portions of articles: *The Journal of Philosophy* ("Causality and General Laws"), LXIII, March 17, 1966; *Nous* ("The Regularity Theory"), II, November, 1968; and *American Philosophical Quarterly* ("Purposive Action"), October, 1970.

CONTENTS

DETERMINISM

INTRODUCTION

ANYONE WHO SEEKS illumination from philosophy on the age-old free will issue confronts an unfortunate division of labor among philosophers. He may read books on free will and moral responsibility; but these books never contain a systematic, in-depth treatment of the doctrine of determinism, a doctrine that must be understood, most would concede, if we are to come to grips with the problems of human freedom.[1] Many works, in fact, relate free will to determinism and say virtually nothing about the latter. On the whole, only philosophers of science have engaged in the sober and detailed inquiry essential to formulating an adequate conception of determinism.[2] But these philosophers have not been primarily concerned to orient their inquiries to questions of human freedom, responsibility, and morality.

This book attempts to bridge the gap. We shall formulate a definition of determinism that can be used in discussions and debates about free will. In the light of this purpose, several desiderata for a definition suggest themselves:

(1) *Determinism is a claim about the world that is true or false, i.e., determinism is a proposition.*[3] Some philosophers have denied that determinism is a proposition and their views will be examined in chapter XI; on the other hand,

---

[1] See, for example, D. F. Pears, ed., *Freedom and the Will* (New York: St. Martin's Press, 1963).

[2] E.g., Ernest Nagel, *The Structure of Science* (New York: Harcourt, Brace & World, 1961), pp. 277-335; and Philipp Frank, *Philosophy of Science: The Link Between Science and Philosophy* (Englewood Cliffs, N.J.: Prentice-Hall, 1957), pp. 207-96.

[3] This use of the term "proposition" is non-controversial. We shall, in fact, reject this concept in the definition of determinism.

1

since many debates centering about free will presuppose that determinism is a proposition, it would be desirable to satisfy this condition. For example, the libertarian believes that human beings have no freedom if determinism is true, whereas the reconciliationist contends that determinism, a doctrine whose truth he accepts or considers plausible, does not rule out freedom. Another group of philosophers we can call "action theorists" maintains that the possible truth of determinism would be irrelevant to human freedom because human actions are not the sorts of things that can be determined. All these positions would have to be rejected if (1) is denied.

Reformulation of the debates might be possible if (1) is denied. Some philosophers who reject (1) consider it possible to prove that an event is determined. What disturbs them is the general claim that all events are determined. Given some event *e* that has been shown to be determined, the three positions mentioned above may be formulated and, therefore, rationally debated. The libertarian asserts that if *e* is some human action, it was not performed freely. The reconciliationist denies this conditional, and the action theorist contends that *e* cannot be a human action. In any case, we shall argue for (1) and, therefore, allow general debates about determinism.

(2) *Determinism is not true in virtue of linguistic or other conventions alone.* We shall discuss several views according to which the truth of determinism is guaranteed by virtue of its definition or its definition together with certain scientific conventions. Indeterminism becomes virtually self-contradictory, then, and this result has devastating consequences for free-will debates.

The libertarian, who accepts indeterminism for some human actions, would find that he is holding an impossible view. Reconciliationists would be foolish both to *argue* for determinism (since this doctrine is analytic) and to *argue* that determinism is compatible with the existence of human freedom (since an analytic proposition is compatible with any non-self-contradictory proposition).

But, it might be argued, the rejection of (2) is desirable since a central free will problem is thereby solved. The reconciliationist is trivially right, and that is the end of the matter. It turns out, though, that all the conceptions of determinism that reject (2) are radically different from the thesis as understood by both libertarians and reconciliationists. For example, Frank argued that determinism is guaranteed by the option scientists have of introducing arbitrary state variables in the light of an apparent disconfirmation of some theory, and assigning these variables the exact values that are required to eliminate the apparent disconfirmation.[4] If we decide to reject the theory, the same option will hold for the new theory. Thus, the truth of determinism is guaranteed by certain scientific conventions. Obviously, a libertarian need not be bothered by the introduction of a "hidden" variable after some decision had been made such that a postdiction of the decision is now possible. If Frank is right, this procedure can be adopted regardless of the nature of human beings and their decisions. A belief in freedom, regardless of the form it takes, does not present even a prima facie incompatibility with Frank's conception of determinism.

(3) *Determinism is prima facie incompatible with human freedom.* I have argued that (3) is violated whenever (2) is. (3) seems desirable since we wish to understand why libertarians accept incompatibilism (the view that determinism is genuinely incompatible with human freedom) and why reconciliationists and action theorists discuss the libertarian position at great length, thereby displaying, often openly, their acceptance of (3).

After examining attempts to define determinism in terms

[4] Philipp Frank, *Modern Science and its Philosophy* (Cambridge: Harvard University Press, 1950), chap. 1.

of various concepts, we shall define determinism in terms of the notion of law. (3) will be demonstrably satisfied because "All human behavior is governed by law (in a certain way)" seems to imply "No human behavior is free." We shall not try to decide whether or not the implication really does hold. To define determinism, however, we must define the notion of law and must, therefore, consider if laws are necessary truths. Our conclusion will be that they are not, and any argument for the implication based on the premise that laws are necessary is consequently rejected. Our discussion, therefore, favors, but does not entail, compatibilism.

Since a definition of determinism must deal with the question of determinism's scope, we face the issue of whether or not human actions can be determined. Hence, our discussion once again bears on a central issue of free will. Our concluding chapters concern the truth of determinism and the question about human action is raised in the context of an examination of the argument that determinism is necessarily false because human actions cannot be determined. (The conclusion of this argument can also be expressed by saying that a priori considerations require the scope of determinism to be restricted—a formulation that leaves open the possibility that determinism is true.)

Since the issues involved in an account of determinism are sufficiently complex, we shall not explore in a systematic way the implications our definition has for the free will debate. Two important implications have been pointed out; but I do not believe that the clarification I am attempting to introduce into discussions on free will will in itself produce solutions.

Two conditions of adequacy of a definition of determinism are not dictated by the desire to make the definition useful for free will discussions.

1. *The univocity condition.* The term "determined" in "All events are determined" must mean the same as it means in "This event is determined." This condition is so plausible

4

intuitively that one might wonder whether it is worth mentioning. We certainly do not want to suppose that a person cannot generalize his belief that some events are determined unless the term "determined" undergoes a change in meaning. But the condition does rule out certain formulations of determinism in terms of rational predictability.[5]

2. *The unicity condition.* Whatever particular determinists may have claimed, one idea they have held in common is this: At any particular time *t*, what occurs in the world at *t*—or, perhaps, what occurs at or prior to *t*—restricts future possibilities to one. A dramatic statement of this position is provided by William James:

> It professes that those parts of the universe already laid down absolutely appoint and decree what other parts shall be. The future has no ambiguous possibilities hidden in its womb: the part we call the present is compatible with only one totality. Any other future complement than the one fixed from eternity is impossible. The whole is in each and every part, and welds it with the rest into an absolute unity, an iron block, in which there can be no equivocation or shadow of turning.[6]

Any definition of determinism must capture this idea. The condition may also be called the deducibility condition because sentences about the future must, in some sense, follow from the information about the past that restricts the future. Otherwise, the future has "ambiguous possibilities."

ONE FINAL, somewhat personal, remark. If I had to choose one short expression that best captures the spirit of Anglo-American philosophy in the last ten years, I would choose "Hume-baiting." Like all great philosophers Hume

[5] See chap. II.
[6] "The Dilemma of Determinism," *The Will to Believe and other Essays in Popular Philosophy* (New York: Longmans, Green, & Co., 1909), p. 150.

said many things that are worthy of criticism and rejection. But I believe that his fundamental views on many key concepts, e.g., cause and law, are basically right; this book turns out to be, to a great extent, a defense of these views. No great philosopher, I believe, has been treated as unfairly as has Hume by philosophers on both sides of the Atlantic. I confess that these strong feelings reveal a zealousness that may, I suspect, carry me in the pages that follow beyond the limits imposed by the credibility of my arguments. But that possible consequence may inspire rebuttal that will eventually lead to a restoration of balance in a picture that is now terribly lopsided.

PART 1

ACCOUNTS OF DETERMINISM

I. FOREKNOWLEDGE

ALTHOUGH MANY EVENTS are never known to occur until they actually happen, a person might believe that, in some sense, these events *could have been foreknown*. A determinist, some have said, is one who believes that *all* events can be foreknown.[1]

This definition is adequate, of course, only insofar as an adequate analysis of knowledge-statements is at hand. There is, however, a great deal of disagreement about such an analysis. Are knowledge-statements descriptive or performatory? Do they entail belief-statements? How much and what kind of evidence must a person possess before he may be said to know something?

One may naturally feel that if it is foreknown by *A* that *B* will perform a certain action or make a certain decision, then *B* does not really act or decide freely. Although the relationship between foreknowledge and free will was discussed traditionally in a theological context, e.g., by St. Augustine[2] and Hobbes,[3] we need not be concerned about the characteristics *A* possesses in addition to his having this particular foreknowledge unless the nature of *A*'s foreknowledge is distinctive.

People have believed that divine foreknowledge is different in kind from the human variety. But if we allow two kinds of foreknowledge, human and divine, what implications does

[1] See, for example, Pears, chap. 4.
[2] St. Augustine, *The Free Choice of the Will,* trans. Francis E. Tourscher (Philadelphia: The Peter Reilly Co., 1937), Bk. III.
[3] Thomas Hobbes, *The Questions Concerning Liberty, Necessity, and Chance, Clearly Stated and Debated between Dr. Bramhall and Thomas Hobbes* (London: Andrew Cook, 1656).

this have for a definition of determinism? Assuming that a definition in terms of foreknowledge is feasible, we might try: All events can be foreknown by humans and are foreknown by God. (Since all God's potentialities are fully actualized, we do not want to say merely that He *can* know everything that will happen.) We shall discard this implication, however, because the conception of determinism in which we are interested does not presuppose theism; moreover, we should have to clarify further the nature of divine foreknowledge. In this context, it is interesting to note that St. Augustine's arguments in defense of the compatibility of free will and God's foreknowledge (Bk. III, secs. 2, 3, and 4) do not presuppose a unique conception of foreknowledge for God.

In order to avoid a commitment to theism, we might change the "and" to "or" in the definition and be able to read the second clause as: If there were a God, He would foreknow everything that happens. Determinism might then be a necessary truth for it would be a disjunction, and one disjunct might be necessarily true. "If there were a God, He would foreknow everything that happens" is necessary if fore-omniscience is included in the divine essence.[4] To discover whether or not it is a necessary truth, one would have to get deeply embroiled in theology.

The truth of the proposition in question may be grounded in God's atemporal character. That is, since God is outside time, one cannot specify the time at which He knows something. But then one should not speak of "divine *fore*knowledge," since God does not know that something will take place at *t, prior to t:* from His vantage point in eternity, the whole temporal process is "non-temporally before God's eyes." If this conception can be rendered intelligible, it would appear that no incompatibility exists between divine foreknowledge and freedom since God knows what Smith will

---

[4] Richard Taylor argues that the proposition is false in "Deliberation and Foreknowledge," *American Philosophical Quarterly,* I (January, 1964), 73-80.

do in a way very similar to that in which Jones, *who is watching Smith do it,* knows. The problem of *fore*knowledge requires that we suppose the knowledge to exist prior to the event known; for it is only when this condition is satisfied that we become concerned about our freedom. And we have adopted a desideratum for a definition of determinism according to which determinism and freedom must be prima facie incompatible.[5] Divine omniscience disturbs us because we view God as *having already* observed us doing things that we have not yet done. If, however, we are precluded from applying temporal predicates to God's epistemological states, then we cannot produce the formulation that disturbs us and must look elsewhere if we wish to satisfy this desideratum.

One might try to ground the proposition in the fact that God makes everything happen and, thus, has foreknowledge in a way similar to the way I know how the chair I am constructing will turn out. But one cannot be concerned about freedom unless one supposes an actual God who makes us do things. That is, no one worries about the freedom of his future actions because he accepts the proposition "If there were a God, He would make us perform the actions we do perform" unless he also accepts the antecedent of this conditional. Again, our desideratum is not satisfied.

Thus, if a person does not want to assume theism, but wants to know why foreknowledge seems to threaten freedom, he obviously cannot cite properties of a hypothetical God that are linked to divine foreknowledge. We may, though, cite properties of the world that, it may be argued, are related to His foreknowledge. For example, one may say that if there were a God, He would foreknow all that happens because the world is deterministic and He would have all the relevant information. Ignoring the fact that we are supposed to be defining determinism in terms of foreknowledge, it is clear that our concern about freedom arises from the assumption that the world is deterministic, not from the

[5] See above, p. 3.

fact that there might be a God who knows the true deterministic theory. Hence, I see no point in referring to divine foreknowledge in the definition of determinism. I further contend that our concern about freedom does not arise from the fact that there might be someone, *human or divine,* who knows the true deterministic theory.

Libertarians emphasize the distinction between free and voluntary actions, insisting that an action may be voluntary and yet not free. If a voluntary action is, roughly, one I perform but am not constrained to perform, they wish to insist that the absence of constraint is, at most, a necessary condition of freedom. It would appear that a person who believes that foreknowledge and freedom are incompatible would be forced to accept this libertarian point. For it would be odd to conclude that B is *constrained* to do something merely because someone else knows that he will do it. Examples bring this point home. If I know that you will give money to a certain charity because I know you are generous, are sympathetic with this particular charity, and are not at the moment pressed for funds, it is very odd to conclude that you will be constrained to give the money as if at the point of a gun. A person who believes that foreknowledge and freedom are incompatible, therefore, would presumably have to argue, like the libertarian, that voluntariness is not a sufficient condition of freedom.

But, in fact, *some* of the persuasiveness of the doctrine that foreknowledge and freedom are incompatible derives from a conception of the relation between the foreknower and the act foreknown that is very much akin to constraint. Why should one have this conception?

Some who have proposed an analysis of knowledge-claims assert that "*A* knows that *B* will do *e*" entails "*A* believes that *B* will do *e*" or a similar psychological fact about *A*.[6]

---

[6] John Hospers, *An Introduction to Philosophical Analysis* (Englewood Cliffs, N.J.: Prentice-Hall, 1953), p. 146.

Even if this inference is so, the strength or weakness of A's conviction concerning the doing of e by B cannot in itself lend any credibility to the proposition that B must do e or that B does not do e freely. We do not judge an action unfree or necessitated merely because we find someone who believed, felt certain, or was absolutely convinced that the action would be done.

But, it may be replied, knowing is a different state from feeling certain or being absolutely convinced. For knowledge is the only state that *guarantees* the occurrence of the event foreknown. Thus if Jones at t really is in the state of knowing that Smith will do e at $t + n$, then it is logically necessary for Smith to do e at $t + n$.

Thus, one has the picture of a state of the knower at one time mysteriously necessitating or constraining some future event. But this is a confusion that is easily cleared up by looking more closely at the term "state."

Some descriptions of the state of an object are true only if certain future events occur. Citation is the winner of the horse race only if the judges later certify that he carried the correct weight during the race. No one believes that this fact lends credence to the belief that some state of Citation's prior to the judges' decision constrained them to decide that Citation carried the correct weight. "Knowing" may be like "winning" insofar as the non-occurrence of the event alleged to be known entails that there was no knowledge. But this certainly does not warrant the conclusion that the knowing brings about or constrains the event foreknown just as Citation's winning does not bring about or constrain the judges' decision. It does show that "knowing" is not like "being in pain" insofar as my now being in pain entails nothing about the future.

Hence the belief that foreknowledge and freedom are incompatible is not supported by consideration of psychological facts about the knower.

If one feels that the basis of the inference from "*A* knows that *B* will do *e*" to "*B* must do *e*" or "*B* does not do *e* freely" lies in the fact that "*A* knows that *p*" entails "p," then he is mistaken. There is, it is true, a relationship of logical necessity between the two propositions "*A* knows that *B* will do *e*" and "*B* will do *e*," the former entailing the latter.[7] Clearly, though, to infer validly that *B*'s action is not free, one would have to show that the act is necessary or that *B* must do *e* in a different way. One cannot say that *B*'s act is necessary in a sense of "necessary" which precludes freedom merely because the sentence describing the act follows necessarily from the true sentence "*A* knows that *B* will do *e*," for there is always a true sentence which entails a sentence describing any particular event. If "Jones washes his car on May 22, 1984" is true, it follows from the true sentence "Jones washes his car on May 22, $1984 \cdot 2 + 2 = 4$" or simply "Jones washes his car on May 22, 1984." But it surely does not follow that Jones does not wash his car freely on May 22, 1984. I am not here denying that foreknowledge and freedom are incompatible. If they are, however, it is not because of the logical necessity which holds between "*A* knows that *p*" and "p." We would have to deal with aspects of the content of the knowledge claim other than this one. If *A* truly asserts today: "Jones washes his car on May 22, $1984 \cdot 2 + 2 = 4$," then, if we assume that *A* has absolutely no reason to believe the first conjunct, we are not in the least inclined to feel that Jones *had* to wash his car; whereas if *A* truly asserts today: "I know that *B* will do *e* tomorrow," we may very well be inclined to view *B*'s action as necessary. Thus, some feature of the knowledge-claim must be responsible for our inclination, other than its being true and entailing the sentence describing the event whose occurrence *A* claims to know.

[7] If this entailment relation is denied, then the argument loses its *prima facie* plausibility.

Many philosophers would assert that knowledge-claims imply the ability to support the claims by reliable evidence or good reasons. There are three major sources of disagreement.

First of all, some have suggested that there are propositions which we know to be true for which the request for evidence is inappropriate. But the propositions in question are not propositions of the kind "*B* will do *e*." They are either logico-mathematical propositions or propositions which are known "directly," e.g., "I am in pain now," "It seems to me that there is a red object before me now," and the like.

Miss Anscombe speaks of "knowledge without observation."[8] For example, I ordinarily know without observation that my limbs are in a certain position or that I have kicked my leg. Let us grant that these cases are correctly described as cases of "knowledge without observation." Let us also grant that non-observational knowledge is knowledge concerning which the request for evidence is inappropriate. But propositions of the form "*A* knows that *B* will do *e*" cannot be cases of non-observational knowledge if *A* is a different person from *B* since non-observational knowledge is always self-knowledge. *I* cannot know without observation the position of *your* limbs. If, on the other hand, *A* is the same person as *B*, there are two possibilities: (1) *A* may know that he will do *e* in the same way other people know that he will do *e*. Although these kinds of cases have been underemphasized in recent literature, they do exist. To the question, "How do you know that you will insult him?" *A* may reply: "People like that always irk me." But, of course, this kind of knowledge is not non-observational or, at least, not non-evidential. *A* is appealing to the same kind of evidence that other people must appeal to. (2) *A* may know that he will do *e* in a way which precludes the necessity of his providing

[8] *Intention* (Ithaca: Cornell University Press, 1957), pp. 13-15.

evidence. For example, if A asserts "I shall wash the car tomorrow," it may be reasonable to infer that he will wash the car tomorrow (although it would be odd for A to say that he knows that he will wash the car tomorrow unless someone suggests to him that there is reason to believe that he will not). It is interesting that, when A does wash the car tomorrow, we are not ordinarily led to feel that he could not have done otherwise. If A's utterance was the expression of a decision or an intention, then we may feel that he could have changed his mind. Moreover, libertarians sometimes contend that decisions, rather than actions, are the proper subjects of the predicates "free" and "unfree." Hence, from the information that A has made a certain decision and has implemented that decision, we are not led to feel that he lacked freedom. When certain information is brought to bear, however, we may begin to feel that A could not have done (or decided to do) otherwise. As we shall see shortly, this information comprises the evidence that would support another person's knowledge claim about the doing of e by A. Thus, even if there is non-observational knowledge, and even if one can say of a person that he can have non-observational knowledge of his own future actions, the cases that induce concern about a man's freedom are those in which knowledge of future action is supported by evidence, either from the person acting or some other person. A second center of disagreement with the assertion that knowledge-claims require evidential support is among those who view knowledge as a special state of mind vis-à-vis the object of knowledge. The untenability of this doctrine has been demonstrated by a number of philosophers, e.g., A. J. Ayer, and it is for this reason that I dismiss it from consideration.[9]

Finally, some philosophers have replaced this condition, viz., the ability to support the knowledge-claim, with the

[9] *The Problem of Knowledge* (Harmondsworth, Middlesex, England: Penguin Books, 1956), pp. 14-26.

presence of some sort of causal relation between either the known fact and the belief, or certain facts related in a specified way to the known fact and the belief.[10] In the case of "A knows that B will do e," the facts that cause A's belief cannot include "B will do e" for this is a future fact. But the present state of affairs that causes B to do e in the future can cause A's belief, and if so, A's belief is knowledge. Generally, philosophers who support this causal theory of knowledge point out that all the conditions of knowledge, including the causal condition, can be satisfied even where the knower cannot specify the grounds of his knowledge.

Let us first consider the consequences of the assumption that "A knows that B will do e" is true only if A has reliable evidence to warrant the proposition "B will do e." Suppose A is a psychologist who has excellent reason to believe that "All people with characteristics a, b, and c, when placed in circumstances s, will do e" is a law; further, suppose he asserts that he knows B will do e on the basis of his knowledge that B satisfies the antecedent of this presumed law. Now, if we are inclined to accept the inference from "A knows that B will do e" to "B does not do e freely" as valid, I suggest that our inclination is due to the existence of such excellent grounds for the proposition "B will do e." We have seen that the inference cannot be supported via a consideration of the other alleged features of knowledge-claims. Its support must lie in the necessity of offering evidence to support knowledge-claims. Consider a knowledge-claim put forth by A, e.g., "I know that B will choose steak at the restaurant tonight." Suppose that A is convinced that B will do this, and suppose that B does it. We also know that A's belief is not based on information about B's eating habits or on any reliable evidence whatsoever. A is asked: "How did you know that B would choose steak?" He replies: "I

---

[10] See, for example, Alvin I. Goldman, "A Causal Theory of Knowing," *The Journal of Philosophy*, LXIV (June 22, 1967), 357-72.

just felt he would." We may then say to A: "You didn't know. You just guessed." The point to be stressed is that we do not view B's action in this situation as unfree or necessitated since A's knowledge-claim could not be supported by information about B. Suppose, on the other hand, A replied: "I have been doing a detailed psychological and physiological investigation of food choices and I have found that they depend on six factors. B, of course, was not informed of these results, in order to avoid the introduction of extraneous factors. I studied B and his situation, and then calculated that his choice would be steak." We might consider that poor B could not have chosen otherwise, and our feeling would clearly be due to the existence of such excellent evidence.

It is important to point out that the grounds of the belief in the validity of the inference from "A knows that B will do e" to "B must do e" lie in the existence of evidence for "B will do e" and not on A's capacity to present such evidence. If, as a matter of fact, food choices are invariably a determinate function of six factors, then our feeling that this information justifies the proposition "No one makes a food choice freely," would neither more nor less incline us to accept the proposition if someone has this information. If someone knows the function and uses it to make predictions, we then know that a person is not making a free choice; but whether or not the action is free clearly depends on the state of the world and not on our knowledge of its state (assuming the validity of the inference).

Now let us consider the consequences of the assumption that the causal theory of knowledge is true. It is clear here, too, that the grounds of the inference from "A knows that B will do e" to "B must do e" lie in the causal relation between the facts causing A's belief and the fact that B will do e, rather than the causal relation between the facts causing A's belief and A's belief. Again, our belief that B must do e is based on a belief about the world outside A.

It follows that there is no point in considering the question "Are foreknowledge and freedom incompatible?" If freedom is really incompatible with certain kinds of facts about a person's character, personality, background, heredity, and/or the existence of psychological laws and true theories, it does not matter which set of facts constitutes grounds sufficient for the label "knowledge." Knowledge becomes a secondary issue independent of the issue of freedom, and all these considerations should be sufficient rebuttal to the opinion that a definition of determinism in terms of foreknowledge conduces to a sharper focusing of the issues arising in free-will debates.

Although the definition lacks this virtue, are there any virtues that it possesses which may justify its adoption?

The most obvious limitation, alluded to earlier, is the difficulty of stating a criterion to decide whether or not a knowledge-claim has been adequately supported. Ordinary language provides far too liberal a criterion for the determinist. If A asserts that he knows that B will do e and B does e, then if we are interested in finding out how A knew this, we often will accept, as sufficient, references to B's wants, motives, and personality traits, although A would be hard pressed to specify with any degree of precision the conditions under which B manifests these characteristics and the conditions under which he does not. For example, if A says that he knows that B will act in a friendly way toward his new collegue because B is a friendly person, it may be that B is occasionally unfriendly and that A cannot distinguish the conditions of B's acting friendly from the conditions of his acting unfriendly. If, however, B does act friendly toward his new colleague, few would deny that A was in possession of genuine knowledge. If, then, ordinary language is our criterion, we have to say that B's action was known prior to its occurrence and, hence, that it was determined. It is obvious, however, that determinism is a stronger thesis. A determinist cannot admit—although, *qua* determinist, he believes it— that sufficient information is at hand for asserting that *B*'s action was determined, on the grounds that no one had ascertained the conditions which make the difference between *B*'s acting friendly and his acting unfriendly. It will be recalled that one of the conditions of adequacy of a definition of determinism requires that the determining factors determine a unique result.[11]

Adopting the causal theory of knowledge does not improve matters. The term "cause" in this context embodies all the above vagueness. If *B*'s general friendliness causes *A*'s belief that *B* will be friendly toward his new colleague, and *B* does act friendly because he is generally friendly, we would say that *A* had knowledge. If the causal theorist of knowledge accepts this, he would have to interpret "causes" not as "is a sufficient condition of," and would generally have to analyze the notion of causation more carefully. Again, however, a determinist cannot allow this sort of liberalization.

We reach a situation reminiscent of the one discussed earlier: the issues which must be dealt with if an acceptable definition of determinism is to be formulated are independent of an analysis of knowledge-claims. Perhaps there are good reasons for accepting *A*'s knowledge claim about *B*'s friendly behavior as genuine knowledge. But an analysis of knowledge has no bearing on the thesis of determinism because we know what a determinist would have to say regardless of the way in which the analysis turns out. Even if we propose an account of knowledge which would satisfy a definition of determinism in terms of foreknowledge, the introduction of the concept of knowledge could only serve as dead lumber since the criteria of adequacy of the definition are independent of an analysis of knowledge-claims.

Finally, notice that a definition in terms of foreknowledge

[11] See above, p. 5.

must use modal terminology. Evidently, a determinist wants to say that events are determined even though no one may actually possess prior knowledge of their occurrence—hence, he says that all events *can* be foreknown. But logical possibility is plainly not the concept being employed here, for consider the following equivalences: "Event *e* can be known to occur prior to its occurrence" = "It is logically possible for someone to know that *e* will occur before it does occur" = " 'Someone knows that *e* will occur before it does occur' is not self-contradictory." Now, there are only a few ways in which "Someone knows that *e* will occur before it does occur" (*S*) might be shown to be self-contradictory for some event *e*.

There are, for example, a few bizarre substitution instances for *e* such as "the birth of the first person (or knower)" and "the discovery of the law that all *X*'s are *Y*'s by *A*" which denote events about which it is impossible to have prior knowledge. The fact that there are such cases would be taken by a determinist as a ground for rejecting the interpretation in terms of logical possibility since he believes that such events, also, are determined.

Or one may accept philosophical arguments alleging proof that foreknowledge of any event is logically impossible. If so, this is simply another good reason to reject foreknowledge as the definiens of determinism.

Suppose, further, that *e* is an undetermined event. Whatever that might mean, suppose for the sake of argument that it entails the logical impossibility of prior knowledge of *e*. But *S* is still not self-contradictory unless one conjoins to it the sentence "Event *e* is undetermined." This conclusion holds unless it can be shown that "*e*" entails "*e* is undetermined," i.e., unless it is of the very nature of the event to be undetermined—as, for example, someone might insist about the nature of a human choice. The circular nature of adding "Event *e* is undetermined" is evident: one is using the concept "undetermined" in a definition of determinism. But if we cannot add "Event e is undetermined," we must accept the absurd conclusion that "is determined" and "is undetermined" always express intrinsic properties, for the decision as to which predicate applies would depend entirely on the analysis of "e." If "e" entails "e is undetermined," then, of course, e is undetermined. But if "e" does not entail "e is undetermined," then S is not self-contradictory and e, therefore, is determined. Determinism would be trivially established for all cases except perhaps the few (human choice and decision) that have been believed by some to be intrinsically undetermined.

Finally, suppose someone asserts: "If we knew the initial state of the world (or some part of it) and all the relevant laws, then we could predict all future states of the world (or some part of it)." Although this is an account of determinism in terms of predictability and will therefore be discussed later,[12] there are some points which should be made now. Consider a set of events whose first member occurs at time t. Now, what would it mean to say that someone at time t knows the laws governing the occurrence of these events? Surely, the utterance of the laws would not be sufficient, for there must be some way of distinguishing a lucky guess from genuine knowledge. If knowledge requires evidence, and if evidence is forthcoming only through observation of the events, then knowledge at this time is impossible. Of course, one may be able to infer the laws from a knowledge of laws governing similar operations; but even if the inference turns out to be true, and we are willing to count it as genuine knowledge when the inference was made (at t), this possibility is precluded when the set of events is sufficiently different from any other set—and, *a fortiori*, when t is the beginning of the world, if such talk makes sense. We can, therefore,

[12] See chap. II.

22

describe a situation in which foreknowledge at t of some event e at $t + n$ is logically impossible, viz., when (a) e belongs to a set of events E the first member of which occurs at t; (b) there exists no other set, any of whose members occurs prior to t, which is sufficiently similar to E to warrant a reliable inference about the laws governing E; (c) knowledge at t of the laws governing E is a necessary condition of knowledge at t of e.[13] The logical impossibility results from the fact that knowledge requires evidence and these conditions entail its absence.

We are, however, again considering a case in which supplementary information must be conjoined to S to derive a contradiction. But if this is allowed, we may as well conjoin "Nobody knows that e will occur before it does occur" and make the derivation simple. In other words, there are many situations which can be truly described by sentences which are incompatible with S, namely, those situations in which S happens to be false. But if this is allowed, then the criterion of being determined really becomes the actuality of knowledge instead of the logical possibility of knowledge, since a search for cases in which S is false is the same as a search for cases in which S conjoined with an appropriate choice of true sentences entails a contradiction. Because a determinist wants to say that events are determined even though no one may actually possess prior knowledge of their occurrence, he must reject this technique of deriving contradictions from S.

Since, except for a few bizarre substitutions for e, there is no legitimate way of showing that S is self-contradictory, S would be true for any event, and determinism would be established in a quite trivial fashion.

---

[13] The bizarre substitution instances cited (above, p. 21), together with so-called organic phenomena, may be construed so as to satisfy these or similarly formulated conditions.

Whereas logical possibility of foreknowledge is too weak for a determinist, technical possibility[14] is too strong. This type of possibility is relative to a particular time and means that at time t, e is technically possible if and only if someone possesses the knowledge and capacity to verify e at t. If we change "verify" to "have prior knowledge of," a determinist will not want to commit himself to technical possibility regardless of the value taken by t. He wants to allow for the possibility of events' being determined although we may never be in a position to have prior knowledge of their occurrence.

Perhaps, then, the possibility is of an empirical nature. That is to say, "It is empirically possible for someone to know that e will occur before it does occur" = "Someone knows that e will occur before it does occur' is not incompatible with a law of nature."

Now, let us suppose that there is a set of events occurring in the interior of the sun whose members and the conditions of these members' occurrences leave no traces detectable by anyone unless he gets fairly close to the interior of the sun. Suppose, as well, that there are no substances, natural or artificially produced, which can protect man from the intense heat in this area. In such a case, no one can know what the events will be before or after their occurrence, and this fact can be deduced from laws of nature and appropriate assumptions. Compare this case with the famous experimental situation in quantum physics. Here, one cannot know the trajectory of a single electron passing through a slit in a diaphragm and hitting a screen parallel to the diaphragm. Now, disregarding for the moment the fact that some view the latter impossibility as, in a sense, logical,[15] we are confronted with two cases which are quite different. No determinist would

[14] Hans Reichenbach, *Experience and Prediction: An Analysis of the Foundations and the Structure of Knowledge* (Chicago: University of Chicago Press, 1938), p. 38.

[15] Nagel, pp. 293-305.

consider the former case as evidence against determinism. He would say that the events in the interior of the sun may very well be determined although we can never know. The latter case, however, can present at least a *prima facie* problem for him. So the important consideration is not whether or not we can know something, but what prevents us from knowing it. Does the limitation reside in the unknower or in the unknown?[16]

Let us see how far we can take the empirical possibility of foreknowledge as the definiens of determinism. We have to say now that event *e* is determined if and only if "Someone knows that *e* will occur before it does occur" is compatible with all laws of nature except those (if there are any) which are incompatible with "Someone studies the conditions of *e*'s occurrence."[17] This is still incomplete because "Someone studies the conditions of *e*'s occurrence," where *e* is one of the aforementioned events in the interior of the sun, is not incompatible with "No person can live in an environment of *x*°F. temperature regardless of protective material" unless one adds such assumptions as "Event *e* and its conditions occur in an environment of *x*°F. temperature," "Event *e* and its conditions leave no traces at any lower temperature," and so on. Similar emendations regarding the compatibility condition must be made.

Let us then try: Event *e* is determined if and only if "No one knows that *e* will occur before it does occur" is not deducible from any set of true sentences which includes, as essential to the deduction, at least one law of nature, except a set (if there is one) which also entails "No one studies the conditions of *e*'s occurrence." If laws are not required

---

[16] A few see the limitation of quantum mechanics as a consequence of the interaction between the knower and the known. See, for example, David Bohm, *Causality and Chance in Modern Physics* (New York: Harper & Bros., 1957), pp. 81-84.

[17] This is admittedly vague. Also, "Someone studies the conditions of *e*'s occurrence" is not meant to imply that *e* is determined.

in an essential way in these sets, then no events actually un-known prior to their occurrence would be determined since "No one knows that e will occur before it does occur" would be true and would entail itself. It could, therefore, be the sole member of the set were it not for the stipulation that a law be essential to the deduction.

Further emendations may be required; but there is a serious difficulty which obviates the practicality of making the definition more rigorous. Consider a hypothetical occur-rence, r, which no one knew about before its occurrence. People had been studying these kinds of occurrences. What would it mean to assert that r is not determined? There must be the appropriate set of true sentences which cannot entail "No one studies the conditions of r's occurrence," for that sentence is false.

Now reference may be made in the set to the fact that r is uncaused, that there is no sufficient condition of r, or that r is not governed by non-statistical laws. In this even-tuality, the "laws" are sentences like "No uncaused events are known prior to their occurrence." But whether or not one is willing to count this sentence as a law, the important point is that the applicability of the concept of the possibility of foreknowledge presupposes concepts like cause and law. Why not, therefore, define determinism in terms of these con-cepts, since nothing is gained by making a more complicated definition in terms of the possibility of foreknowledge? In other words, if "caused" (or "lawful") and "knowable" are extensionally equivalent, and if explanation of the latter ul-timately makes reference to the former, why not eliminate the latter altogether?

If the set does not explicitly refer to such concepts, it will contain sentences which, if they appear in a theory, make the theory indeterministic in certain respects. For example, from Heisenberg's uncertainty principle together with other sentences we can deduce "No one knows the trajectory of electron *e*." Here again, though, it is because of an indeterministic situation that we do not have knowledge. We must, then, be able to identify those characteristics which preclude foreknowledge. In other words, the identification of a situation as deterministic or indeterministic is logically prior to the identification of that situation as one in which we can or cannot have foreknowledge. Is it not a prior and more interesting concern to examine exactly what makes a theory deterministic or indeterministic?

We arrive again at the conclusion that a determinist is one who has certain beliefs about events that might render foreknowledge possible, but that these beliefs are not *about* the possibility of foreknowledge. They may not even coincide if we decide, for example, that we can have foreknowledge where we do not have causation or lawfulness. Foreknowledge therefore, is not a suitable definiens of determinism.

II. PREDICTABILITY

A MORE COMMON PROPOSAL for the definiens of determinism is predictability or predictability in principle.[1]

One key difference between foreknowledge and predictability is the following: A may predict that p, even if he does not know that p. If A says, "I know that p," one can demand that he support the assertion of "p"[2]; but support is not necessary in order to predict that p. To be sure, ordinary language is not entirely firm on this point. One may say, "No one can predict how it will turn out," meaning, of course, that no one can have sufficient information to warrant the present assertion about the outcome without meaning, obviously, that no one can now make a true assertion about the outcome. At any rate, for a determinist who employs predictability as the definiens of determinism, "Event e is predictable" cannot mean simply "Someone can assert a true statement about e before it happens," since one can assert all possible statements about some future situation—assuming that there are a finite number of them. Thus, victory in a tennis match tomorrow between A and B is determined simply because I can assert today, "A will win tomorrow" and "B will win tomorrow." Since predictability in this sense is inadmissible as the definiens of determinism, let us designate by the expression "rational predictability" the concept a determinist has in mind.

Another problem always faced by determinists adopting this approach is the difference they are inevitably com-

---

[1] See, for example, Richard B. Brandt, *Ethical Theory* (Englewood Cliffs, N.J.: Prentice-Hall, 1959), pp. 506-07.

[2] Unless a causal or similar theory of knowledge is correct.

28

pelled to acknowledge between rational predictability in fact and rational predictability in principle. "Event e at $t + n$ is rationally predictable in fact at t" might mean "There is someone at t who has sufficient information—or who has the ability and knowledge to acquire sufficient information at that time—to warrant a prediction of e which occurs at $t + n$." Granted the vagueness of this definition, it is clear that there are always events which are not in fact rationally predictable just as there are always events of which it is not technically possible to have prior knowledge. This difficulty makes the determinist turn to rational predictability in principle. Let us first consider the concept of rationality embodied in this account.

Plainly, rational predictability in principle as a criterion must be criticized in much the same way foreknowledge was. We are often prepared to say either that we know that e will take place or that a prediction that e will take place is rational where we do not have sufficient reason for saying that e is determined. Hence, rational predictability requires the *same* increase in rigor as foreknowledge. Once this requirement is recognized, we again find ourselves dealing with issues which the introduction of the concept of predictability does not help to solve. Just as the nature of the evidence for a knowledge-claim is the relevant consideration in deciding whether or not an event is determined, so is the information upon which a prediction is made. If we want to know why we do not have sufficient information for saying that e is determined although a prediction of e made on the basis of this information would be considered rational, we must have a definition of determinism that is independent of predictability.

It may be thought that rational predictability can be saved by stipulating that the evidence warranting the prediction must be strong enough to entail the sentence describing the event in question. In fact, we shall want at least three condi-

29

tions for the truth of "*A* rationally predicts that *h* on the basis of *e*."

First, "*e*" entails "*h*." If this condition is omitted, we will not have demonstrated that *h* is determined. There remain alternatives to it that are not ruled out as causally or nomically impossible. Thus, let us demand the inclusion in "*e*" of all relevant causal and nomic statements.

Second, "*e*" is true. If "*e*" is false, it is *not* evidence. Or if we allow it as evidence, we shall want independently to add that "*e*" is true if we wish to say that a rational prediction that *h* on "*e*" shows *h* to be determined. These first two conditions imply that all rational predictions are successful, an implication not contained in the ordinary notion of a rational prediction. That is to say, an unsuccessful prediction made on the basis of the best available information is not considered irrational just because it is unsuccessful. Strictly speaking, then, the concept that must be employed for the purpose of defining determinism is the concept of a successful rational prediction.

Finally, *A* knows or has good reason to believe "*e*" prior to *h*. Since *A* is predicting on the basis of "*e*" he must accept "*e*" prior to *h*; and since the prediction is rational, he must at least have good reason to believe "*e*."

These conditions are clearly insufficient as an explication of rational prediction for a number of reasons.

First of all, if one has no way to rule out so-called "accidental" generalizations from "*e*," then all events are rationally predictable in a trivial way. If, having observed that two of the three persons in room *A* are redheaded, I form the hypothesis that all persons in room *A* are non-blonds, but the third person is a brunette, have I rationally predicted that the third person is a non-blond? No. But to show that I have not, one must deal with many issues that are central to a definition of determinism. And in so doing, the concept of a rational prediction, like the concept of foreknowledge, plays no role.

Furthermore, one can show that the conditions may be satisfied (with only *bona fide* laws) although *h* is not determined. In order to do this, one must first show that it would be too strong to demand that a person know all the sentences in "*e*" in order to make a rational prediction.

Often, we make rational predictions on the basis of well-confirmed lawlike sentences that we are not prepared to say we know to be true. Also, it seems clear that the cause or part of the cause *c* of some event *h* may be simultaneous with that event.[3] If so, let us suppose that *c* is not determined. There may be only statistical laws governing the occurrence of *c*. Prior to *h*, therefore, we cannot know that *c* will occur. But since "*e*" must entail "*h*," we might require the inclusion of "*c*" in "*e*." In that case, we cannot know "*e*" prior to *h*. We may, however, have good reason to believe that *c* will occur if we know that some condition is present that precedes *c* ninety percent of the time. We can then rationally predict *h* on the basis of evidence we have only good reason to believe. The third condition of rational prediction, therefore, is not too weak insofar as it allows rational prediction on grounds that we have only good reason to believe.

But it can now be shown that the third condition *is* too weak inasmuch as undetermined events can be rationally predicted. Let "*n*" describe an event *n* that is prior to and that renders *c* highly probable. *C* is, again, part of the cause of and simultaneous with *h*, and is not itself determined.[4] Suppose we know "*n*" and "*d*" where "*d*" designates all the conditions of *h* other than *c*. We, then, have good reason to believe "*c*" since we know "*n*" and know that *n* renders *c* highly probable. Moreover, since we know "*d*" and know

[3] Many people believe that cause must precede effect. We shall return to this question in chap. viii.

[4] To say that *c* is not determined is not to say that it has no conditions, which is absurd. *C* is not determined if there are only statistical laws governing its occurrence. "*C* is not completely determined" is one way of expressing what I wish to say; but I reject this usage.

that $c \cdot d$ is a sufficient condition of h, then we have good reason to believe "h". Then "h" can legitimately appear in "e". Finally, if we suppose that "$h \supset c$" is a law that we know or have good reason to believe, we may deduce "c," a sentence describing an undetermined event.

It may, however, be objected that the conditions of the above case are self-contradictory, for if "$h \supset c$" is a law, then c must be determined. This objection is not valid.

Suppose the makers of pendulums report that the altitudes of their pendulums keep changing, and that no reason or discernible pattern can be discovered. Let us suppose that we are forced to conclude that these altitude changes are "undetermined." Statistical laws can be formulated, however, and they achieve a high degree of predictive success. Now, given the altitude of the pendulum at any time, one can calculate the period of the pendulum at that time. But it is also true that one can calculate the altitude from information concerning the period. Hence, the altitude "has a sufficient condition" although it is undetermined. Any adequate account of determinism must define the difference between "deterministic laws" and mere "sufficient condition laws," a point we shall deal with later.[5] I mention this example because it shows that the conditions of the case in which c, an undetermined event, is rationally predicted are not self-contradictory, and because it shows again that the important issues do not revolve around the concept of a rational prediction.

Perhaps examples like the prediction of c can be ruled out by stipulating that "e" contain no sentence describing events subsequent to the time the rational prediction is made. But this stipulation is inappropriate, for "c" is required in order to deduce "h," a sentence describing a determined event. But c is simultaneous with h and subsequent, therefore, to the time of the prediction.

It will also not be possible to demand only non-statistical

[5] See chap. VIII.

laws in "*e*." This requirement may eliminate the deduction of "*c*" since we require the statistical law "Wherever *n*, then probably *c*". But we require the same statistical law just as much for the deduction of "*h*."

An interesting recourse for anyone who wishes to define determinism in terms of predictability is to point out that if determinism is true, then this critique is of only academic interest. Since there will be no undetermined events, all events will be rationally predictable. There always is sufficient evidence prior to any given event.

But this path is not open to us because we have adopted a desideratum of univocity for a definition of determinism.[6] That is, "determined" means the same in both "All events are determined" and "This event is determined." If determinism is false, then, as we have just seen, we cannot take "This event is determined" to mean "This event is rationally predictable." Nor can we, therefore, take "All events are determined" to mean "All events are rationally predictable." And it is surely absurd to rebut by saying that "This event is determined" is defined on the supposition that determinism is true. We may be forced to surrender determinism in physics; but we may have reason to accept it in psychology, and we surely want to understand "All human behavior is determined" or just "Jones's decision is determined." But "Jones's decision is determined" does not mean "Jones's decision is rationally predictable."

There are, therefore, very serious problems in the explication of "*A* rationally predicts that *h* on the basis of 'e' " as the potential analysans of "*H* is shown to be determined." But there are equally serious problems in the explication of the concept of predictability in principle. This explication is necessary since the actual rational prediction of *h* is, at most, a sufficient condition of "*H* is determined." The rational prediction need only be possible.

[6] See above, pp. 4-5.

But the problems involved here are identical with the problems which appeared when the analogous issue arose in the analysis of foreknowledge. First of all, if "Event *e* is rationally predictable in principle" is analyzed as " 'Someone rationally predicts *e*' is not self-contradictory," all but a few bizarre cases will turn out to be undetermined (cases which determinists claim are determined) and determinism will be established in a trivial fashion (for all other cases). Furthermore, if "Event *e* is rationally predictable in principle" is analyzed in terms of the empirical possibility of rational prediction, it either presupposes concepts like cause and law or the capacity to identify theories as deterministic or indeterministic. This circularity suggests the uselessness of introducing the predictor into a definition of determinism. Finally, we have seen the impossibility of appealing to the technical possibility of rational prediction.

The discussion of foreknowledge, then, suggests that any *prima facie* plausible account of "predictability in principle" will turn out to be circular or useless in that it will presuppose the concept of determinism or concepts which can themselves be used to define determinism without the unnecessary trappings of notions like "predictability." Even if this is not so, however, the explication of "rational prediction," a concept which must still be retained, runs into very serious difficulties.

For these reasons, we must reject predictability as the definiens of determinism.[7]

---

[7] I have not commented on a series of discussions in the literature concerning certain types of conceptual restraints on predictability. Believing that these discussions were not proceeding along fruitful lines, I nonetheless felt obliged to say something about them until I came across a commentary in R. L. Franklin's *Freewill and Determinism* (New York: Humanities Press, 1968), pp. 127-35. Franklin, too, is unimpressed, and I can do no better than simply to refer the reader to his excellent discussion.

III. EXPLANATION

DETERMINISM HAS OCCASIONALLY been construed as the view that all events can be explained.[1] By now, however, it must be evident that the difficulties unique to the view that this definition is adequate must be added to the familiar problems raised by the presence of a modal term in this definition.

The inclination to link determinism and explanation is due in many cases to the prior acceptance of the deductive nomological (covering law) theory of explanation,[2] for the model of explanation advanced by the advocates of this theory looks very much like a traditional model of a deterministic account. An event e is explained, roughly, if "e" (the explanandum) is deducible from sentences which refer to antecedent conditions and general laws (the explanans). If we call any argument that satisfies those conditions a lawful account of e, the covering law theory says that explanations are provided by producing lawful accounts. And since many people think that deterministic accounts are lawful accounts, the tendency to identify determinism with the view that all events can be explained is understandable.

Criticisms of the deductive model are many. But if any of these criticisms is sound, it serves to divorce explanatory accounts from lawful accounts and has no bearing on the

[1] The discussion of determinism in chap. 4 (pp. 51-52) of Pears includes several accounts of determinism, one of these being explicability.

[2] See Carl G. Hempel and Paul Oppenheim, "The Logic of Explanation," *Readings in the Philosophy of Science,* ed. Herbert Feigl and May Brodbeck (New York: Appleton-Century-Crofts, 1953), pp. 319-52.

view that deterministic accounts are identical with lawful accounts.

Thus, for instance, the apparently contextual character of explanation has been cited as a sufficient reason for rejecting any single model of explanation. The analysis of "the explanation of e," it is argued, must give way to a set of analyses, each one of which would be appropriate under different conditions. The choice would be a function of factors like the level of understanding of the person who requests the explanation and restrictions on type imposed by that person. Evidently, however, whether or not some event is determined depends not at all on context. If a chemist asks me to explain why a particular house is burning down, he obviously is not asking me to tell him that sufficient heat was applied to a combustible material in the presence of oxygen. This excellent context-independent deterministic account would be considered an inadequate explanation in all but a small number of contexts. A determinist need not be concerned, therefor, with the complexities in the concept of explanation if he identifies deterministic and lawful accounts. Most, but not all, criticisms of the covering law theory can be dealt with similarly.

Some critics have pointed out that, even if the covering law model expresses one type of scientific explanation, others, such as genetic explanations in biology and history[3] and statistical explanations, are equally legitimate. Again, these complexities are irrelevant. For even if there are genetic and statistical explanations and, therefore, the view that the covering law model is the only model of explanation is false, genetic and statistical explanations cannot be deterministic accounts. They violate the unicity requirement since it is impossible in both cases to deduce the explanandum

[3] W. B. Gallie, "Explanations in History and the Genetic Sciences," *Theories of History*, p. 387.

from the sentences providing the explanation. Hence, even if explanatory accounts include lawful and non-lawful accounts, deterministic accounts are always lawful. Again, why not define a deterministic account as a (certain kind of) lawful account and forget about explanation?

Scriven argues that the requirement that explanandum be deducible from explanans is generally too strong a condition for explanations.[4] Even if he is right, this deducibility condition must be met by deterministic accounts for, in this way, the unicity requirement is satisfied.

Another criticism Scriven makes is that reference to laws normally constitutes the *justification* that an explanation is correct rather than a part of the explanation proper.[5] The explanation itself can consist simply in the citing of the cause or antecedent conditions.

But since we are really concerned with the meaning of "Event *e* is determined" rather than "*D* is a deterministic account of *e*," we are, therefore, interested in the analysis of "Event *e* can be explained," not "*F* is an explanation of *e*." And if "Event *e* can be explained" means or entails "Event *e* is caused," it may be that an analysis of the latter refers to laws or the existence of laws even if the explanation of *e* contains no reference to laws. In fact, Scriven admits that the isolation of the cause of some event may involve the assumption that *some* law connects cause to effect.[6]

Matters are not so simple if we turn to criticisms of the covering law theory that concern the status of the laws that are supposed to be involved in explanations. For example, Scriven believes that the demand for true laws is, like other

[4] Michael Scriven, "Explanations, Predictions and laws," *Minnesota Studies in the Philosophy of Science,* ed. Herbert Feigl and Grover Maxwell (Minneapolis: University of Minnesota Press, 1962), III, pp. 194-96.

[5] Scriven, pp. 196-97.

[6] "Truisms as the Grounds for Historical Explanations," *Theories of History,* p. 456.

demands of covering law theorists, unnecessary.[7] Since scientific laws are almost universally known to be in error, i.e., false, adherence to this covering law requirement forces us to say that science has produced virtually no explanations. No one would want to say this.

But if we define determinism in terms of the concept of law we shall have to concern ourselves with the nature of laws and the relation between law and truth anyway. Scriven has touched upon an issue that bears on our interest; but the use he makes of his conclusions is of no interest to us. How the relation between law and truth affects a theory of explanation is interesting if we are concerned about explanation, not if we are interested in the nature of laws merely.

There is, in fact, only one way explanation can enter the picture to an important degree, and that is if the concept of explanation has to be referred to in the analysis of law rather than vice-versa. It may be argued, for example, that a generalization that meets certain conditions will be refused the status of law if it fails to explain the phenomena covered by it. If deterministic accounts are a subclass of lawful accounts, it follows that deterministic accounts must be explanatory. We shall want then to understand how lawful (and deterministic) accounts achieve explanatory power.

This possibility is suggested by critics of the covering law theory who charge that restrictions must be placed on the generalizations that may appear in explanations.

We must, for example, rule out accidental generalizations. Scriven points out that we are in an excellent position for prediction if we discover that whenever cows lie down in the open field by day, it always rains within a few hours. But the earlier event is hardly an explanation of the latter.[8]

[7] "Explanations . . . ," pp. 190-92, 212-14 and "The Key Property of Physical Laws—Inaccuracy," *Current Issues in the Philosophy of Science,* ed. Herbert Feigl and Grover Maxwell (New York: Holt, Rinehart and Winston, 1961), pp. 91-104.

[8] Scriven, "Explanations . . . ," pp. 176-77.

There are also, as Hempel points out,[9] predictions made on the basis of statistical regularities that are not formulable as statistical laws.

Between accidental generalizations at one extreme and full-blown laws at the other, there are many interesting examples of generalizations that Nagel calls "developmental laws."[10] If we consider the simple form "$(x)(Px \supset Qx)$," then developmental laws are true generalizations in which Px is a genuine condition of Qx. But we believe that, although there are no instances contrary to the generalization, there are other important conditions of Qx which, perhaps, we do not yet know. These other conditions are always present when Px is present and if they are not, "Qx" will not be true. Nagel's examples are "The formation of lungs in the human embryo never precedes the formation of the circulatory system" and "Consumption of alcohol is always followed by a dilation of the blood vessels."

Developmental laws evidently afford little explanation of the phenomenon in question. For this reason, critics of the covering law model often cite such generalizations to support their contention that the covering law theory does not state a sufficient condition of explanation. An example is Scriven's "The appearance of sun-spots is followed by widespread radio disturbance."[11]

Sometimes the trouble is created by the fact that "Px" does not make entirely clear what conditions that hold of all P's are relevant to Qx. An example is "Copper is a good conductor of electricity." One may construe the question "Why does this piece of copper conduct electricity?" as neither a request for the generalization about all copper nor

[9] Carl G. Hempel, "Deductive-Nomological vs. Statistical Explanation," *Minnesota Studies in the Philosophy of Science,* ed. Herbert Feigl and Grover Maxwell (Minneapolis: University of Minnesota Press, 1962), III, p. 119.
[10] *Structure,* p. 6.
[11] *Theories of History,* p. 468.

even a request for any higher-order generalization, e.g., "All metals are good conductors of electricity." The inquirer may want to know what it is about the structure of all these objects that accounts for their ability to conduct electricity. In other words, he wants a theoretical account. He wants to know more than he needs to know in order to guarantee the conductivity of electricity. Sufficient conditions for prediction are at hand although they do not state the entire set of determining conditions.

This proposed restriction is not a matter for concern. If an event is determined, developmental laws can always be replaced by laws that spell out the complete set of determining conditions. We may simply rule out developmental laws, therefore, from deterministic accounts.

Another troublesome group is comprised of laws that explain phenomena other than those referred to by the explanandum. The law of the pendulum may legitimately be used to explain some pendulum's period. But, as we saw earlier[12] one can just as easily deduce the pendulum's altitude from the law together with initial conditions (including the period). But no one would maintain that we now know why the pendulum has the length it has.

Hempel admits that he cannot deal with cases like this.[13]

There are problems, then, in the notion of a lawful account. We want to eliminate the three types of generalization just described from deterministic accounts. In order to understand the meaning of "is determined," therefore, we shall have to understand the difference between these types of generalization and the *bona fide* variety. Now, it is surely no accident that these generalizations that fail to explain *also* fail to provide deterministic accounts. I prefer to devote this part of the book to a critique of explications of determinism, however, and reserve a substantial portion of the second part

---

[12] See p. 32.
[13] "Deductive-Nomological . . . ," pp. 108-110.

to an analysis of law. There we shall define the type of law that is legitimate in deterministic accounts and discover what role is played by the concept of explanation in the definition.

Also, from the point of view of one who is concerned about the existence of free will because he believes determinism might be true, determinism is not thought of as a thesis about the possibility of explanation. He sees determinism as possibly implying that no one can act or choose differently from the way in which he does as a matter of fact act or choose. What is it, then, in the nature of the deterministic thesis which suggests such an implication? If we may relax our analytic vigilance for the moment, the answer to this question may be expressed in the following way: Determinism says that: (1) the past dictates the future; (2) an omniscient observer could predict everything we do; (3) everything that we do is governed by inviolable laws; and (4) there is universal causation in the world. Indeed, concepts such as these have dictated the traditional accounts of determinism. The dominant concept and the one which induces concern about free will is the notion that there are rules which dictate that, given the past at any particular time, only one future is possible. It is the intention of this book to formulate more precisely the content of this concept. If, in proving that some event is determined, one also explains the event, all well and good. If, on the other hand, no explanation is thereby offered, we cannot criticize the concept of determinism. All that one need specify to satisfy determinism is the rule which reduces the future possibilities to one. The concept of explanation seems to play no role here; rather, we must turn to concepts like cause and law. Although the latter concepts are often explanatory, their being so is of no interest to determinism.

But until the analysis of law is completed, we cannot really be sure that the concept of explanation does not reappear in the very definition of "is a law."

41

IV. CAUSALITY

DETERMINISTS AND OTHERS have frequently maintained that determinism is identical with the doctrine of universal causation, i.e., the doctrine that all events have causes.[1] Now, if a particular debatable proposition is correct, we may include the doctrine that all events have causes as one of the formulations of determinism under the concept of law, and reserve discussion of these formulations until we examine laws. The proposition is: To say that an event is caused is to say that it is subsumable under laws of a certain type.

Let us call this theory the generality theory of causation. It is distinguishable from the regularity theory of causation, since the latter entails the generality theory, but not conversely. The additional claim of the regularity theory has to do with the analysis of laws—it is denied that laws are necessary in some relevant sense of "necessary."

When people think about the Humean theory of causation, they normally have both these elements in mind. There is good reason for coalescing the two, since it would be odd to accept generality and reject regularity. What would a generality non-regularity theory look like?

We introduce the sentential connective "*ni*" (nomic implication) which is supposed to represent the relation between the terms of a genuine law according to the non-regularity theorist (the necessitarian). It is non-truth-functional and "$(x)(Px \ ni \ Qx)$" entails but is not entailed by "$(x)(Px \supset Qx)$."[2] Laws are supposed to be propositions of the form "$(x)(Px \ ni \ Qx)$."

[1] Hospers, pp. 263-64.
[2] See, for example, the Principles of Modal Ordering in the

42

What constitutes a confirming instance of "$(x)(Px\ ni$ $Qx)$"? No mere truth-functional expression, such as "$Pa \cdot Qa$," will do because the conjunction confirms "$(x)(Px \supset Qx)$," and "$(x)(Px\ ni\ Qx)$" is stronger. Even if we allow that "$Pa \cdot Qa$" confirms sentences like "$(x)Px \cdot (x)Qx$" and "$(x)(Px \equiv Qx)$," we are still not entitled to say that "$Pa \cdot Qa$" confirms "$(x)(Px\ ni\ Qx)$."

This consequence can also be established if one assumes Hempel's definition of confirmation.[3] The development of the hypothesis "$(x)(Px\ ni\ Qx)$" for the class $\{a\}$ is "$Pa\ ni$ Qa." Since "$Pa \cdot Qa$" does not entail "$Pa\ ni\ Qa$," then on Hempel's definition, "$Pa \cdot Qa$" does not directly confirm "$(x)(Px\ ni\ Qx)$." Nor is there a hypothesis directly confirmed by "$Pa \cdot Qa$" and entailing "$(x)(Px\ ni\ Qx)$." Therefore, "$Pa \cdot Qa$" does not confirm "$(x)(Px\ ni\ Qx)$."

It is necessary, therefore, to have "$Pa\ ni\ Qa$" as part of the instance, at least. A question that remains and that we shall not here deal with is whether or not it is necessary to include "Pa" in addition. The question cannot be answered by defining "ni" in such a way as to have "$Pa\ ni\ Qa$" entail "Pa"—and, therefore, "$Pa \cdot Qa$"—for then "$(x)(Px\ ni\ Qx)$" would entail "$(x)(Px \cdot Qx)$," which is absurd. Putting the point in a different way, necessitarians would like to use "ni" as the connective in counterfactual conditionals that are warranted by laws.

(The epistemological issue to which the above discussion of confirmation is intimately linked concerns whether or not it is necessary to observe some substitution instances of "Px" and "Qx" in order to know of some object a "$Pa\ ni\ Qa$." In other words, is our knowledge of necessary connections

conclusion of chap. 5 of Arthur W. Burks, *Cause, Chance and Reason* (Ann Arbor: University of Michigan Press, forthcoming).

[3] Carl Hempel, "Studies in the Logic of Confirmation (II)," *Mind,* LIV (April, 1945), 97-121.

a priori? If not, in what way is experience necessary to our knowledge of necessity?)

The upshot of this discussion of confirmation is that, according to the necessitarian, laws must be thought of as generalizations of facts (or truths about individuals) each of which is or includes a necessary truth in its own right.

We defined the generality theory as a view about the meaning of propositions of the form "Event *e* is caused." But we may formulate it also as a view about the meaning of "Event *c* is the cause of event *e*." Roughly, it would claim that the latter statement means that some law of a certain type connects *c* to *e*.

We can begin now to see the oddity of a generality, non-regularity view. A necessitarian sees laws as generalizations of necessary facts. Causal laws would be understood, then, as generalizations of causally necessary facts. One may, therefore, completely understand the relation of causal necessity as holding between two particulars in a given situation without bringing in the fact that this situation may be generalized. There would be as much reason to refer to the fact that all the men in the room are bald in order to give the meaning of "One of the men in the room is bald." The notion of causality would, so to speak, have meaning in single cases.

But the situation is more complex because it is not clear that the relation between "*Pa ni Qa*" and "$(x)(Px\ ni\ Qx)$" is the same as the relation between "$Pa \cdot Qa$" and "$(x)(Px \supset Qx)$." Necessitarians usually conceive of the former relation as stronger. If we can establish "*Pa ni Qa*," we are more entitled to generalize to "$(x)(Px\ ni\ Qx)$" than we are to generalize to "$(x)(Px \supset Qx)$" from "$Pa \cdot Qa$." Indeed, says the necessitarian, his position's superiority lies in its power to solve the problem of induction. For if we are entitled to infer from "*Pa ni Qa*" to "$(x)(Px\ ni\ Qx)$," but not entitled to infer from "$Pa \cdot Qa$" to "$(x)(Px \supset Qx)$," then inferences to unexamined cases are warranted only if necessitarianism is true.

On the other hand, although some necessitarians believe that it is impossible for *"Pa ni Qa"* to be true and *"(x)(Px ni Qx)"* to be false, others are more cautious. Burks, for example, denies this impossibility, maintaining that generalizations of this sort presuppose "some factual, synthetic assumptions . . . about the general nature of the universe."[4] Thus his insistence upon the use of the causal modalities does not rest on the belief that this use solves the problem of induction.

Consider the necessitarian who rejects Burks' view and sees the generalization as a necessary inference from a single case of necessary connection. He agrees with the generality theorists that causal propositions entail that some law connects cause to effect; but he denies any connection of meaning between particular causal propositions and propositions asserting the existence of a law connecting cause to effect.

This necessitarian holds a generality, non-regularity theory. But this is nothing like the generality we associate with Hume. Must we, therefore, in order to define a Humean position, demand the strong meaning-connection? Or ought we to see the real issue between Humeans and non-Humeans as the one concerning the introduction of *"ni"*? Many necessitarians are willing to concede that what Humeans like to see as a meaning-connection is at least some kind of necessary connection. If the Humean is willing to give up the strong claim, therefore, then the only argument is the one about necessity.

It is also advantageous for a Humean not to have to defend a view that many would regard as unclear, viz., that the generality theory must demand synonymy rather than logical equivalence between causal propositions and propositions asserting the existence of laws.

One may try to preserve the debate over generality by formulating the generality theory in terms of the notion of

[4] Arthur W. Burks, "On the Presuppositions of Induction," *The Review of Metaphysics*, VIII (June, 1955), 574.

a criterion.[5] The generality theorist is then seen as affirming that one establishes causal connections by discovering that cause and effect are connected by law. This establishment is achieved by examining cases other than the one in which cause and effect occur, an approach supported by the fact that one of the most powerful arguments of the Humean is his claim that one cannot tell which of the preceding events is the cause without introducing information from other situations. This formulation is inadequate, however, because we do not always wait upon the results of examining other situations before affirming a causal connection. To say that a causal proposition commits one to certain results if an examination were to take place, however, is to revert to an entailment position. Many necessitarians would, under this reversion, have no disagreement.

One might save the criterion approach by viewing it genetically as Hume did. We do not in fact affirm causal propositions until we perceive a number of cases, and when it looks as if we are affirming causal propositions *a priori,* two explanations are possible: (1) we are guessing and do not really believe or have much confidence in the causal proposition; (2) we are asserting the causal proposition on the basis of previous cases similar to the present one. The theory would be a theory of belief inasmuch as it would provide a partial account of some of the beliefs a man has at a given time.

Many necessitarians have, on this point too, echoed agreement. We do not, they say, believe that one can perceive certain necessary connections without a certain amount of experience. Experience puts one in a position to "see" or believe with confidence that cause necessitates effect. They may restrict the requirement of past experience to certain

[5] R. Harré accuses Hume of failing to distinguish meaning from criterion in "Concepts and Criteria," *Mind,* LXXIII (July, 1964), 357.

connections, in order to maintain that at least some causal connections are perceived the first time the terms are experienced.

Thus, there have been necessitarians who agree with Humeans on all issues except the issue of necessity. They agree that we do not formulate causal beliefs *a priori* and that when we do, we are making a commitment of a general nature.

On the other hand, there are necessitarians who disagree more extensively with Humeans.

Some of them say that some causal connections are known independently of prior experience. The claim that such connections are necessary seems to follow, because, assuming that cause and effect are logically independent, then the only way to explain this knowledge is to suppose insight into a special connection between cause and effect. And this special connection would have to have the key properties of causal necessity.

If a necessitarian so believes, but rejects the Burks view according to which causal propositions do not even entail the existence of a law connecting cause to effect, then his position can be refuted by proving the truth of the regularity view. For if no laws are necessary, but every causal proposition entails the existence of a law, then the connection between cause and effect is not necessary.

The Burks view represents the second area of disagreement with Humeans that is *prima facie* different from the area of necessity. Since necessitarians themselves differ on this issue, unless some necessitarians entertain unintelligible views, the issue would appear to be distinct from the necessity question.

Some necessitarians maintain that the necessity we sometimes perceive in particulars is perceived merely as connecting the particulars. Others believe that we see the necessity as connecting kinds through the particulars. It is true that a rejection of necessity *in toto* would destroy both positions. But if we deal with the question of the necessity of laws only, we do an injustice to the Burks view, for even if the regularity theory is right about laws, there may be particular necessary causal propositions that resist generalization.

It may be considered that I have made too much of the difference among necessitarians. For example, it is not Burks' view that we perceive necessity as merely connecting particulars, but rather as connecting kind-instances. That is, necessity is a relation among particulars of a certain kind, and the only worry in generalization is the same worry that is called the problem of induction. So if we allow ourselves some form of the uniformity of nature principle, we may generalize any causal proposition. And then, if no laws are necessary, there are no necessary causal propositions.

Almost all of this discussion of the two aspects of the Humean theory leads to the conclusion that it is difficult to separate one issue from the other. On the other hand, there are some critics of Hume who have emphasized one or the other aspect. We shall, therefore, concentrate here on criticisms of generality; but we shall construe the generality theory in entailment, not meaning, terms. Although some necessitarians agree with this formulation, we shall not in our discussion suppose any necessitarian views.

Generality is not the only issue relevant to an analysis of causation, however. For example, any adequate discussion of causation should deal with the question of how we make the distinction between cause on the one hand, and condition, occasion, etc., on the other. Thus, even if causal propositions entail that some law (of a certain kind) connects cause to effect, the converse is impossible. Although the law that connects the striking of the match with the fire is the same as the law that connects the presence of oxygen with the fire, we normally and unhesitatingly choose the striking of the match as the cause. According to the generality theory, both would be causes unless we conceived the theory as a one-way entailment-claim. The theory will, therefore, be construed as the claim that causal propositions entail, but are not entailed by, propositions asserting the existence of laws.

It does not seem to matter, then, that there are some interesting distinctions to be made among the conditions mentioned in the law since a determinist demands a sufficient condition and is apparently not interested in how that sufficient condition is constituted.

But someone may argue that the relation between the causal condition and the effect is fundamentally different from the relation between other conditions and that effect, even if the two relations share a general commitment. He may demand that a determinist spell out the difference or even present two or more conceptions of determination. It is necessary, therefore, to consider the difference between cause and condition.

A more fundamental point against the sufficiency of a defense of the generality theory in this context is simply the fact that, since singular causal sentences are sometimes true, an individual event causes another individual event, even if this fact requires the truth of some general laws. If a determinist believes that all events are law-governed, does he not ignore the relation of causation that individual events have to one another?

Assuming we may ignore for the moment the distinction between cause and condition, and assuming we have a clear notion of causal law, a generality theorist might say, "I am not ignoring the relation of causation—I am analyzing it. 'C causes e' is logically equivalent to 'There is a causal law connecting c to e.' "

It is not clear that this response is not adequate. Of course, we do face serious problems in the specification of the connection between the law and the events, as we shall see.

There is, however, a simpler and more clear-cut response the determinist might make. He might reject the point and say that, although singular causal sentences are sometimes true, causation is *not* a relation between events. "*C* causes *e*" really affirms the result of an operation on the sentences "c" and "e" together with the truth of the constituent sentences. Thus, radical Humeanism can be maintained: the only relations that individual events have to one another are spatial and temporal. (Thus, although Hume said that causation relates events, we surrender this tenet and thereby preserve more important aspects of Hume's theory.)

This approach would appear to work, however, for only one sense of "causes." Several writers have pointed to an ambiguity in this term.[6] Sometimes the term is used in an explanatory context. We say, "What caused the billiard ball to move was not the fact that it was struck by an orange object, but rather that it was struck by an object with a certain mass and velocity." Since "being struck by an orange object" and "being struck by an object with a certain mass and velocity" designate the same event, the causal relation being affirmed cannot connect events *simpliciter,* and, therefore, can be plausibly construed as connecting certain sentences that describe these events. Moreover, the generality theorist can plausibly argue that the explanatory role of certain event-describing sentences is bound up with their connection to the general laws that might also be invoked to explain the effect. The law explaining the movement of the billiard ball would mention the mass and velocity of the other ball rather than its color.

In another sense, it is true that the fact that the billiard ball was struck by an orange object or by a product of a company formed in 1888 caused it to move. Here, causation

---

[6] See, for example, Donald Davidson, "Causal Relations," *The Journal of Philosophy,* LXIV (November 9, 1967), 691-703.

seems to be simply a relation between events, and the manner of description of these events is irrelevant. Can "causes" here also be construed as a sentential connective?

We introduce the term *"ca"* to designate this operation. Thus, "*a* causes *b*" is read *"a·b·a ca b."*[7] *"Ca"* is, thus, a nontruth-functional sentence-forming operator since "*a* causes *b*" is true for some cases in which both "*a*" and "*b*" are true, and false for other cases in which both "*a*" and "*b*" are true. This fact should not disturb a Humean. For although *"ca"* is not truth-functional, it implies no necessity (between events or sentences). Suppose, for example, we define a weaker relation "*a ca' b*" to mean "$(x)(Ax \supset Bx)$." *"Ca'"* is not truth-functional although its analysis, and, therefore, its truth conditions, use no nontruth-functional or modal operators. Hence, the fact that *"ca"* is not truth-functional should not in itself disturb a Humean just so long as a regularity analysis of laws succeeds.

There is a serious objection to the above reading of "*a* causes *b*." Davidson argues that it can also be proved that *"ca"* must be truth-functional, and concludes that the construal of "causes" as a sentential connective is basically incoherent.[8] He says we must accept the principle of extensional substitution because "if the fact that there was a fire in Jones's house caused it to be the case that the pig was roasted, and Jones's house is the oldest building on Elm Street, then the fact that there was a fire in the oldest building on Elm Street caused it to be the case that the pig was roasted."[9] Granted. He then applies the Fregeian idea that the extension of all true sentences must be identical in order

---

[7] Although we shall speak, in the discussion that follows, of causation as a sentential operator or a relation between events, nothing here hinges on whether or not the latter option is liberalized to include states and conditions as terms of the causal relation.

[8] Davidson, 694-95.

[9] Ibid., 694.

to conclude that the substitution of any true sentence for "a" in "$a \ ca \ b$" (assume both a and b are true) should not affect the truth value of "$a \ ca \ b$."

There is an objection to the proof that it is helpful to examine, because the response to it will actually strengthen Davidson's case. It may be said that the commitment to the principle of extensional substitution demanded by our use of causal language is not the total commitment Davidson requires to complete his proof. To use his example, suppose we analyze "The short circuit caused the fire" as "There was a short circuit and there was a fire and (There was a short circuit ca there was a fire)." For "There was a fire" we substitute the logically equivalent "$\hat{x}(x = x \cdot \text{There was a fire}) = \hat{x}(x = x)$." The left side of the identity is replaced by the coextensive singular term "$\hat{x}(x = x \cdot \text{Nero fiddled})$" and the resultant sentence is then replaced by the logically equivalent "Nero fiddled." We seem, then, to be committed to the position that "There was a short circuit ca Nero fiddled," and since the proof prevails if "There was a fire" is replaced by any true sentence, the absurd conclusion that "ca" is truth-functional is reached.

Consider again what causal language commits us to. If we replace a sentence describing an event with a singular term designating that event under that description, we are obliged to allow replacement of this singular term by any other coextensive one. For example, if "F" is "a fire on Elm Street at t_1," then "$(\imath x)(Fx)$" is replaceable by, for example, "$(\imath x)(Gx)$" where "G" is "the occurrence on the oldest street in Canton, Ohio, that made Mrs. Jones faint." Then we must allow the conversion of "$(\imath x)(Gx)$" into a sentence that replaces "There was a fire" in "There was a short circuit ca There was a fire." If, instead of "There was a fire," we use "$\hat{x}(x = x \cdot \text{There was a fire}) = \hat{x}(x = x)$," our commitment does *not* require us to allow replacement of the left side by any coextensive singular term because the left side does *not* designate "$(\imath x)(Fx)$."

Notice that we are not objecting either to the view that the left side is coextensive with "$\hat{x}(x = x \cdot \text{Nero fiddled})$" or to the general claim that all true sentences are extensionally equivalent. We are saying that since *"ca"* is not truth-functional, not just any true sentence may replace a true term of this relation, or, if Frege was right, that *"ca"* is not an extensional context. And we bar Davidson's inference by disallowing replacement of "$\hat{x}(x = x \cdot \text{There was a fire})$" by "$\hat{x}(x = x \cdot \text{Nero fiddled})$" even if they are coextensive and the constituent sentences "There was a fire" and "Nero fiddled" are, too. The perfectly natural reason again is that the fire, although it is many things, e.g., *G,* is not Nero's fiddling.

Davidson need only change his example to respond to this objection. Let "Px_{t_n}" be the form of a sentence describing an event. "$Ra_{t_0} \ ca \ Pb_{t_1}$" is a true sentence. "$(\imath x)(x = a\text{'s being an } R \text{ at } t_0)$" refers to the event described by "Ra_{t_0}." "$(\imath x)(x = a\text{'s being an } R \text{ at } t_0 \cdot Ra_{t_0}) = (\imath x)(x = a\text{'s being an } R \text{ at } t_0)$" is, therefore, logically equivalent to "Ra_{t_0}." Again, the left side is coextensive with "$(\imath x)(x = a\text{'s being an } R \text{ at } t_0 \cdot \text{Nero fiddled})$" and substitution of it would result in a sentence that is logically equivalent to "Nero fiddled."

This new example *seems* to satisfy our demand that referring expressions refer only to the events described by sentences of the form "Px_{t_n}." I say "seems" because it is obviously not clear whether or not "$(\imath x)(Rx \cdot p)$" (where "p" is any true sentence) refers to the same thing as "$(\imath x)(Rx)$." Unless I am prepared (which I am not) to provide a theory that shows that these expressions are not coextensive, however, I have no right to use this uncertainty against Davidson.

Moreover, if we wish to quantify into causal contexts, and if we allow as legitimate (and true) "There was a short circuit *ca* $(\imath x)(Px \cdot \text{There was a fire}) = (\iota x)(Px)$," we may say "$(\exists y)(\text{There was a short circuit } ca \ y = (\imath x)(Px))$."

And then, are we not allowed to instantiate this sentence by replacing y with any term that is coextensive with "$(\imath x)$ $(Px \cdot \text{There was a fire})$," including "$(\imath x)(Px \cdot \text{Nero fiddled})$"? Does not quantification, in other words, reinstate the general principle of extensional substitution?

Follesdal suggests a way out of the quantificational dilemma by the imposition of a strong restriction on singular terms that would have the effect of ruling out all definite descriptions.[10] If we can adopt this restriction, we can rule out these troublesome cases.

But Follesdal is dealing with the explanatory sense of "causes" (hereinafter "causally explains"). He wants to rule out sentences like "It is causally necessary that the man from Canton, Ohio, got poisoned" even though it was that man who drank the water containing arsenic, and it is causally necessary for any man who drinks the water that contains arsenic to be poisoned.

His argument for the restriction on definite descriptions is based on a general requirement for quantification, to wit, identity of reference for all referring expressions in all causally possible worlds.[11] In other words, if we interpret a causal sentence "Pa_{t_0} causally implies Rb_{t_1}," as one that is true in all causally possible worlds, and if we introduce quantification, e.g., "$(\exists x)(Px_{t_0}$ causally implies $Rb_{t_1})$," we ought to instantiate only with expressions that maintain identity of reference in all causally possible worlds. Definite descriptions fail to do so because "man who drank the poisoned water" may be true of one person in our world, but a different person (or none or many) in other causally possible worlds.

<hr />

[10] Dagfinn Follesdal, "Quantification into Causal Contexts," *Boston Studies in the Philosophy of Science,* ed. Robert S. Cohen and Marx W. Wartofsky (New York: Humanities Press, 1965), II, pp. 263-273.

[11] I agree with Follesdal that talk about causally possible worlds is a heuristic device and should not, therefore, perturb the reader.

Although the argument is tenable for "causally explains," should it be adopted for *"ca"*? After all, we wish to allow, as true, sentences like "There was a short circuit *ca* there was an occurrence on the oldest street in Canton, Ohio, that made Mrs. Jones faint" although they will obviously be false in other causally possible worlds.

I think we ought to look at this matter in the following way. "Causally explains (*ce*)" is the primary relation and *"ce"* sentences are established with the restriction on definite descriptions. *"Ca"* sentences are parasitic in that their truth requires the truth of some *"ce"* sentence. (The only *"ca"* sentence that " 'Pa_{t_0}' *ce* 'Rb_{t_1}' " "requires" is "Pa_{t_0} *ca* Rb_{t_1}.") Since *"ca"* sentences are a more liberal class, why not drop the restriction on definite descriptions? The answer is that *"ca"* sentences are still "about" other causally possible worlds (for they would be false if certain *"ce"* sentences were). *"Ca"* sentences are hybrids. They involve tacit reference to other causally possible worlds and yet can be false in those worlds. The retention of the restriction on definite descriptions will sort this matter out in the following way.

Consider the following example:
1. b = Brutus
2. c = Caesar
3. S = stabs
4. D = dies on March 15, 44 B.C.
5. bSc *ca* Dc

We want to allow (6) bSc *ca* Wa (*"Wa"* means "Calpurnia is widowed.") But we cannot include the following step in light of the restriction on definite descriptions:
7. $(\imath x)(x = $ the death of Caesar$) = (\imath y)(y = $ the widowing of Calpurnia$)$.

We introduce variables ranging over events, say, s, t, and u and a stock of event names e_1, e_2, and so on. (Davidson, of course, requires such variables, too.)

    8. $Ys = s$ is a dying of Caesar on March 15, 44 B.C.

    9. $It = t$ is a widowing of Calpurnia on March 15, 44 B.C.

Now (5) entails (10) $bSc\ ca\ Ye_1$. We capture uniqueness in the familiar way:

    11. $(u)(Yu \supset u = e_1)$, and (11) is conjoined to (10). It is also true that

    12. $(s)(Is \supset s = e_1))$

If

    13. Ie_2,

then (12) and (13) entail

    14. $e_2 = e_1$

and (14) and (10) entail

    15. $bSc\ ca\ Ye_2$.

We then adopt the principle that distinguishes *"ca"* from *"ce."*

    16. $(x)(s)(F)((Px\ ca\ Rs \cdot Fs) \supset (Px\ ca\ Fs))$[12]

(15) and (16) entail

    17. $bSc\ ca\ Ie_2$

and (17) in turn entails (6).

Thus, we can derive the *"ca"* sentences we wish to derive without definite descriptions. Notice, also, that we need not worry about bizarre properties of events. For example, if *"Ze_1"* is defined as *"$Ye_1 \cdot$ Nero fiddled"* (we might describe an event as the dying of Caesar that preceded the fiddling of Nero), then we must say *"$bSc\ ca\ (Ye_1 \cdot$ Nero fiddled)."* It does not follow that *"$bSc\ ca$ Nero fiddled"* because e_1 is still not Nero's fiddling. (Recall again that Davidson also needs to analyze the notion of event identity.)

We cannot, of course, read *"$bSc\ ca\ (Ye_1 \cdot$ Nero fiddled)"* as "Brutus's stabbing of Caesar caused e_1 *to be* the death of Caesar and Nero to fiddle." We must rather construe the right term as "e_1 is the death of Caesar and Nero fiddled,"

---

[12] The principle for converting the first term is, of course, "$(x)\ (s)\ (F)\ ((Ps\ ca\ Rx \cdot Fs) \supset (Fs\ ca\ Rx))$."

or, more colloquially, "the death of Caesar which was accompanied by (no temporal restrictions) Nero's fiddling." Since conjunction is commutative, we do have to allow "BSc ca (Nero fiddled $\cdot Ye_1$)"; but this is not serious since we disallow inference to "bSc ca Nero fiddled." Hence, the idea that an event causes two effects must be expressed in *two* causal sentences.

I think we can, therefore, treat "ca" as a sentential connective and analyze "ca" sentences the way a Humean would like, i.e., as sentences that are derivable from "ce" sentences, perhaps with the aid of the principle embodied in 16. "Ce" sentences, of course, would be analyzed in terms of the existence of laws connecting the terms of the "ce" relation, viz., sentences, and "ca" sentences would be parasitic on "ce" sentences in that one would be entitled to derive a "ca" sentence from any "ce" sentence in which the sentences that are *connected* in the "ca" sentence are *named* by the terms of the "ce" relation. For example, " 'bSc' ce 'Dc' " entails "bSc ca Dc."

There is one final objection to radical Humeanism. Surely, temporal relations exist between events. It would be absurd to attempt to replace "before" and "after" by sentential connectives. Yet, as Davidson has shown, the logic of temporal terms is very similar to the logic of "ca." If we could, therefore, carry out the above program for temporal terms, would we have to draw the analogous conclusion, viz., that "before" is a sentential connective?

We might be able to carry through the program for "befores"; but we no longer have any justication for eliminating definite descriptions (except the *ad hoc* one that their elimination solves problems). Temporal sentences are about this world only and involve no tacit reference to other possible worlds in the way "ca" does. They do not have as truth-conditions sentences that clearly are about other possible worlds ("ce" sentences). Moreover, from the very nature of an

57

event it follows that events must be before, after, or simultaneous with one another. If there were an analogously compelling argument about causal relations, I would have to surrender radical Humeanism.

As far as I can see, therefore, a determinist may ignore the causal relation between individual events either on the grounds that the analysis in terms of the existence of causal laws enables him to construe the sentence "*a* causes *b*" as "There is a causal law connecting *a* to *b*" or on the stronger grounds that no such relation exists.

CAUSES AND CONDITIONS

Before we spell out in greater detail the nature of the connection between causal laws and individual causal sentences, we must see if there is anything special in the relation between cause and effect that is not present in the relation between condition and effect. (Since nothing hinges on it here, we shall talk as if these relations related individual events.)

Mill's well-known position on this subject is that "nothing can better show the absence of any scientific ground for the distinction between the cause of a phenomenon and its conditions, than the capricious manner in which we select from among the conditions that which we choose to denominate the cause."[13] If this view is correct, a determinist may feel free to ignore the distinction, opting, if the generality theory is correct, for a single definition of determinism in terms of the concept of law.

The assumption that underlies this discussion is that the determinist is advancing a metaphysical thesis and is, therefore, free to put aside the many pragmatic and contextual components that should be mentioned in a complete account of the notion of causation.

But the term "capricious" is too strong for Mill's purposes, because he goes on to specify several principles accounting

[13] John Stuart Mill, *A System of Logic* (London: Longmans, Green & Co., 1843) p. 215.

for the selection of the cause. He used this strong term because he probably believed: that we are free to select from the various principles of selection the one we shall use on a given occasion; that one of these principles is the "requisiteness to the production of the effect we happen to be insisting on at the moment";[14] and that none of the principles indicates some feature of the cause-effect relation that shows it to be closer, stronger, and more intimate than the relation between condition and effect.

This third point deserves further discussion. Some principles or rules are relative in the sense that the selection of the cause is in part a function of some fact about the person, his beliefs, interests, even his values. Let us call such a principle an *R*-principle. It is evident that *R*-principles are of no interest to the determinist. Given that *A* and *B* are each necessary and jointly sufficient for *C*, then the fact that *A* is designated the cause because, to take one of these principles, the presence of *B* was obvious to Jones hardly justifies a second definition of determinism.

Nor is a second definition justified if we admit a second type of principle which might be called "objectively relative" (*OR*). Here, an objective feature of the causal relation is selected. But (1) it is possible to explain its selection in the same psychological terms that account for *R*-principles and (2) the selected feature in no way suggests that the cause-effect relation is more intimate, binding, or necessary than the condition-effect relation.

Interestingly enough, however, almost all the principles suggested by philosophers for distinguishing cause from condition fall into one of these two categories. Mill, himself, suggests at least six, five of which are *R* or *OR*-principles:

1. The cause is the non-obvious condition (*R*-principle).[15]

2. The cause is the condition we happen to be interested in (*R*-principle).[16]

---

[14] Ibid., p. 216. [15] Ibid., p. 217. [16] Ibid., p. 216.

3. The cause is the temporally latest condition (*OR*-principle).[17]

4. The cause is an event rather than a state (*OR*-principle).[18]

5. The cause is selected on the basis of certain moral principles which enable us to assign responsibility.[19]

6. The cause is that condition that exercises force or exerts activity.[20]

Mill remarks that the use of the fourth principle is always in accordance with the third principle, for an effect is brought about by some change (event) in some pre-existing state of affairs. But the use of the third principle and, derivatively, the fourth, is precarious, for there is a tendency to infer that a connection is stronger and more intimate if it is closer in time. This, Mill correctly says, is a mistake. The psychological account of the use of these principles would probably refer to the fact that changes, especially any contiguous to the effect we are interested in, are more noticeable or obvious than other conditions of that effect.

Ducasse accepts a weakened version of the fourth principle, maintaining that *if* the effect is an event (it may however be an unchange), then its cause must be an event (change). The cause of some change *B* is a change *A* which is sufficient in the state of affairs in which these changes occur to the occurrence of *B*.[21] We shall discuss Ducasse's theory in detail shortly, but I wish here simply to point out that there are changes that fit the definition that are not considered causes, and instances of causation that do not fit the definition. Gorovitz points out that no omissions can be considered causes on Ducasse's definition. As an example of the former

[17] Ibid., p. 215. [18] Ibid., pp. 214, 216. See also Harré, 358.

[19] Mill, p. 215. See also William Dray, *Laws and Explanation in History* (New York: Oxford, 1957), p. 99.

[20] Mill, pp. 216-17.

[21] C. J. Ducasse, *Nature, Mind, and Death* (La Salle, Ill.: Open Court, 1951), p. 108.

type of counterexample, Gorovitz cites the case of a man whose car blows up as he turns on the radio because a bomb had been planted the night before. According to Ducasse's definition, the cause of the explosion was the man's turning on the radio.[22]

Since Mill was neither arguing for these principles nor claiming universality for any of them, these counterexamples would not perturb him. Of course, one can criticize these principles in ways other than the citing of counterexamples. One may point out, for example, that none of them guarantees a unique cause. But I am interested neither in attacking nor in defending any of them. I simply wish to argue that if the distinction between cause and condition is made in terms of these principles, it is a distinction that determinists may ignore.

Smith says to Jones, who, knowing that Green could have been saved by proper medical attention, nonetheless sat by and watched Green die, "It was really you who caused Green's death." The truth of Smith's accusation has as a necessary condition the truth of some moral principle in accordance with which it was Jones' duty to help Green. Ergo, the fifth principle.

Whether or not this principle is R or OR depends upon whether or not "is a duty" designates an objective characteristic of action. This is, of course, a central question of ethical theory. Again, though, this principle is of no interest to a determinist.

Mill does not offer the sixth principle. An unidentified critic does, and Mill rejects it after examination. It deserves special treatment because it is the only principle we mention that would perhaps require us to offer two definitions. It is maintained that the relation between cause and effect is more intimate than the relation between condition and effect, be-

[22] Samuel Gorovitz, "Causal Judgments and Causal Explanations," *The Journal of Philosophy*, LXII (December 2, 1965), 696-97.

cause the former includes the relation of acting upon. This view is sometimes known as the activity theory of causation.

Almost all advocates of the activity theory agree with Hume that we never perceive in sense-experience activity in the manner required by the theory.[23] They usually argue that the presence of activity is a matter of inference from the experience of ourselves as causally active. Are we really aware of a unique kind of causation in our volitional activity?

That we sometimes know ourselves as agents, i.e., as beings who are acting, often voluntarily and with specific intentions, is evident. We are also effective agents insofar as the effects of our actions are often as we intend or wish them to be.

The line between an action and an effect of an action is to a great extent a matter of convention. One says: "I shot the deer." But one can also say: "I fired the rifle and, as a consequence, shot the deer (or the deer was shot)." But the activity theorist does not find the special connection between an action and its effect when a description in these terms is appropriate. Rather he finds activity in those cases in which the action is basic or primitive—it need not, of course, be basic merely—and we think of the cause as being simply ourselves or, perhaps, our will.

Let us first consider the view that we know a special causal connection between ourselves and actions, a view often advanced by philosophers who see its truth as a condition of free will. Two typical presentations of this libertarian position are those of C. A. Campbell[24] and R. M. Chisholm.[25]

[23] See, for example, George Berkeley, *The Principles of Human Knowledge* (Dublin, 1710), secs. 25-27; C. D. Broad, *Perception, Physics, and Reality* (Cambridge: Cambridge University Press, 1914), pp. 79-80 (Broad ultimately rejects the activity theory); G. F. Stout, *Mind and Matter* (Cambridge: Cambridge University Press, 1931), p. 16; A. C. Ewing, *Idealism* (London: Methuen and Co., 1934), p. 172.

[24] C. A. Campbell, "Is Free-Will a Pseudo-Problem?" *Mind,* LX (October, 1951), 441-65.

[25] R. M. Chisholm, "Freedom and Action," *Freedom and Determinism,* ed. Keith Lehrer (New York: Random House, 1966), pp. 11-44.

If some action we perform was determined, then it was inevitable: given the antecedent conditions and laws of nature, the action could not have been otherwise, so we were not free in performing it. This conclusion holds even if the antecedent conditions are our own desires, beliefs, character traits, or whatever.

But if the action was determined by nothing, then it was a mere chance or random happening and in no sense an expression of us. It merely came to pass, and nothing governed or controlled its happening how, when, and where it did.

But if being determined and not being determined exhaust the logical possibilities, and if we are free in neither case, we seem to be depriving the term "free" of any meaning. The alternatives have not been exhausted, however, for agent causality ("creative causality" is Campbell's term and "immanent causation" Chisholm's) is a third alternative. What is agent causality?

We often cite as the cause of some event an object, substance, or person. We say, for example, "The stone broke the window." But we are prepared to replace the substantive reference by an expression that denotes an event, condition, or state of that object. We are prepared to say, "The motion of the stone broke the window." Moreover, we feel that the replaced sentence is more accurate: it really tells us the cause. Similarly, we would be prepared to replace "Smith broke the window" with "Smith's throwing the ball in the way that he did broke the window."

Agent causality is causality in which a person (in his role of actor, i.e., agent) is the cause of an action and reference to that person cannot be replaced with a reference to some event in him or state of him. If we could make such a substitution, we would be back to normal causation, which is claimed to be incompatible with freedom. Thus, according to agent causality the act is determined, but not in the ordinary way—and it is only the ordinary way that precludes freedom.

Two questions may be raised: (1) Is agent causality really a necessary condition of freedom? (2) Does agent causality exist? It seems to me that the answer to both is "No." Consider the second question.

Broad has objected to agent causality (although he gives an affirmative answer to the first question) on the grounds that the cause of any event must include a factor that has a date.[26] We can always ask why an event happened at the time that it did and, if the event is determined at all, the answer can only be given by specifying the date of one of the determining factors. But then, if some action is determined at all, it must be determined by an event (or at least a condition or state). It cannot be determined by the agent, for agents do not have a date. The existence of an agent has a date; but that date cannot be the cause for then the agent would always be performing the action in question.

It seems to me that the libertarian can reply adequately if he is willing to surrender the notion that the agent is the *entire* cause, which seems the reasonable thing to do anyway. We can say of almost any act we perform why we did it at the time that we did. Chisholm grants that agent causality is not incompatible with the presence of desires or motives upon which the agent may choose to act.[27] But these desires "incline without necessitating" if the agent can resist the temptation to act upon them—and he can only resist the temptation if there are no psychological laws according to which people invariably act in a certain way, given these desires and beliefs (and undoubtedly other conditions). If, on the other hand, the desires necessitate action in accordance with psychological law, there is no agent causality. For Campbell, too, the agent is in a position to say why he acted in the way that he did. And his answer may include

[26] C. D. Broad, "Determinism, Indeterminism, and Libertarianism," *Ethics and the History of Philosophy* (New York: Humanities Press, 1952), pp. 215-16.
[27] Chisholm, pp. 25-28.

64

reference to a belief (state) that the action was his duty.

Thus, Chisholm and Campbell would probably not be averse to including reference to desires and beliefs in a full account of the action. Moreover, it seems natural to describe the situation by saying that *the* cause is the agent; but the *conditions* of the action are desires, beliefs, the situation, and so on. Hence the temporal considerations that Broad demands are provided by the conditions, and the cause remains atemporal.

Given any action, there are three possibilities. The first is that it is random and I am not, therefore, free. Now whatever a "random action" is, any action has *some* conditions. I cannot randomly raise my arm unless I have an arm. Thus, even random actions are "partially determined." But if "undetermined" is the contradictory of "determined," then random actions are undetermined. Second, the action may be (completely) determined, and none of the determining factors is me. Again, I am not free in performing this action. Finally, I am the cause of my action even though the action has conditions distinct from me.

Are these exclusive? If (1) holds, then neither (2) nor (3) can. If (2) or (3) holds, then (1) cannot. But are (2) and (3) incompatible?

The libertarian stresses their incompatibility: if the action is completely determined, there is no room for the agent to maneuver, and conversely. Agent causality is necessary and sufficient for freedom.

Here we have an implication of another unique feature of agent causality, to wit, the impossibility of overdetermination. If I set out to murder Smith, I might play safe by simultaneously stabbing and shooting him. Moreover, each may be a sufficient condition of Smith's death (given that Smith has a normal body, etc.). But, says the libertarian, it is impossible for an act to be determined both by the agent and by a sufficient condition that does not include the agent, for the presence of this sufficient condition does not make it possible for the agent to prevent the event from happening.

Thus, in order to know that I am the cause of an act, I must make sure that the act is not completely determined. Since there might be a law governing my action of which I am ignorant, however, I can never be certain that agent causality is a fact. Campbell accepts this conclusion.[28]

Traditionally, the activity theory of causation was introduced to account for the unique phenomenon of doing. We all can tell the difference between doing and undergoing, action and passion. We know that some happenings are "under our control" or "governed by us" whereas others merely come to pass in us. Now, *this* distinction is one we can all recognize (even if there are borderline cases) without appeal to matters distinct from the experience. I do not undertake a causal inquiry to tell that I am raising my arm as if it were possible for me to discover that it is rising of its own accord.

It follows that the difference between action and passion in this sense has nothing to do with agent causality since, to tell that agent causality is present, I must guarantee that my "action" has no sufficient condition.

One might say that the belief that I am acting is a sign of agent causality. But (1) it is a very unreliable sign since many actions are probably governed by law[29] and (2) I cannot tell how this view would be defended.

Another rebuttal is that when we do discover a sufficient condition of our actions, we then tend to think of them as not quite fullblooded and ours: they lose their status as clear examples of actions.

This change in attitude may be true if we discover, for example, that we are acting as the result of post-hypnotic

[28] Campbell, 464-65.
[29] If it can be shown, as I shall try to do in chap. XIII, that there are no conceptual barriers to the inclusion of actions in the scope of determinism, it will be extremely implausible to maintain still that no actions are determined.

suggestion. But, on the one hand, there is an important distinction that is independent of the results of causal inquiries. In one sense, I can be quite sure now that I am raising my arm. When I begin to explicate this distinction (as I did) in terms of "being under my control," I use terminology that does seem liable to rejection if I am acting as the result of post-hypnotic suggestion. The problem lies in the explication of the distinction, however, not in its existence. Moreover, I in no way preclude the conclusion that the action is not *free* merely on the grounds that it is determined. An action that is not freely performed, however, is an action that is performed. On the other hand, it is highly implausible to say that we were really not acting at all if the cause consists of our desires and beliefs rather than the actions of the hypnotist. But the rebuttal supposes that *any* sufficient condition makes an action not the agent's. (Again, the *freedom* of the action is not at issue.)

The sequence of my argument is: Agent causality is sufficient for freedom → Agent causality precludes ordinary determination by law → Agent causality can only be detected by causal inquiries → One central distinction between action and passion has nothing to do with agent causality.

The libertarian now has two options: (1) He can accept this argument; (2) he can revise his conception of freedom so that the premiss of the argument is rejected.

Consider the second option. The libertarian is willing to say, we shall suppose, that agent causality is only a necessary condition of freedom, for we shall allow for the possibility of overdetermination. That is, agent causality can coexist with normal determination; but under those conditions, it is not free. It is as if a man plunged a knife into someone who had just been shot. Since the victim's death was determined by the shot, the man who did the stabbing was not free in regard to that death, even if the stabbing alone would have sufficed. But if the shot was not fatal (analogous to motives that incline, but do not necessitate), then the act of the stabber had a point.

The libertarian is now free to identify agent causality with the ordinary experience of acting. Or is he?

The whole point of introducing this notion of agent causality was to reply to the charge that the only alternative to determination is randomness. The libertarian goes to great lengths to work out a sophisticated and difficult theory that ends up by saying:

    1. Free actions and unfree actions have conditions.

    2. Free actions are not completely determined.

    3. In the case of a free action, in addition to its conditions, there is agent causation that is detected as action rather than passion.

But it is clear that the libertarian could have said the same thing without introducing agent causation. All he had to do was to unmask all the confusions involved in the charge of randomness. Fortunately, this has been done most creditably by Mrs. Foot[30] and only a few remarks are necessary here.

The libertarian had to concede that all actions have conditions. The typical randomness charge confuses contrariety with contradictoriness. If an act is not determined, it is said, then it can happen anywhere under any conditions. This conclusion is absurd. All the libertarian needs is the absence of a *sufficient* condition, and this does not imply "absolute chance," and so on.

The libertarian had to concede that we can tell the difference between action and passion whether or not we link this distinction to agent causality. But another move of the randomness people is to give the impression that actions without sufficient conditions appear to the person acting as states that he undergoes.[31] This contention, too, is wrong, for I may

[30] Philippa Foot, "Free Will as Involving Determinism," *The Philosophical Review,* LXVI (October, 1957), 439-50.

[31] See, for example, R. E. Hobart, "Free Will as Involving Determination and Inconceivable Without It," *Mind,* XLIII (January, 1934), 7.

first identify an action, and *then* search for its conditions. I may, therefore, fail to find a sufficient condition.

Sometimes it is said that a random action would be completely out of character with the agent. First of all, an act may be in character even though acts of this type are only governed by statistical laws. Secondly, I may freely decide, with good reason, to act out of character. Again, if there is no sufficient condition, is my decision "random" or an "accident"?

There are a number of properties that might be meant by "random" or "accident," and for each of them we may suppose that an undetermined action lacks it.

1. An undetermined action has conditions.

2. An undetermined action may be experienced as an action.

3. An undetermined action may be in or out of character.

4. An undetermined action may be performed intentionally, deliberately, with good reason, and with full commitment. Even if we suppose deliberation to precede decision to precede action, we need not suppose deterministic laws governing this process.

An example of this fourth property may be the case in which Smith must choose a career. He would like to be a poet; but the law attracts him too. He is dimly aware of the fact that the law attracts him because of the prestige attached to that profession and because it would please his father. But he has become sufficiently independent and mature to be wary of such motives. After thinking about the matter, he says to himself, "To hell with prestige. I must act not for others, but rather for myself. I shall be a poet."

We take the matter to an omniscient psychologist who says, "No deterministic laws governed Smith's decision. Some who are identical to him in all relevant respects do just the opposite."

Some would have us believe that the psychologist's judgment makes Smith's decision an accident. He cannot be held responsible. But why? He knew what he was doing. He deliberated. This deliberation had some bearing on his decision.[32] (For example, his recognition of the motives inclining him to the law rendered his decision more probable. Also, his desire to be a poet was a necessary condition of the decision.) People do in fact hold him responsible. Furthermore, he is not absolved from responsibility on the grounds that his decision is determined for, by hypothesis, it is not.

The conclusion here is that the introduction of the concept of agent causality is pointless. The "determined-random" dichotomy was bogus. The libertarian can get by with a conception of freedom of action which includes the absence of a sufficient condition, and the absence of all those features (passivity, surprise, unintentionality) that are mistakenly supposed to be present when a sufficient condition is denied. (Of course, this is so different from what we normally think of as libertarianism that a different label might be preferable. The position includes the libertarian view that determinism implies the absence of freedom.)

The point here is quite simply that there is no reason to construe "I raise my arm" as a causal proposition. It describes an action I perform (I know quite well that it is an action) and the action may be caused. Reference to the person acting does not provide the cause of the action: the cause, if there is one, is a desire of the agent. On the contrary, reference to the person indicates the *subject* of the action. Only persons can act; only heavy objects can fall. When I tell you *which* heavy object fell, I do not tell you the *cause* of the fall. So the fact that only persons can act (and know they are acting) does not mean that persons *cause* their actions.

Of course, we say that Jones made the match light. But,

[32] If the bearing is causal, then if the generality theory is true, it follows that some laws involved in causal propositions can be statistical. We shall consider this possibility later and, at that time, reconsider this point.

70

in the first place, as we have already established, we are often prepared to replace reference to an agent with reference to an action of his; besides, we use this language to locate subjects. "*That* tree made the damage" does not warrant agent causality for trees.[33]

Our reply here to the libertarian who is willing to say that agent causality is only a necessary condition of freedom applies as well to the libertarian who refuses to make that statement. The latter, as we have seen, has additional problems.

To show that it is unnecessary to introduce a concept is not to show that the concept has no application. But if the concept is admittedly a difficult one to accept in the first place, it is comforting to know that we are not constrained to accept it.

G. F. Stout, one of the most prominent advocates of the activity theory, argues for agent causality independently of considerations of free will.[34]

We are aware of active tendency when we initiate activity, even if we fail in our goal. Each phase of the process is indissolubly united with the entire process via our will or initiative. Besides the primary tendency we apprehend as will or endeavor that unites the process, there are various partial or secondary tendencies that stand in relations of determination to one another precisely because they are united with one process. For example, suppose I am pressing one hand against the other. The primary tendency uniting this process is my effort or will to do it. The various secondary tendencies are the pressures at the various points on my hands that are initiated by me. The relations among the pressures are a function of my will.

Must we, then, attribute will to external objects if we

[33] I do not mean to imply that the notion of action is univocal for trees and persons. (In the previous paragraph, I allow that there may be a sense of "action" that is distinctive for persons.) Nor have I presented an analysis of this concept. I am here simply rejecting an argument that human action should be understood in terms of the notion of self-causation.

[34] *Mind and Matter,* Bk. I. chap. 2, Bk. IV, chap. 6.

project this model? Yes and no. What we do attribute to inanimate nature are secondary tendencies. We talk of the tension of a bow; but this is like the tension we feel in our hand, not the striving to set the bow. Thus, we do not directly attribute will to nature. But, says Stout, the existence of a secondary tendency presupposes a primary tendency. Hence causal relations in nature do imply will. Animism is, therefore, true even if many specific forms of animism take on a superstitious cast.

I do not wish to deny that we act and endeavor to act and know that we do these things. I am concerned only with causation. Nothing that Stout says leads me to believe that a case of action is *ipso facto* a case of causation. It is true that we do and feel certain things because we are working toward some goal, and that the characteristics of the things we do and feel are causally connected to our overall effort. For example, because I am trying to get a pack of cigarettes, I press my hand on the doorknob of the drug store. We shall later consider the question of the relationship between accounts of behavior in terms of goals or purposes and accounts in terms of causal laws.[35] Stout is not arguing, as some have, that the former (teleological explanation) is not reducible to the latter. He is saying that teleological accounts imply that the causal connections involved must be understood on activity lines. In fact, as he suggests, unity is achieved by human beings via a range of activities such as attention, interest, set, and so on.

All that Stout really shows is that a complete causal account of certain features of our experience and facets of our activity must include reference to an activity or condition that is relatively permanent. For example, to explain each act involved in doing a crossword puzzle, one must refer to a persistent desire, set, or striving in the absence of which the person would stop doing the puzzle. What is noteworthy

[35] Chap. XIII.

about this situation? If it is the fact that it is an instance of teleological behavior, we shall postpone discussion of it. If it is the fact that an action or activity (striving) has effects, we are dealing with the obvious. It does not follow that, because activities have effects, the causal relation is special. (No one has propounded an alcoholic theory of causation although the drinking of gin has effects.) If, finally, it is the fact that a permanent background condition modifies the course of things, why is the way that modification takes place unique? Perhaps there is the assumption that the Humean view of causation can be sustained only if the cause is an event preceding another event. But regardless of Hume's views, the basic features of generality and regularity are quite independent of either the view that cause must precede effect or the view that causes are only events.[36] I have no wish to defend either of these views. The fact that is supposed to be special is the same as the fact that the presence of oxygen is a necessary condition of fire, including its continued existence (what the medievals called a cause *in esse*). Are we to suppose that this fact is evidence for the activity theory?

Since we have found no evidence for the activity theory in volitional activity, there is little point in examining Stout's arguments that something akin to activity must be a feature of external causal relations; his arguments obviously presuppose that the activity theory applies at least in the sphere of volitional activity. But if our arguments have not thus far been convincing, it may be helpful to consider briefly Stout's further arguments.

Both Broad[37] (who rejects the activity theory) and Ewing[38] (who is sympathetic) agree that the activity theorist

[36] We shall eventually reject both views, at least in the form they shall appear in the definition of determinism.

[37] *Perception, Physics, and Reality*, p. 81.

[38] A. C. Ewing, *The Fundamental Questions of Philosophy* (London: Routledge and Kegan Paul, 1951), p. 170.

may be able to avoid the charge of anthropomorphism by distinguishing act and content. Thus, what I feel (tension) is different from my feeling it. We would be guilty of attributing feeling or consciousness to nature only if we wished to attribute to nature the act of feeling (tension) or the state of being conscious (of tension). But the activity theorist need not make this attribution: he can be content with the attribution of concept (the tension that is felt).

It is not clear that the use of the distinction will defeat the charge of anthropomorphism since some mental contents (e.g., pain) seem to imply consciousness or awareness. Besides, although Stout carefully restricts himself to the language of contents, he shows that he wants to have his cake and eat it too when he goes on to argue that secondary tendencies (e.g., tension) presuppose will or striving. I cannot see that he has presented sufficient reason here.

Stout argues that the awareness of self-activity presupposes knowledge of objects other than the self, especially one's own body: we are aware of other factors as supplementary and completing our own agency in one continuous transaction. Hence, he says, we apprehend the other as involving active tendencies akin to our own.

But we may accept that awareness of self and self-activity presuppose knowledge of objects, including our own body, and that our continuous transaction with the other implies active tendency in the other. This active tendency is secondary (Stout does not use this argument to show that we apprehend will in nature for he does not believe that we do), and we are still faced with the problem of getting to primary from secondary tendency.

Assuming, at this point, that volitional activity does not provide warrant for the activity theory, we may nonetheless accept animism and still be Humeans about causation. That is, the activity theory is not a consequence of the proposition that nature is alive.

Some theorists see the activity relation as holding between an act of will (or a volition) and, say, a bodily action.[39] Broad has pointed out that some of Hume's arguments to show that there is no special causal connection in this kind of case are inapplicable to the weaker claim that acts of will are the *necessary* conditions of bodily actions.[40] (Hume notwithstanding, they are evidently not sufficient conditions, since our nervous system must always be intact if some bodily action is to occur.) But they are evidently not necessary conditions of arm-movements, for example, since arms sometimes move without acts of will. There remain two possibilities: (1) Volition V_1 is a contributory condition of A's moving his arm (or the motion of A's arm); (2) Volition V_1 is a necessary condition of A's moving his arm.

With respect to (2), it is evident that bodily actions cannot be distinguished from "mere behavior" in terms of the fact that bodily actions are caused in part by volitions, for (2) would then become an analytic truth rather than a causal proposition. The proposition must assert, therefore, that, although it is logically possible for bodily actions to occur without volitions, they never do. (2) is still untenable, even with this interpretation. For if it is maintained that actions never occur without volitions, some of Ryle's arguments are very much to the point.[41] There is something odd about the claim that every act we perform is preceded by a volition. Ryle shows that we do not have a language which can be used to describe volitions, that certain questions which are legitimate to raise about actions in general cannot be answered when raised about volitions. Moreover, although some actions are preceded by conscious deliberation, consideration of alternatives, and the like, many actions are not;

[39] See A. C. Ewing, *Idealism,* p. 164.
[40] C. D. Broad, *The Mind and Its Place in Nature* (New York: Humanities Press, 1951), pp. 101-103.
[41] Gilbert Ryle, *The Concept of Mind* (New York: Barnes & Noble, 1949), pp. 62-74.

and so, even on introspective grounds, there is no basis for the view that all actions are preceded by volitions.

Moreover, the criteria by which we distinguish voluntary from involuntary actions, regardless of the subtleties embodied in this distinction, make no appeal to the presence or absence of volitions. Even if the presence of a volition were the characteristic making an action voluntary, the relation between volition and voluntary action would then be logical, not causal.

Finally, if every action requires a volition, then volitions require volitions, *ad infinitum*.

The only way to avoid some of these criticisms is to change (2) to read: Volition V_1 is a contributory condition of A's moving his arm. Thus volitions can be contributory conditions, whether or not they are contributory conditions of movements or the moving by someone of something. Let us not concern ourselves with the status of the event of which volitions are contributory conditions, for the untenability of Ewing's position can be shown without consideration of this issue.

The notion of a contributory condition can be understood in one of several ways.[42]

We may say that A is a contributory condition of B where A and B are classes of events. For example, "Stepping on the accelerator is a contributory condition of the movement of automobiles." It is not sufficient, for a car will not move if the brake is on, nor is it necessary, for one can push a car and cause it to move without stepping on the accelerator. Ewing does not have this notion in mind, for when we experience ourselves as cause, as active, we are not experiencing a general fact (although one may argue that an inference to a general proposition is legitimate). Ewing wants to say

---

[42] For a detailed discussion of this notion, see J. L. Mackie, "Causes and Conditions," *American Philosophical Quarterly,* II (October, 1965), 245-64.

that we experience the efficacy of a particular volition for a particular action and must, therefore, have a different notion in mind.

Further, we may infer from the general proposition "Stepping on the accelerator is a contributory condition of the movement of automobiles" that any particular pressure on the accelerator is a contributory condition of a particular movement of an automobile. But, surely, when our car is being towed, stepping on the accelerator makes no contribution to its movement. Formally, A_1 is not a contributory condition of B_1, if there is some other contributory condition which is part of the same sufficient condition that A_1 is part of which is absent in the situation of which A_1 and B_1 are a part.

Another account is that "A_1 is a contributory condition of B_1, where A_1 and B_1 are particular events" means that in the particular situation of which A_1 and B_1 are a part, B_1 would not have occurred without A_1 (although other A's occur without B's sometimes).[43] But Ewing cannot mean this either since we cannot infer from the "experience of ourselves as cause" that a sufficient condition of B_1 which did not include A_1 was not present. Since A's are not necessary conditions of B's, how can we be sure that, in the particular situation of which A_1 and B_1 are a part, B_1 would not have occurred without A_1, unless we also know that a sufficient condition of B_1 which did not include A_1 was absent? We may know this; but it cannot be inferred simply from this special experience.

"A_1 is a contributory condition of B_1" may mean "There exists a necessary condition of B that is described by a disjunction one disjunct of which is A and no disjunct of which

---

[43] Davidson finds talk about events as conditions bewildering in "Causal Relations." Some accounts are bewildering; but the above counterfactual account is only as bewildering as counterfactual accounts in general.

is vacuous, i.e., no proper subset of the disjunctive set is a necessary condition of B." Thus, B_1 would have occurred without A_1 if some other disjunct had been satisfied. But there are conditions, e.g., when no disjunct other than A is satisfied, under which B will not occur without A. How are we to infer the preceding sentence from this special experience only? Since we do not know that a sufficient condition of B that does not include A is not present, this experience may not even be one of those cases in which A is necessary to B. Yet we are supposed to be able to infer that A is necessary under some conditions to B.

But this sense is too weak anyway for Ewing's purposes. For if S is any set of conditions which constitutes a sufficient condition of B and includes A, S may contain contributory conditions other than A. If it does, then the occurrences of A_1 and B_1 do not, in themselves, guarantee the efficacy of A_1, since some other contributory conditions may be absent. If they are absent, then some other sufficient condition of B_1 produced B_1. If, on the other hand, S contains only necessary conditions (besides A), one cannot know this simply from the experience to which Ewing refers. Hence, in order to guarantee the efficacy of A_1 we must know either that S contains only necessary conditions (besides A_1), or that all other contributory conditions, which together with A_1 and the necessary conditions of B_1 constitute a sufficient condition of B_1, are present. Surely, we cannot discover what we must know in order to affirm that A_1 is a contributory condition of B_1 merely from the "experience of ourselves as cause" or any other experience like this.

Although the rejection of antecedently acquired information renders the experience insufficient for Ewing's purpose, we shall *not* take the view that causal propositions are never known "on the basis of" one experience. The position that causal knowledge is possible on the basis of a single experience is compatible with the generality theory and, therefore, there is no reason to postulate a special sense (activity) of causation.

One final criticism of the activity theory. It is common to cite as causes absences, failures, omissions, and so on. If such talk is legitimate, and I see no reason to think that it is not, it may be difficult to see how such causes can "act on" the effects in the way required by the theory. Moreover, it cannot be said that "negative causes" cannot be sufficient conditions for, although this claim is true, it is irrelevant. Since we are considering how we extract the cause from the other conditions, causes will not usually be sufficient. If the activity theory is intended to apply to all cases, therefore, negative causes, although not sufficient, pose a serious problem.

Unless future discussions that bear on the activity theory prove otherwise, I conclude that the theory is groundless and cannot, therefore, provide a principle for distinguishing cause from condition.

Another principle that has frequently been mentioned as distinguishing between cause and condition is that of manipulability:[44] the cause is that condition which is amenable to control by human beings. We may be interested in producing the effect, in which case the cause is that condition we have the power to introduce into a situation in which all the other conditions of the effect are present. Or we may be concerned to prevent the effect, in which case the cause is that condition we can remove from a situation that might produce that effect.

[44] See, for example, R. G. Collingwood, "On the So-Called Idea of Causation," *Proceedings of the Aristotelian Society*, XXXVIII (1938), 85-112, and the same author's *An Essay on Metaphysics* (New York: Oxford, 1940), p. 302; and Harold Ofstad, *An Inquiry Into the Freedom of Decision* (Oslo: Norwegian Universities Press, 1961), pp. 56-57.

79

The power to manipulate or control some condition depends on features both of the condition and of the controller. Moreover, the use of this principle indicates no feature of the condition that makes its relation to the effect more intimate. We have again an *OR*-principle that is of no interest to the determinist.

One of the most sophisticated discussions of the distinction between causes and conditions is that of Hart and Honoré's.[45] Regarding the distinction between causes and conditions, two contrasts are of prime importance, according to Hart and Honoré: "These are the contrasts between what is abnormal and what is normal in relation to any given thing or subject-matter, and between a free deliberate human action and all other conditions."[46]

The second contrast is of importance in our context here because it plays a role in the decision concerning transitivity of causes. For example, transitivity will hold in a causal sequence if that sequence can be traced back to a deliberate, voluntary action. But the causes of this action are not deemed the causes of the action's effects. And a condition that would normally be considered the cause reduces to "mere means" if it is caused by a voluntary action. Clearly, the most this contrast can produce is an *OR*-principle.

The first contrast, however, is of far greater importance. The principle is presented to account for causal ascriptions in ordinary life where the effect is a departure from the normal or expected course of events. We see already, therefore, the relative character of the account, a relativity determinists may ignore.

The cause, then, is the difference between the normal and abnormal situations, and the conditions are the factors present in both. Hart and Honoré show how the other princi-

[45] H. L. A. Hart and A. M. Honoré, *Causation in the Law* (Oxford: Clarendon Press, 1959), pp. 8-41.
[46] Ibid., p. 31.

ples we have mentioned may be seen as subordinate to this principle.

We need go no farther, for Hart and Honoré explicitly admit the relative character of this criterion. The application of the principle, i.e., the decision as to what is and what is not abnormal, depends upon practical interests, attitude, the presence or absence of human institutions, the assumptions we make, and the questions we ask. Gorovitz, recognizing that there are all sorts of problems in the distinction between normality and abnormality, believes that the most fruitful line this approach can take is in the direction of complete and explicit relativization:[47] the normal class of situations is that class that happens to be contrasted with the actual state of affairs. If this general approach is accepted, we repeat, determinists need not worry about the possibility of two definitions.

One final principle that would show that the cause is more intimately linked to the effect is the principle of necessity. Unfortunately, however, that principle must fail here. There is only a necessary connection, if there is any at all, between the effect and the sum total of the conditions. If any condition is absent, then the effect will not take place. Hence necessity cannot distinguish some conditions from others.

Almost every writer on this subject points out that the term "cause" becomes lost as scientific investigation reaches a relatively sophisticated level of theory-formation. This loss is accounted for in terms of the practical interests that permeate the language of cause and effect. The line we have taken lends support to this commonplace observation.

GENERALITY THEORY DEFINED

We no longer need fear that a separate definition of determinism is required by the special relation that some condi-

[47] "Causal Judgments . . . ," 700-701.

tions have to their effects (barring the possibility that subsequent discussions have implications to the contrary).

At this point, there is an ambiguity in the generality theory that must be cleared up. Determinism is clearly false if the only law governing some kind of event is statistical. For this means that the event sometimes fails to occur, under conditions that are identical in all relevant respects to conditions under which the same kind of event does occur. Assuming the truth of the generality theory, one might argue that the law involved in some causal relationships is statistical. If so, then the proposition that c causes e would not entail the proposition that e is determined. We would presumably have to drop causality as a potential definiens of determinism.

Whether or not the stronger version of the generality theory, viz., that causal propositions entail the existence of nonstatistical laws only, is tenable, presents a very interesting question. Persuasive arguments can be mustered on both sides of the issue. But it is not an issue that requires our attention. For we are only concerned with causality as a potential definiens of determinism if the generality theory is false. If the generality theory is true, we shall turn to formulations of determinism in terms of the concept of law. Hence, whether we defend a weak or strong version of generality is beside the point. If we can defend a strong version, all well and good. But if we can only defend a weak version, then we are forced to recognize that the ordinary concept of causality must be tightened or eliminated if an adequate definition of determinism is to be provided. In either case, we need not offer two definitions—one in terms of cause and the other in terms of law—and that is the sole preoccupation justifying this chapter. We shall define the strong version and see how far we can take it. If we are forced to shift to a weak version, then so be it. If, on the other hand, we are forced to reject generality completely, that is a serious matter.

C. J. DUCASSE

For Ducasse, the sentence "A_1 is the cause of B_1," where "A_1" and "B_1" denote particular events, means "A_1 and B_1 are the only changes which occur in a state of affairs S_1, B_1 immediately following A_1."[48] Causation, then, is a triadic relation, all of whose terms viz., the two changes and the state of affairs, are individuals. The analysis of the causal proposition contains reference neither to classes of events nor to events of the same kind as A_1 and B_1.

Ducasse claims that his theory is in agreement with our version of the generality theory. For, he argues, given that two events A_1 and B_1 in S_1 of kinds A, B, and S respectively are in accordance with the definition, it follows logically that all other instances of A, B, and S will be in accordance with the definition. That is, the uniformity of causation is logically necessary although the analysis of causal propositions makes no reference beyond the individual case of causation.

Ducasse presents a *reductio ad absurdum* proof of the necessity of the uniformity of causation. The assumption that causation is not uniform is self-contradictory, for "this would be to suppose that a change having identically the same nature in each case, in a state of affairs also having identically the same nature, *at one time is and at another time is not etiologically sufficient*[49] to occurrence of a later change having identically the same nature . . . , *notwithstanding that etiological sufficiency was defined in a manner wholly independent of times*."[50] Or, "by the very definition of causation . . . , the difference between the two instances . . . , which *ex hypothesi* is solely a difference of absolute dates, is wholly irrelevant to causal necessitation."[51]

To assert that etiological sufficiency is defined in a manner

[48] *Nature, Mind, and Death,* p. 105.
[49] Etiological sufficiency is, roughly, the same concept as causal sufficiency.
[50] Ducasse, pp. 156-57.
[51] Ibid., p. 156.

wholly independent of times is to assert that the criteria for the use of this concept contain no restrictions on the applicability of the concept to two events and a state of affairs based on date of occurrence. The only temporal considerations are contained in the stipulation that the cause must occur immediately before the effect. It does not follow, however, that if A_1 is etiologically sufficient to B_1 at t_1, another event qualitatively identical to A_1 is etiologically sufficient to an event qualitatively identical to B_1 at t_2. The criteria for the use of the concept of spinsterhood make no reference to father-daughter relationships; but it does not follow that the quality of such relationships has no bearing on the prevalence of this property. If Ducasse's point were accepted, we would have the foundations of a version of idealism, to wit, that all the "facts" about the reference of some concept are actually included in the definition of the concept.

Since this proof fails, Ducasse does not establish that his analysis is consistent with our version of the generality theory.

Because many changes that precede a given change B_1 are causally irrelevant to B_1, some device must be provided for eliminating these changes from the state of affairs S_1 that contains B_1. For, on Ducasse's theory, any change in S_1 preceding B_1 is the cause or part of the cause of B_1. I contend, however, that the specification of S_1 can be made only by inferring causal irrelevance from laws or general considerations derived from other situations. So general considerations enter in a fundamental way.

Ducasse concedes that more than one experiment[52] is required to discover the necessary and sufficient conditions of some event when that event is described as a member of a certain class of events, that is to say, as an instance of a certain kind of event. If, however, we do not abstract from

[52] An experiment is an example of a causal situation where a person introduces the earlier change.

the whole of the completely determinate change, but rather consider the event in its full concreteness, then a single experiment suffices to provide us with a causal fact. If, in other words, we want to know the cause of the event (total change) which occurred at location l_1 at time t_2, the answer is quite simple: The cause is the event (total change) which occurred at location l_1 at t_1. Or, if we can describe an event completely, making sure that we have abstracted all of its descriptive features, we can specify cause and effect in terms of complete descriptions of the changes at t_1 and t_2. If we wish to restrict the length of a description of a particular causal fact to 40 volumes or under, though, many conventions will have to be imposed on the descriptions of these events. The problem of length, however, is not solved that easily, for once a complete description of the effect is provided, there can be no guarantee that we have included all the causally relevant features in the description of the changes at t_1 until we have described all the changes in the entire universe at t_1. Ducasse still has no method for restricting the features admissible into the state of affairs because he does not consider spatial proximity (ascertained by ordinary visual or tactual methods) as a necessary condition of causal interaction.[53] Hence we may not restrict the location of the cause to l_1 unless l_1 is the universe. We, then, are left with two kinds of causal facts ascertainable by a single experiment: (1) the total change in the state of affairs at t_1 is the cause of the total change in the state of affairs at t_2 (where t_2 is a time immediately following t_1); (2) all the changes in the universe at t_1 (actually specified) cause some total change at t_2 (actually specified).

There is a third kind of causal fact ascertainable by a single experiment except that the word "cause" in the description of this fact means only "sufficient condition," whereas in the first two kinds of causal facts, it means "necessary

[53] Ducasse, pp. 134-38.

and sufficient condition." If we abstractly describe some particular effect which occurs at t_2, thereby omitting many features of it, we may still view as its cause either the total change in the state of affairs at t_1 or all the changes in the universe at t_1 (actually specified). Strictly speaking, since there is no way of guaranteeing that some omission is not causally relevant, the state of affairs referred to by the first alternative cannot be arbitrarily restricted in any way; the reference has to remain sufficiently open in order to include potentially any change in the universe at t_1. The inclusion of this kind of causal fact is justified by a rule which states that if A is a sufficient condition of B, then $(A \cdot C)$ is a sufficient condition of B. In other words, we are bound to include the "cause" of this event if we refer to or describe the total situation at t_1.

All other causal facts—for example, that some event is necessary but not sufficient, or sufficient but not necessary—require more than one experiment.

It is important to realize that these remarks do not depend on whether we read "cause" as *"ca"* or *"ce."* It might be thought that Ducasse is using the notion of *"ca"*, since this is in a sense the more inclusive notion: the truth of *"ce"* sentences depends on the way events are described, whereas the relation Ducasse is talking about does not. But even *"ca"* sentences pick out *certain* events at a location and at a time. Even though it does not matter how we refer to the fire in the building, the short circuit did not cause all the events in the building at the time. The relevant changes are determined through general considerations even if we are completely free to describe those changes in any way.

Ducasse is the first to admit that we rarely use the concept of causality in these ways. But, says he, the fact that practical interests dictate our concern with the kind of causal facts which require more than one experiment does not imply

86

there are no facts of the kind ascertainable by a single experiment.

I do not wish to deny the "facts" which Ducasse refers to and I would certainly not deny their existence on the grounds that a knowledge of them serves no practical end. What I do deny, though, is the right to call such facts "causal." Ducasse insists that the problem of the nature of causality is the problem of finding a definition of the term "cause" which reflects the way in which the term is actually employed.[54] Can he seriously contend, though, that the term is actually employed in the manner in which he states it is? He says that the concept is rarely used in the way he delineates; I would contend that it never is. Ducasse does not deny the legitimacy of labeling facts as causal when more than one experiment is required to ascertain them. He does claim, however, that certain other facts are causal, and this claim is incompatible with his prior statement of the purpose of a philosophical investigation into the nature of causality.

Consider the first kind of causal fact viz., "The total change in the state of affairs at t_1 is the cause of the total change in the state of affairs at t_2." In the first place, most people would not say that particular causal judgments are *a priori;* yet these are, since no empirical knowledge is required to confirm or disconfirm them. Thus, not even one experiment is required. Moreover, it is always fair to demand of someone who raises a causal question or undertakes a causal investigation that he specify the event or kind of event whose cause he is interested in discovering. Disregarding for the moment the fact that ignorance of the cause in such cases cannot exist since it is always the same non-descriptive reference, one cannot even offer an acceptable answer to this demand. Surely, "that which occurred at t_2" or "the total change in the state of affairs at t_2" is not acceptable unless

[54] Ibid., pp. 102-104.

it can be supplemented by a description of the changes at t_2.

The difficulties associated with the second kind of causal fact are, in a sense, just the reverse. Whereas ignorance of the first kind of causal fact is impossible, knowledge of the second kind of causal fact is impossible, since one must list all the changes in the universe at some moment. I contend that no causal knowledge is acquired even if such an account can be given: all that one has done is list the changes in the universe at two adjacent times. Moreover, if the part of the universe chosen as the effect is relatively circumscribed, then we again have the problem of defining causal relevance, for no one who understands causal language would say that every change in the universe immediately prior to the effect is causally relevant to it. Even if one assumes total ignorance of the causal relations in the world, no one would say that it has been *demonstrated* that all the changes in the universe are causally relevant. The most one can say under the assumption of total causal ignorance is that all the changes in the universe *may be* causally relevant. After all, some of the changes that occurred in the universe may have had effects outside the domain of the effect in question.

I have, of course, suggested the reply to the claim that there is a third kind of causal fact. If the effect in question is the breaking of a windowpane, than a complete description of the prior state of affairs and all its changes is not the cause. In other words, it is consistent with ordinary usage to assert the possibility of changes which are causally irrelevant to this effect. It is true that, if A is a sufficient condition of B, $(A \cdot C)$ is a sufficient condition of B in the sense that, if all occurrences of A are followed by an occurrence of B, then all occurrences of $(A \cdot C)$ are followed by an occurrence of B. But this sense of "sufficient condition" does not reflect the ordinary concept of causation, for no one would say that the presence of heat, a combustible material, oxygen, and a Roosevelt dime caused the fire merely because the first three did. One is entitled to include as part of the cause necessary or contributory conditions only.

I conclude, then, that Ducasse's attempt to avoid a serious difficulty in his account, to wit, that he cannot define the causal relation by one experiment, fails for two reasons: in the first place, the resultant theory is an untenable one; furthermore, the resultant theory is incompatible with Ducasse's professed claims about the purpose of a philosophical investigation into causality.

Ducasse cites an experiment which he performs with students to confirm his thesis that ordinary causal judgments do not conform to the generality theory. He places on the desk a parcel, puts his hand on it, and at once the face of the parcel glows. The students say that the glow was caused by his placing his hand on the parcel. Ducasse concludes that "they based their judgment of causation upon, . . . not repetition of a certain act of mine followed each time by the glow, but *one single case* of sequence of the latter upon the former."[55] When asked why they chose what they did as the cause, the students replied," . . . because nothing else happened to the parcel at the time."[56] Hence, by the cause " . . . they mean the only change introduced into the situation immediately before the glowing occurred."[57]

It may be the case that Ducasse has here confused the concept of confirmation with the concept of meaning. It is true that the students based their causal judgment on, or found their causal judgment confirmed by, this single case. It does not follow, however, that the causal judgment entails nothing beyond this single case. If Ducasse insists that the students considered the causal judgment completely verified by this single case, on the assumption that the change introduced immediately before the glowing was the only relevant

[55] Ibid., p. 95. [56] Ibid.
[57] Ibid. (Ducasse has this in italics.)

change, I would reply that they are also working on the assumption that determinism is true.[58] In other words, the causal judgment is considered completely verified by a single case only if it is assumed that, under identical conditions, the same result would ensue, or that, under conditions which are identical in all relevant respects, the same result would ensue. Of course, this is a very rough and, ultimately, unacceptable formulation; but I trust that the point is not contingent on a precise formulation. We do ordinarily assume determinism to be true and, hence, feel entitled to make causal judgments on the basis of a single case when we are reasonably convinced that only one relevant change has been introduced prior to the event in question. The evidence for the view that more than the single case is involved is that subsequent cases could have a bearing on the causal judgment. If, for example, we never again find that the glowing occurs when a hand is placed on the parcel in experiments which occur under conditions so similar to the first as to shake our belief in determinism, we will certainly question or reject our original causal judgment. I conclude that the assumption of determinism accounts for the fact that we may make an inherently general causal judgment on the basis of a single experiment.

Consider another case. As I shave one morning, I feel a sharp pain at a spot the razor touches. The next moment blood appears at that spot. I know very well, without having to perform subsequent tests, that I cut myself. What would a generality theorist say about this case?

In the first place, the mere fact that I do not perform subsequent tests before affirming that the bleeding was caused by the razor blade does not, as we indicated in our discussion of the notion of a criteria, prove that the generality theory is wrong. One may have great confidence in the general con-

---

[58] Cf. Arthur Pap, "A Note on Causation and the Meaning of 'Event,' " *The Journal of Philosophy,* LIV (March 14, 1957), 157.

nections that are tacitly affirmed as the result of past experience.

The generality theorist would argue that the causal claim entails some connection of a general kind between blades (sharp object) and skin (soft object). The razor blade was chosen rather than, say, splashing water because the water, unlike the blade, is not connected by law to skin openings. Moreover, although we may not be in a position to specify the applicable sufficient condition of this skin opening, we know that the conditions other than the action of the blade may have prevailed in this case. We have, therefore, tacitly adduced general considerations to limit the possibilities, have no reason to believe that any other possible cause is present (a strange skin disease), and have many positive instances of a law connecting the motion of sharp blades and skin openings (or a general theory of which this law is but one of many lower-order generalizations). We therefore have a great deal of evidence for "There is a law connecting A to B" and, *therefore,* are entitled, given information about this particular case, to affirm "A is the cause of B." So if we have enough background information, we are entitled to make a causal judgment on the basis of a single experiment.

The generality theorist also maintains that the causal judgment must be surrendered if one comes to learn that no law connects A to B. And this is so.

There are at least two kinds of discovery that would require the rejection of the causal proposition. The action of the blade was not of a kind, e.g., it was too light, to produce the opening. (It is difficult to see how one might be sure of this—but there might be a lot of indirect evidence.) The opening was actually caused by a strange skin disease, and so on. Or, we may discover that, although the action of the blade was of a kind to produce skin openings, other conditions of this general connection were absent. In this case, the causal proposition is not rejected because no law connects A to B. It is rejected because this situation is not an instance of that law. (For example, the striking of the match did not cause the fire for the match was wet.)

A genuine problem facing the generality theorist is that he must often say that a person's causal knowledge depends on his having observed cases that are similar to a given one. But "similarity" must be defined because, if no restrictions on class membership are imposed, everyone is in a position to make any causal judgment at all. To deal with these questions is to get embroiled in the central issues of confirmation theory, e.g., how do certain observations confirm certain generalizations and not others? We shall not have to do this here, for anti-generality theorists face the same problem. The problem may be stated by comparing two men, A and B, who attend a football game for the first time and agree that the ball's motion at the beginning of the game is caused by a kick. A is a normal person who in the past has observed football-like objects being put in motion by kicks and other forces. But B is a strange individual who has not made the "relevant" observations. Through the use of strange predicates, however, he has generalized from "irrelevant" situations to the present case, and it happens that his inference is correct in this case. For example, let "cick" mean "is copper or a kick" and let "motec" mean "conducts electricity or produces motion." B, having observed cases of copper conducting electricity, generalizes to "all cicks are motecs" and thereby infers correctly that the kick caused the football to move. How can a generality theorist distinguish A's legitimate inference from B's illegitimate one?

But an anti-generality theorist is faced with the same problem, since he must explain why the change distinguished as the cause is described as a "kick" rather than a "cick." He too determines a class by the predicate chosen to describe the cause. If, on the other hand, the generality theorist can explain why "kick" is preferable, he can explain why prior kicks rather than prior experiments with copper warrant the present inference.

Suppose, however, that A's inference was based on the observation of cases of the application of external force other than kicks. (We are considering inferences from only similar cases.) Here, too, the inference is legitimate. But again this fact does not confer superiority on the anti-generality theory.

Either the anti-generality theorist is prepared to describe the cause more generally as "application of external force" or he is not. If he is, the justification for the step from "kick" to "application of external force" is the same as the justification a generality theorist would have to give for the inference from prior cases of applications of external force other than kicks to the present case of a kick. If he is not, then ignorance is the only explanation. The anti-generality theorist must eventually concede as the evidence pours in that this redescription of the cause is appropriate. And if so, he is faced with the same problems of class restriction that the generality theory faces.

In order to formulate the generality theory, let us look more closely at the football case. First of all, the nature of the causal account is a function of the properties of the object whose activity constitutes the effect which we select. The property selected in this case is, let us say, hitting the ground fifty yards from the point of impact. It is axiomatic that the instantiation of this property is a function of certain forces acting on the object which possesses this property, e.g., the force of the kick, the force of gravity, and the force of air pressure. The effect is also a function of the angle of the kicker's foot, the point of its contact with the ball, the air pressure within the ball, the weight of the ball, and the nature of the material out of which the football is made. There are more; but I can see no theoretical reason which precludes the discovery of all the factors that have a bearing on this kind of effect. The work is facilitated by the tacit stipulation that only independent properties are to be chosen. Thus, we need not refer to the material out of which the shoe of the kicker is made since that only bears on the force of the kick, a property already included. Now, there are evidently great practical barriers to the specification of the particular conditions that would enable a deduction of the sentence describing the effect together with appropriate laws, i.e., to the assignment of values to all the relevant variables. For example, the effect is a function of air pressure which varies slightly from point to point during the flight of the ball. Clearly, then, only an approximation to the actual pressure can be made by calculating the average from samples of the air over the field. This figure may be erroneous, for the ball travels in a specific arc, and the average pressure on points along this arc may be slightly different from the average as calculated for the entire field. Hence, although it seems to be practically possible to discover all the relevant variables, it is virtually impossible to assign true values to all of these variables in this and analogous cases. How does this situation affect the claims of the generality theory?

The causal sentence in question is: The kicking of the ball caused it to travel fifty yards in the air. As is customarily the case in ordinary causal sentences, the event chosen as the cause is a contributory condition of the effect. That is to say, it is a member of a class of events (external force applied to the ball) a disjunction of whose members is a necessary condition of the effect and no proper subset of which is disjunctively a necessary condition of the effect. It is possible to formulate the relations of dependence between the property of the object whose activity constitutes the effect and its conditions in the form of equations—since we are concerned with magnitudes. Thus, a law is formulable although it may contain no expression logically equivalent to "kick." It may contain an expression (like "external force") which is connected to "kick" via rules of logic and, perhaps, meaning-postulates or rules of correspondence.

The relation between the terms of a causal sentence and the terms in the law whose existence is entailed by that sentence varies, depending on whether or not "cause" means *"ca"* or *"ce."* The term "because" typically indicates *"ce."* For example, in the (false) causal sentence "Harry got ptomaine because he ate fish whose taste he did not like," (T), it is supposed that there will be a term in the law that is connected by logic and convention only to the term "dislike." Two weaker possibilities will not do. For example, suppose we say that "c is the cause of e" entails "There is a law one of whose antecedent condition terms is true of the same event as c and whose consequent term is true of the same event as e." We surely do not want to say that a law about worms (the real culprits) can be a candidate for a law whose existence is asserted by T. The person asserting T means to locate the trouble elsewhere—in Harry's psyche. But such is the consequence if, as may be the case, Harry did not like the taste of the fish that contained worms. For then, "Harry's eating fish that contained worms" is the same event as "Harry's eating fish whose taste he did not like." Hence, a law about worms would contain an expression that is true of the same event as "Harry's eating fish whose taste he did not like."

We can strengthen the connection between terms by demanding that there be some connection of law between them. But it may be entailed by laws plus antecedent conditions that Harry likes the taste of no fish that contains worms. Assuming this, however, we still feel that a law about worms cannot be involved in the first causal sentence. We must, therefore, demand that the event descriptions be connected by logic and convention.

On the other hand, if a coroner reports: "The tea killed

95

him," (A), after learning that the tea contained arsenic, we do not suppose the coroner to be implying that the involved law mentions "tea" or any expression related by meaning postulates to "tea." We can explain his use of "the tea" rather than "the arsenic" without supposing that he believes tea to be in itself a deadly beverage. We do suppose T to imply that Harry's disliking the fish was causally relevant. Why else would the fish be identified in this way?

There are in fact three possibilities: (1) the person intends his causal description to be connected by meaning postulates only to a conjunct in the antecedent of the law (*"ce,"* e.g., T); (2) the person makes no such commitment (*"ca,"* e.g., A); (3) the person makes a commitment weaker than (1) and stronger than (2). For example, someone might believe that something that causes illness happens to fish that is two weeks old. But he might not know what that is. He attributes Harry's illness to his eating two-week-old fish. Now, we would accept the statement as true if the connection between age and worms is lawful. But if the presence of worms has nothing to do with age, and it is merely a coincidence that this two-week-old fish contains worms, then the statement is false. Hence a generality theorist must offer three analyses and claim that one of the three applies to any causal sentence; the decision as to which applies in any given case depends upon the speaker's intended meaning.

$G.T._1$ will be: "C causes e" entails "There is a set of conditions described by some conjunction 'S' (one conjunct of which is 'c') each conjunct of which holds of the situation in which c and e occur and a set of laws L and a set of meaning postulates M (definitions, linguistic rules, rules of correspondence) such that $S \cdot M \cdot L$ entails e, and e is not entailed by any of the following: S, M, L, $S \cdot M$, $M \cdot L$, $T \cdot M \cdot L$, where T is any proper subset of S."

$G.T._2$ is identical with $G.T._1$ except for the following addition: "or there is a sentence 'D causes e' that entails 'There is a set of conditions described by some conjunction "S" (one conjunct of which is 'd') . . . ,' and 'c causes e' is derived from 'd causes e' in accordance with the procedures described earlier for converting "ce" sentences into "ca" sentences."

$G.T._3$ is identical with $G.T._2$ except that the procedures for converting "ce" sentences into "ca" sentences are strengthened thus: the key principle in the derivation to "ca" sentences (in terms of conversion of the first term) is: $(x)(s)(F)((Rs\ ca\ Px \cdot Fs) \supset (Fs\ ca\ Px))$. Here, we require in addition that "Fs" be derivable from "Rs," other sentences about the situation, laws, and meaning postulates (such that each is essential to the deduction).

On this account of the generality theory, to say that some condition is causally relevant is to say that it appears in some form in the law; for, if it does not appear there, then the deduction of "e" does not require it and it would not, therefore, appear in "S."

Since laws are empirical propositions and since the inference from c to e is mediated by laws, there exist procedures for the identification of all the properties, except the e-property, mentioned in the laws that are independent of the procedure used to identify the e-property. In the case in question, there are procedures for the assignment of values to the variables force, air pressure, gravity, etc., that are independent of the procedure (or some procedure) used to assign a value to distance traveled.

These laws may mention only "relevant" conditions. Thus, only variables whose values make a difference to the values of the variable representing e may be included in the equations appearing in the laws or, if the laws do not include equations, then only properties necessary or contributory to e may be included. But this principle merely defines rather than solves any problem.

For example, if the laws include equations, then the inclusion of some variable in a particular equation requires that its values "make a difference to the values of the variable representing e." If this is interpreted to mean that a functional relationship holds between the two sets of values, there is a sense in which it is true of any two sets of numbers, since the two lists of numbers are sometimes said to be the specification of the function. If the laws do not include equations, we do at least eliminate properties which are always absent when e is present; we have not, however, stated a criterion which will eliminate properties always or sometimes present when e is present, but which are causally irrelevant to the instantiation of e. We shall take up these questions later.

According to *G.T.*, a person who asserts a causal proposition commits himself to the existence of a set of laws which applies—in the senses specified by the analyses—to the case about which the causal sentence is made, but does not claim to be able to specify the content of these laws. Insofar as the laws need not be specified, we seem to be making a concession to anti-generality theorists; but anti-generality theorists are surely right in maintaining that ordinary causal sentences do not contain an actual law. Surely, one may assert that the kicking of the football caused it to travel fifty yards without including in that assertion the fact that the distance traveled is a function of air pressure; indeed, one may know nothing about air pressure. I am aware that one may not know all the propositions entailed by an assertion; but it is absurd to maintain that this causal sentence entails reference to all the factors which are relevant to distance.

Notice that the proposed analysis does not stipulate that the generality involved in the causal proposition concern only instances in which the actual values of all the variables are repeated. A football may never again be kicked fifty yards; but a causal sentence is possible, for there is a set of laws (of the appropriate type) each of which has many instances,

98

and one of these instances refers to the present case. Hence, an event may be unique in one respect and yet be subsumable under a generalization, thereby permitting a causal claim to be made about it.

One reason for the exclusion of an actual law from the analysis of causal sentences is that we are often ignorant of all the conditions which must be mentioned in the law. The proposed analysis does not require, on the other hand, that the causal sentence refer to any of the values of the variables mentioned in the set of laws which applies to the case about which the causal sentence is made. Hence, the practical impossibility of specifying all of these values is not a difficulty for this analysis. The causal sentence does imply that, if these values are given, they will be in accordance with the laws. Clearly, the laws can be confirmed through observation of simpler cases than the one in question and, then, be held to apply to the latter.

Scriven, a critic of generality theories, admits that "in certain cases we are in a position to judge, not that certain specifiable laws apply, but that *some* laws must apply."[59] He goes on to say that it is *very* odd to make this assertion rather than that we can be sure of causal statements even when we do not know any relevant laws. I do not agree because, first of all, there is admittedly no incompatibility between the two statements and because, secondly, it is important to emphasize the element of generality in causal sentences. In so doing, for example, we imply the disconfirmability of causal sentences by subsequent observation.

It is true that almost any law-like statement which is claimed to apply to the present case may be subsequently disconfirmed without affecting the truth of the causal sentence. But there is still no incompatibility with the generality theory as I see it, for there are ways of disconfirming the causal sentence by subsequent observation. One might show,

[59] *Theories of History,* p. 456.

for example, that the laws governing the occurrence of the effect make no reference to the existence of an external force applied to the objects belonging to the class of which footballs are a member. Thus, one would have to show that football-like objects do not require an external force in order to be accelerated. Our certainty in the causal sentence derives from the certainty we afford this general fact as a result of the most naïve observations of the world. If we were to discover that footballs could animate themselves, and if we were able to confirm some theory about the mysterious internal composition of a football which explains this phenomenon, we might very well question our causal sentence. If footballs were capable of self-animation and animation by an external force, then we would have to discover which was operative in the case in question and we could describe conditions under which the original causal sentence would have to be rejected. Hence, although we may be more certain about our causal sentence than about any law-like statement we may claim to apply, we are not more certain of the causal sentence than we are of the general fact that football-like objects cannot animate themselves.

Scriven develops an interesting argument against the generality theory.[60] He points out that there are cases in which we would assert that A_1 is the cause of B_1 although A (the type) does not even accompany B (the type) frequently. The examples he offers are cases in which B has several causes of which A is the most common. That is to say, B is usually accompanied by A rather than some other possible cause; but, given A, B does not usually follow. For example, given that a man who has been exposed to radiation of a certain kind develops cancer, we say that the exposure (together with some other conditions) caused the cancer, although

<hr />

[60] "Explanation and Prediction in Evolutionary Theory," *Science,* cxxx (August 28, 1959), 477-82.

most people do not develop cancer after such exposure. But—let us suppose—people who develop cancer have usually been exposed to radiation of this kind. Thus, we are willing to assert that A (exposure to radiation) is the cause of B (cancer) although we know that B does not usually follow A; nor do we even know if there exists a sufficient condition of B. He also cites cases in which A is the only cause of B, and these two conditions hold. Of course, the fact that A_1 is said to be the cause of B_1 although B does not usually follow A is not incompatible with $G.T.$ for the latter does not claim that "A is the cause of B" entails that all A's are B's. Also, we explain the fact that A_1 is the cause of B_1, even if A is usually not accompanied by B, in terms of the fact that A is not usually found together with the other necessary conditions of B. Thus, the important point made by Scriven is that we assert that A_1 is the cause of B_1 even if we do not know that B has sufficient conditions. Although this is true, it is not a criticism of $G.T.$, unless it is taken to imply that "A is the cause of B" does not entail that B has a sufficient condition one of whose components is A. We stated this problem earlier, remarking that a strong or weak version of $G.T.$ is formulable, depending on whether or not one is willing to countenance the existence of statistical laws as entailed by causal sentences. We also stated at that point the most important consideration for us, to wit, that since we are interested in causality as the potential definiens of determinism, then if some form of the generality theory is true, we must accept only a strong version even if it is contrary to some usage. For if we do allow statistical laws, then an event's being caused will not suffice for its being determined.

But in our discussion of the activity theory of causation, we said that even if the deliberative process is in part non-deterministic, it may be that the stages are all causally linked.

101

It follows that if laws are involved at all, some must be statistical.

My own feeling is that the strong version is an idealization of principles and tendencies that are but partially realized in the everyday language of cause and effect. The idea is that if we surrender our belief that a relevant difference can be found between the case in which B follows A and the case in which B does not follow A, we would be more prone to revoke "A is the cause of B." Its retention is a function of our belief that relevant differences can be found between the two situations. Another way of formulating this belief is contained in the strong version's requirement that the sentence describing the effect be deducible from the law and all the sentences describing antecedent conditions (the deducibility-requirement). For then, if the effect is different (e.g., the ball is really kicked fifty-five yards rather than fifty), we must change the value assigned to at least one of the variables when we believed the effect to be fifty yards.

Alternatively, the point of the strong version may be stated by saying that, to the degree that one gives up deducibility, the selection of causally relevant factors becomes more and more arbitrary. (Of course, deducibility is not a relative matter. But, one may drop it and require, say at least 95% statistical laws. The point of the strong version is that as we liberalize the requirement on statistical laws, the claim of causal relevance becomes more and more absurd. Given that B and C are the only other conditions of D and that D occurs 50% of the time under those conditions, is it not absurd to suggest that A is another condition if its presence does not increase this probability at all?)

But it is a fact, I think, that the above principles are only partially realized, as I have said. For example, if A accompanies B 97% of the time and satisfies all the other conditions requisite for its being labeled the cause of B, then we may dismiss as "a quirk of nature," and without upsetting the proposition that A is the cause of B, the fact that there are isolated cases of $(A \cdot -B)$ which do not seem to differ in an important respect from the cases in which A accompanies B.

This desire for systematization plays an even more interesting role when we consider the powerful influence of theoretical assumptions. For example, we are even less inclined to surrender causal judgments (although no appropriate deterministic law can be discovered) if indirect evidence supports our belief that the causal judgment is correct. In other words, we may have a highly confirmed theory in accordance with which the factor we judged to be a cause was correct.

Such is the case in our deliberation example. We are prepared to acknowledge that Smith's awareness of the nature of his motives for choosing the law (prestige, the desire to please his father), his desire to be a poet, and his relative maturity are causally connected to his decision to be a poet. Evidently, this belief is in accordance with our imprecise, pre-scientific psychological theorizing. If we had to surrender this belief, we may have (there may be) no plausible replacement.

I do not mean to build into the definition of causal relevance psychological considerations (our attitudes, inclinations, beliefs). But it is true that, as we use this concept, it allows for cases in which the concept applies although deterministic laws may not. But if the violation of the principle embodied in the strong version is not minor, we are entitled to charge ascriptions of causal relevance with arbitrariness.

Hence, to adopt the strong version is to accept the everyday criterion, but in an idealized form. There is evidently nothing illegitimate about doing this so long as we know what we are doing. Thus, a definition of determinism in terms of causal law is possible even though it does some violence to

103

ordinary usage. The point is that no *principles* are violated—they are rather idealized. From here on, then, we shall accept the strong version.

GENERALITY THEORY IN PSYCHOLOGY DEFENDED
H. L. A. HART AND A. M. HONORÉ[61]

Many critics have concentrated their attacks on generality interpretations of three classes of causal propositions in psychology: (1) An agent performed a certain action because he had a certain desire, reason, or motive; (2) he had a physical reaction (gasp, start) because of some stimulus (pain, loud noise); (3) his reaction *to* or *at* some object (fear of the face in the window, amusement at a joke) was caused by that object.

Hart and Honoré offer an anti-generality analysis of a subclass of the first class. Interpersonal causation is defined by them as a transaction between A and B in which A's words or actions—in the form of persuasion, coercion, advice, command, or threat—are the reason or part of the reason why B acted. Thus, A's words or action must be known to B (who must understand the words if used), and B must make up his mind to act after the occurrence of A's words or actions.

Consider this case: Tom threatens to take John's life unless John gives Tom his money. John then decides to give Tom his money. When asked why he did this, John asserts, "I gave Tom the money because he threatened to take my life if I did not" (S).

Hart and Honoré claim that only in one way can S be disconfirmed by the introduction of independent information: if we possess a highly confirmed, law-like proposition according to which no individuals with characteristics $a, b, c,$ and d are amenable to threats of the kind Tom made,

---

[61] H. L. A. Hart and A. M. Honoré, *Causation in the Law* (Oxford: Clarendon Press, 1959), pp. 1-55.

and if John possesses characteristics *a, b, c,* and *d,* we may find it necessary to reject *S.* But, they continue, the appeal to this generalization merely indicates that John lied about or forgot the real reason for his action, which implies that John did at one point know the reason for his action, and no subsequent information can upset that. In other words, causal knowledge in such cases is acquired from the single case alone and commits one to nothing beyond the single case. After all, to ask someone his reason for acting is to ask him how he reached his decision to act. In such cases, his declarations are of primary importance. Indeed, they are so "primary" that subsequently introduced information can never show that John did not know the reason for his action; it can only show that he forgot the real reason or lied about it.

"John asserts *S*" and "John is neither lying (nor committing a verbal error) nor has he forgotten the reason for his decision" (*L*) entails, according to Hart and Honoré, the falsity of "No individuals with characteristics *a, b, c,* and *d* are amenable to threats of the kind Tom made, and John is an individual with characteristics *a, b, c,* and *d*" (*G*). Thus, if John asserts *S, G entails* ∼*L.* But this means that if John asserts *S,* there is no criterion which can be used to discover whether or not he is lying or has forgotten which is independent of the criteria used to confirm *G.* If there were, then the assertion of *S* together with the truth of *G* would not entail ∼*L* in which case John could assert *S* without lying, making a verbal error, or having forgotten and yet be mistaken since *G* is true. It follows that ∼*L* can only be used as an *ad hoc* hypothesis. It is introduced whenever sufficient evidence has been compiled to confirm *G,* and we wish to use *G* to refute *S.* In other words, it is a device to save the theory against counterinstances. It certainly does not mean what it ordinarily does—"In saying *S,* John lied (forgot, made a verbal error)" is taken to be logically inde-

105

pendent of G. Thus, the position of Hart and Honoré on the disconfirmation of S is untenable.

It may, of course, be a *fact* that L is always false when someone asserts an S-type proposition and the corresponding G-type proposition is true. Even if we say "almost always," the generality theory must explain how a person can be reasonably convinced that a proposition describing an interpersonal transaction is true since the proposition is supposed to entail the existence of a general fact. A number of considerations collectively provide the explanation.

First of all, John knows that there is a law that has as one of its antecedents "y threatens to take x's life" and has as its consequent "x decides to surrender his money to y" on the basis of evidence acquired prior to the confrontation.

Further, John is equipped with many generalizations which rule out as possible causes many other events simultaneous with the occurrence of the threat.

Besides, the fact that John may not be quite sure as to the relevance of certain factors, e.g., his belief that Tom desperately needs the money, does not render S dubious. Even if John intends S to be analyzed by $G.T._1$, the truth of S is independent of the relevance of this belief. If the belief is relevant, it may appear in the law as a conjunct separate from "y threatens to take x's life." But it may even appear as "x's life is threatened by a person y whom x believes desperately needs money" for $G.T._1$ prevails if the conjunct in the law only entails the sentence specifying the cause. $G.T._1$ simply demands the presence of the conditions whose descriptions enable deduction of effect-description from cause-description—not reference to the conditions by the cause-description. And if the belief is irrelevant, it will not appear in the law. But John's uncertainty regarding the exact content of the law does not make S less certain.

Again, John's past experience may even enable him to rule out with some conviction psychoanalytic alternatives to his causal account.

Finally, when John gives Tom the money, he may be simultaneously aware of the threat, but not aware of any other possible cause. Generally when a man is acting on a desire, he may be conscious of the desire as he acts.

When Hart and Honoré assert that the question "What is the reason that *A* acted?" is really the question "How did *A* reach his decision to act?" the suggestion that lends credence to their position is that the latter question is answered by an introspective inquiry, or by an inquiry into matters which are all at hand in the present case. If so, then it would appear that these causal propositions cannot in any way be general. Although it may be true, however, that from a phenomenal or introspective point of view, we do not ordinarily appeal to any information beyond the present case in order to specify the reason that we acted, it does not follow that the generality theory is false. As Hancock has pointed out, there are cases of physical causation in which we do not, from a phenomenal point of view, appeal to matters beyond the present case, e.g., "The pin-prick caused my pain."[62] Propositions describing cases of physical causation, however, are, according to Hart and Honoré, supposed to be inherently general. (We have not presented the details of their account of physical causation.)

It is not difficult to reconcile these cases with the generality theory. We would have to say that the entailments of *S* are not exhausted by the propositions which simply describe the individual facts of the case, e.g., "John understands Tom's words · John feels frightened · John believes that Tom means what he says · etcetera," although *S* may be asserted on the basis of a knowledge of the individual facts of the case. In order to prove our case, we must show that the additional information entailed by *S*, although it may never become part of John's "phenomenal field," satisfies the conditions of the generality theory. If we simply take as the

[62] Roger Hancock, "Interpersonal and Physical Causation," *The Philosophical Review,* LXXI (July, 1962), 374.

causal property "having one's life threatened," then $G.T._1$ claims basically that the causal proposition entails the existence of a law whose consequent is "x surrenders his money to the person threatening x (y)" and one of whose antecedents is "y threatens to take x's life." Moreover, this antecedent occurs essentially in the law, and the present case is an instance of the law. Hence, the causal proposition can be disproved by showing either that there is no such law or that there is and the present case is not an instance of it. The latter method may be conjoined with a demonstration that the present case is an instance of some other law. Another possibility is that the present case is an instance of more than one law relative to this consequent, i.e., overdetermination.

Let us take an example in order to illustrate one method of disconfirmation. John is a wealthy man who "cannot give of himself" to other people. In order to avoid recognizing this unpleasant fact, he is very generous. Thus, whenever he feels that he must give something to someone else, he gives money. He is also plagued with severe guilt feelings which he tries to alleviate in almost any way that he can. Now, Tom used to be a friend of John's; but John hurt Tom very deeply. John is plagued with such severe guilt feelings and feelings of obligation toward Tom that he can alleviate them only by surrendering everything to Tom. Thus, John would have given his money to Tom regardless of the threat Tom made on his life. Assuming that John is unaware of this fact, it is plausible for him to ascribe his surrender to the threat. Finally, in order to show that the event was not overdetermined, let us suppose that we have good evidence to believe that the absence of a certain type of masochism is a necessary condition for surrendering one's money under the assumption that the surrender will not accomplish certain specifiable goals, e.g., relief of severe guilt feelings. John, of course, is a masochist of this type.

The fact that accounts like the above are so rare explains our reliance on the account of interpersonal transaction given by the person whose action constitutes the effect. The advent of psychoanalysis has made us somewhat less reliant on the person's own account of such transactions. In effect, then, the acceptance of psychoanalysis is some evidence that the generality theory is true. If propositions describing interpersonal transactions are considered disconfirmed by psychoanalytic evidence, then we tacitly acknowledge the claims of the generality theory. It should be mentioned in this context that some writers believe that psychoanalytic accounts are not really causal.[63] But if so, then neither are accounts of interpersonal transactions. In other words, propositions of the form "(Part of) the reason why A did Q was C" (R) are sometimes incompatible with certain psychoanalytic evidence. Now, if R represents, as Hart and Honoré say, a causal proposition, then psychoanalysis must provide causal accounts in which case their acceptance is evidence for the generality theory. If, on the other hand, R is not a causal proposition, then perhaps psychoanalysis does not provide causal accounts; but in that case, R should be dismissed as irrelevant since we are discussing causality.

It is not uncommon to claim that R is not or does not entail a causal proposition. Although we are not here interested in that thesis, we shall later be interested in it when we discuss the possibility that human actions are determined.[64]

The belief in human freedom is often considered supported by the position that R is not causal. If such accounts of human behavior are not causal, then perhaps they do not

[63] A. C. MacIntyre, *The Unconscious: A Conceptual Analysis* ("Studies in Philosophical Psychology"; London: Routledge & Kegan Paul, 1958), pp. 60-61. There are causal accounts in psychoanalysis according to MacIntyre; but he does not consider the accounts in which we are interested as causal.

[64] See Chap. XIII.

even present a *prima facie* case against free will. But unless it can be shown that a causal account cannot be given or that *R*-type accounts are incompatible with any possible causal account, then the fact that such accounts are not causal is not interesting from the point of view of the free-will problem. Obviously, there are many true statements about human behavior that are not incompatible with free will. But if one is concerned about free will because of the possibility that determinism is true, the existence of such statements presents no comfort.

An argument against the generality theory is that, although psychoanalytic accounts may overthrow some propositions describing interpersonal transactions, they cannot overthrow all of them. For our ability to understand the psychoanalytic explanation presupposes acquaintance with simple "paradigmatic" cases of reason-giving which the psychoanalyst uses as a model to undermine other cases of reason-giving. But the generality theory claims that all causal propositions are theoretically disprovable.

If a paradigm case of reason-giving is simply a standard we use to judge the acceptability of other cases of reason-giving, I have nothing against the notion. But if a paradigm case is one that cannot possibly turn out to be wrong, or if the term "standard" is supposed to imply that it cannot turn out to be wrong (I do not use the word with this implication), then the notion of a paradigm is unacceptable and naïve. We would not consider as a paradigm a situation in which a psychotic girl sincerely claims that she murdered her parents because they would not give her money for bubble-gum, because we have excellent reasons derived from general considerations about human beings which indicate that she must be mistaken. Thus we consider a case paradigmatic only when we are reasonably convinced that subsequent information will not disconfirm the proposed causal proposition. But we may be wrong.

Moreover, there is something strange about the claim that

a causal proposition that cannot be disconfirmed is a paradigm for the use of causal language if causal propositions are normally discomfirmable. Whether or not a class of propositions is disconfirmable by subsequent evidence may be a reflection of meaning. If so, then the meaning of "cause" may be different in the paradigm cases from what it is in the other cases. But then the claim that the cases are paradigms is absurd. To say that no causal propositions are capable of disconfirmation, on the other hand, is also absurd, given the original assumption, viz., that the capacity of psychoanalysts to disconfirm causal propositions presupposes the existence of paradigm cases.

This point may be and has been generalized in the following way: the choice of objects as paradigms is problematic, for then the claim that they have the paradigmatic property is analytic whereas the claim that other objects also have it is synthetic. Again, though, there is nothing harmful in making the point that unclear cases are often adjudicated by appeal to clear ones, just so long as philosophers do not get their puritanical hands on the word "clear."

An interesting rebuttal to the claim that psychoanalytically grounded rejections of reason-giving accounts support a *G.T.* analysis for at least some propositions describing interpersonal transactions is based on the feeling that these rejections are not total. There must be a sense in which the girl who said she murdered her parents because they would not give her money for bubble-gum was giving her reason. The "real" or "underlying" reason does not completely replace the given reason—it simply provides more insight and greater explanatory power. We can see how the stated reason fits into the large picture provided by the "real" reason. Surely the stated reason has more to do with the action than a desire that the girl may have had that was completely irrelevant, e.g., a normal desire for a glass of water that happened to be present at the time.

But just as the real reason may show how the given reason

111

is, in some sense, a reason, it may also show how completely irrelevant it is. Or it may show nothing about the given reason, and we disprove its irrelevance independently: the girl saw something on television that unconsciously led her to produce this excuse. If the real reason is explanatory, it may explain the belief (mistaken) that the given reason is the reason.

There are, of course, many cases where the stated reason is a genuine reason even if another reason is deeper. The compulsive hand-washer is, perhaps, motivated by the belief that his hands are dirty even if a deeper motivation is also present. If so, he would not wash his hands were the belief that they are dirty absent. It does not follow that there is a reason-giving proposition which is immune from subsequent rejection. For, since there is a genuine distinction between a given reason that activates and one that is simply an excuse, any stated reason may turn out to be simply an excuse. We may discover that the person would have acted in the way that he did even if the desire given as the reason had been absent.

The intimacy between reason and action that is sometimes alleged to give a person direct and incorrigible knowledge of the relation has been argued for on the following basis. It is impossible to understand the relation between a reason, say a desire, and an action done out of that desire as a normal causal relation that has features like generality, etc., because "P performs action a out of desire d" says more than and cannot, therefore, be analyzed as "P's doing a is caused by desire d."*

But is it not absurd to suppose that the man who has not had water for three days might be wrong when he attributes his grasping the glass of water to extreme thirst? Yes it would

---

* This question is a large one we shall discuss in the context of the general possibility of psychological determinism. See Chapter XIII.

be absurd—as absurd as it would be to think that the football is moving from some cause other than its being kicked.

I would go so far as to say that a man might theoretically be mistaken even if he simply says that he acted for *some* reason. My position sounds strange because commonsense accounts of intentional actions are almost invariably in terms of reasons. In those cases in which no conscious reason is present and we do not consider the possibility of unconscious reasons, common sense just lets the matter rest. We thus do not have at hand a stock of causal, non-reason accounts of actions. We must turn to the psychologist, who may help us by suggesting causal factors such as subtle environmental cues, conditioning, complicated learning mechanisms, and physiological states. For example, Maier has shown that problem-solving behavior is often aided by the presentation to the subject of clues that give him the right direction or slant on the problem, even though they do not tell him how to do any particular feature of the problem.[65] This conclusion is in no way upset if the subject is not aware of the value of this stimulus and/or the subject gives as a reason for his success some desire or motive (e.g., strong desire to please experimenter) that may be worthless. Psychologists do not have to be Freudians to recognize causal elements in behavior of which the subject is unaware. And since these causal elements need not be motives or reasons,[66] it is quite possible to suppose that the reason a person gives for his behavior may be mistaken for it has no reasons. I conclude that Hart and Honoré have not shown that causal propositions describing interpersonal transactions require an analysis incompatible with the generality theory; and if reason-giving

[65] N. R. F. Maier, "Reasoning in Humans: On Direction," *Journal of Comparative Psychology,* X (1930), 115-44.

[66] There is, of course, a broader sense of the term "reason" so that these factors would count as *the* reason for success since they explain it. But they are not reasons in the sense expressed by "That was my reason for doing it."

generally is a species of causal explanation, a generality analysis is appropriate to it.

INTENTIONALITY

Much recent discussion of mental causation has received its impetus and form from Miss Anscombe's comments in *Intention*.[67] There, the term "mental cause" was introduced to designate a special causal relation that is allegedly non-Humean. I shall not undertake a detailed critique of the relevant sections of this book for, with one exception, such of the book's claims about causation as bear on the generality theory have been dealt with. Criticisms of Miss Anscombe's views along lines I generally agree with may be found in the middle section of "Mental Cause and Effect" by J. Teichmann.[68]

In the previous section we dealt extensively with the first class of causal propositions in psychology, viz., cases of reason-giving, that critics of the generality theory have pointed to. That a generality analysis applies to the second class, viz., reports of reactions to stimuli, may be seen by considering the following case: I assert sincerely, "I gasped because of the sharp pain." It will suffice in defense of the generality theory to show how this proposition can be refuted.

Suppose I wake up one morning and discover that I have a strange malady. Every half-hour I find myself (involuntarily) gasping, exactly as if I had just experienced a sharp pain. After a while, I form the expectation that I will gasp shortly before each seizure. Near the end of the day, an irate neighbor comes up to me and, just about the time I expect to gasp, he punches me in the stomach. I experience a sharp pain and gasp. But I say to my neighbor, "If you thought I gasped because of the pain you caused, you are mistaken."

---

[67] Anscombe, pp. 13-25.
[68] *Mind*, LXX (January, 1961), 36-52.

I then describe my malady to him, only to gasp in the middle of the description. I then realize that he had struck me only twenty-five minutes after the previous seizure and that I had really gasped because of the pain of the blow.

There remains the third class of causal propositions in psychology (this being the exception mentioned above in the remarks about Miss Anscombe). Unique problems for the generality theory are raised by the fact that mental states take objects, i.e., by the intentional features of mental activity.

The problem for the generality theorist is stated well by Pears:[69] we must consider those mental states whose objects are known for certain by the person in that state. Every argument against the generality theory is based on an example of this kind. One can, as Pears points out, order mental states along a corrigibility continuum. At one end is depression, a mental state whose object may be mistakenly identified, and at the other end amusement, whose object cannot fail to be known. I am in fundamental agreement with Pears' detailed defense of the thesis of the corrigibility of reports of objects of depression.

Since the identification of the cause of some state is guided by identification of its object, the possibility of mistake with respect to an object transfers to the identification of its cause. Hence, problems for *G.T.* are created only by states whose objects are infallibly known, such as amusement.

Pears suggests several features of this continuum that might be relevant to the corrigibility variation. One is the length of reaction. Depression is a steady state, while amusement is relatively momentary. If a state lasts, it seems plausible that one may be wrong concerning its object. A second feature concerns the necessity for an object. Depression may

---

[69] D. F. Pears, "Causes and Objects of Some Feelings and Psychological Reactions," *Philosophy of Mind,* ed. Stuart Hampshire (New York: Harper & Row, 1966), pp. 143-69.

115

be free-floating; but amusement must have an object. Hence, a person cannot retract a statement concerning the object of amusement as readily as in the case of depression, for *some* candidate must fill this position. It seems to me that this fact is the key to the solution. Pears, however, disagrees with the solution I shall offer.

As Pears says, amusement is the best test case. For if *G.T.* is not upset by this example, no other will disturb it.

The problem is this: identification of the object of amusement is incorrigible. In the case of amusement, the object is always a causal factor, or simply the cause. In fact, to say that some remark amused me entails that the remark caused or was part of the cause of my being amused. But then, since the object-statement is incorrigible, so must the causal statement be. *G.T.,* therefore, is wrong, at least in some cases.

Notice that this argument does not confuse the notions of cause and object. Some states, such as free floating depression, have causes, but no objects. Statements about the cause of states imply nothing about their objects. The argument requires only that some object statements entail causal statements. I reject this argument because I reject this premise. I shall state my reasons, consider why we may be led to think it true, and assess Pears' arguments for it.

Being amused is like eating in that both *must* have objects. If I am amused, there must be something I am amused about; if I am eating, there must be something I am eating. Let us use the expressions "object of amusement" and "food" for the general object of these states. Furthermore, there are states closely associated with these that do not require objects (being in a good mood, making eating motions).

Suppose Mr. Jones sets out to starve Mrs. Jones by locking her in a room he believes to contain no food. Several hours later his child reports that he just saw his mother eating an apple. "How can that be?" asks Mr. Jones. "There was actually food in the room," replies his son. (Mrs. Jones had hidden some there for such a contingency.) One might say that the availability of food explains the fact that Mrs. Jones ate, although it is also a logical consequence of that fact. Thus, in certain contexts a logically necessary condition of some event may be considered (part of) the explanation of that event.

As to the *cause* of Mrs. Jones' eating, one would normally cite hunger. But there is nothing objectionable in saying that the presence of food was the cause. (It *is* a condition.) This use of the term "cause" clearly violates *G.T.*, for causal propositions become logical truths, given the existence of the effect. Since a determinist is not interested in this special use of "cause," let us stipulate that the generality theory be construed to apply only to causal propositions in which the cause is not a logically necessary condition of the effect. (The claim that causes necessitate their effects is not involved here.)

"Cause" does mean "logically necessary condition" in: (1) "An object of amusement caused my amusement (at an object of amusement)"; (2) "An object of amusement caused my amusement at your remark"; (3) "Your remark caused my amusement at your remark." For in each of these, the existence of the cause follows logically from the existence of the effect.

Consider, then, (4) "Your remark caused my amusement (at an object of amusement)." This move is recommended by Pears in order to avoid the problem. He says: "Nor is it any good saying that hearing the remark or thinking about it cannot be regarded as causes of the person's amusement because his amusement cannot be separated from these events. For it is only necessary to describe his amusement in a more abstract, general way that makes no references to these events, and then it can be regarded as their contingent effect."[70] Hence, the only genuine, i.e., contingent,

[70] Ibid., p. 161.

causal proposition that follows from "Your remark amused me" is one that is compatible with "Your remark did not amuse me," for (4) in itself may be true because your remark, which did not amuse me, reminded me of an amusing story.

(Notice another interesting fact about Pears' position. Pears' view implies that "Amusement is always caused" is a necessary truth, for amusement necessarily has an object and, in the case of amusement, it is necessary that the object be also the cause. Hence, it is necessary that amusement have a cause. But Pears may not find this conclusion disturbing.)

Is there something unique about amusement, or is there another way to explain the fact that an apparently causal proposition follows from an incorrigible one?

The latter alternative is the right one. Suppose that soldiers are marching near an oak tree. There is no apparent causal implication yet. At most, one has a relation (nearness) between an object and an event. But it is true that the marching of soldiers is a (logically necessary) condition of the oak tree's being near the marching of soldiers. If one wishes to drop the logical connection, there is no difficulty: one simply says that the marching of soldiers is a condition of the oak tree's being near the marching of men. It would, of course, sound incredible if the word "cause" replaced "condition" in this sentence. Nonetheless, the logic is similar. Knowing that a relation holds, we are always able to derive a contingent proposition that asserts that one thing is a condition of something else. Of course, we are inclined to think that the marching of soldiers is not a condition of the oak tree's being near the marching of men in the same sense that oxygen is a condition of fire. We want to say that it is a *term* of the relation, not a condition of it. But we *can* say this since the relation "is next to" is extensional. That is, if a is next to b and $b = c$, then a is next to c. Since this marching of men = this marching of soldiers, then this marching of soldiers is a term of the relation.

But this does not help very much. "Your remark" is a term of the relation "is amused by"; if Pears is right, though, the term in *this* case is also the cause.

In one sense, however, a term of some relation is *always* a condition of it. For if the soldiers had not been marching, the oak tree would *not* be next to the marching of men. Or, to take an example similar to amusement, if there had been no girl walking down the street, then Jones would not now be looking at a girl. (It is similar because of its intentional character and because we would readily say that the presence of the girl caused Jones to look at her.) If the lengthy battle of Waterloo had not occurred, then Wolfgang would not have fought in the Battle of Waterloo.

We can establish these condition propositions without establishing the truth of ordinary causal propositions. All we have to do is establish the relational proposition and an identity proposition (this marching of men is the marching of soldiers, this girl is a girl walking down the street, the battle of Waterloo is the lengthy battle of Waterloo, the object of amusement is your remark). Now causal knowledge *may* be required to establish the relational proposition. You may not be sure whether I am amused at your remark or at your tie, and you may want to appeal to your general causal knowledge to come to a decision. But *I* know what I am amused about, in the same way that I know what I am looking at without appeal to general causal knowledge. That is, because of my special position, I know immediately the truth of certain relational propositions. I then derive a causal or condition proposition by citing the second term of the relation as the cause and a generalized relation as the effect. *But the point to be emphasized is that this derivation can be performed on any relational proposition.*

I would, therefore, go farther than Pears and say that there is a very large class of propositions that are in a sense "causal," but which are contrary to *G.T.* To do this, however, is to take the sting out of these cases. For if we can demonstrate that there is nothing peculiar to the intentional context, we may look at this class in a very general way and find reason to omit it from consideration. In fact, it is easy to establish this hypothetical. Let us do that first and then return to the consideration of the antecedent.

First of all, there is something contrived about the way these propositions are obtained. We feel that in the case of some of them (and we are supposing that the intentional examples are not special), we are just expanding our non-causal information concerning the terms of the relation.

Another important consideration is that nothing is lost if we exclude these cases. Consider again "The girl's walking down the street causes Jones to look at the girl." All the information contained in this proposition is derivable from a normal causal proposition "Jones looks at the girl because she is pretty" and a non-causal identity proposition "The girl Jones is looking at is walking down the street." (It is improper here to claim that the latter proposition is tacitly causal on the ground that the existence of the subject as characterized presupposes the very sort of causal relation we are excluding. For since this claim is indisputably false in non-intentional cases—"The men marching near the oak tree are soldiers"—the claim supposes that intentional contexts are special.)

I conclude that if there really is nothing peculiar to the intentional context, we may ignore these bizarre condition propositions. If someone wants to say that the generality theory has been shown to be false, he may. But for our purposes, *G.T.* is "still" true. Are there, then, any reasons to think that intentional contexts are special?

There is the fact that we find it natural to use the word "cause" for the relation between the remark and the amusement as well as for the relation between the girl's walking and Jones's looking. Several facts may help to explain this.

We can produce amusement by making a remark, and the girl can produce glances by walking. But this is not a sufficient explanation, for the soldiers can "produce" the fact of being near the oak tree by walking near it. The artificiality of the expression designating the product, though, suggests a second feature.

The expressions "is amused" and "is looking" are grammatically self-sufficient. Thus, the necessity for objects is hidden grammatically. We are, therefore, more likely to look for causes, since "being amused" and "is looking" appear to designate simple states of the person. When, on the other hand, the relation is spelled out, we tend to use the word "cause" less in the explanation of the relation. The remark *caused* his amusement; but some feature of the remark *explains* why it amused him. It sounds odd to speak of the cause of the soldiers marching near the oak tree; but we may ask for an explanation of this fact.

But, it may be objected, there is good reason for this grammatical distinction. "Being amused" is, in a sense or in part, an intrinsic property of the person, whereas "being next to an oak tree" is strictly relational. Hence, it is legitimate to speak of the cause of amusement, but not of the cause of being near an oak tree.

This point is an interesting one. We do think of the remark as one thing and the amusement, a property of the listener, as another; but we do not think of nearness to the soldiers, a property of the oak tree, as distinct from the soldiers in the same way.

First of all, there is, once more, nothing unique to the intentionality of mental states here. Eating must have an object; but we think of the apple as one thing and of the eating as another.

The important point is this, however: there is excellent

reason for thinking in these ways, for being amused includes activities that *are* logically distinct from its object, e.g., smiling. Likewise eating includes chewing, salivating, and similar operations, and these are logically distinct from the object of eating. Hence, although activities like eating and being amused must take objects, they involve activities that do not take objects and are, therefore, logically distinct from them. If, however, we try to drop the suggestion of a connection between cause and effect, we drop as well the suggestion of infallibility. That is, if smiling is just a certain type of facial expression, then my belief that it is produced by your remark can be upset in ways similar to those described in the pain-gasp case. When we think otherwise, we think of smiling not as a purely distinct phenomenon or bodily activity, but rather as an object-taking characteristic. One may speak of smiling *at* a joke just as one speaks of being amused at a joke.

Pears agrees with these remarks for the case of "The explosion made me jump." He says: "For if the statement simply reported a reflex movement, it would be vulnerable to parallel negative instances; and if, on the other hand, we regard it as immune from parallel negative instances, and so credit the person himself with a high degree of certainty about it, it seems that this can only be because it carries the implication that the explosion was the object of his reaction of shock."[71]

If, as seems to be the case, Pears' analysis here works as well for "Your remark amused me," then the fact that there are *bona fide* causal relations involved is irrelevant, for these causal relations are in accordance with the generality theory. But their existence is probably a partial explanation of the use of the language of cause and effect here.

Let me make it plain that I do not mean to imply that amusement has no cause: it is indeed a state that is produced by causes. My amusement at your remark may be caused

[71] Ibid., pp. 150-51.

by features of the remark (of which I may be ignorant), by the way you said what you did, and so on.

But can I not be amused at the way you said what you did, for example? If so, then the way you said it would not, in our view here, be the cause. This is no problem for, if I am amused at the way you said something, the genuine cause does lie elsewhere. The cause may be some humorous association (perhaps unconscious) between your manner and certain past experiences of mine. If I report that I am amused at your remark because I am amused at the way you said it, no problems arise for *G.T.* because the "because" here is logical, i.e., the explanans logically entails the explanandum.

What then is Pears' basic reason for believing that the relation between amusement and object is causal? He says that if the causal implication is dropped, then the object report "would mean no more than that he merely happened to feel amused when he heard or thought about the remark."[72] There is, Pears says, a weak sense of "about" that is applicable if I hear or think about something *with* amusement. When I say "I am amused about your remark," however, I obviously mean more than just "I am amused [weak] about your remark."

But this argument will not do for several reasons. First of all, I do not think that "about [weak]" is an intelligible notion. Pears says that amusement must take an object. When I hear something *with* amusement or feel amused when I hear it, what am I amused about? If Pears says "nothing," he can only be referring to the non-intentional effect of the remark, e.g., laughing, feeling good, and so on. If so, it is simply not the case that "I am amused [strong] about your remark" minus "Your remark caused me amusement" equals "I am amused [weak] about your remark."

[72] Ibid., p. 160.

That dull remark of yours always reminds me of an amusing story.

So the addition of a causal relation between the remark and the amusement does not convert the weak sense of "about" into the strong sense. And if Pears rejects my reading of his weak sense on the grounds that it is too weak, the burden is on Pears to produce an interpretation that will satisfy the equation "about (weak) + cause = about (strong)." I do not think this can be done and am, therefore, reinforced in my conviction that the object relation is not an implicitly causal one.

I can say nothing constructive about the object relation. But if, for example, all the statements that contain reference only to "intrinsic" properties of me and the water do not entail "I drink the water," this is no reason to construe this relational proposition as also causal.

I have chosen to use Pears' article as a springboard for this discussion because the issues he raises provide a real test for the generality theory and it displays a respect for the Humean conception of causality not usually found in critiques of this conception.

Pears does not simply reject the generality theory on the basis of his position regarding object and cause. He thinks that our present concept of amusement does not admit of a Humean interpretation; but one can describe conditions under which the present concept would be changed, in such a way that reports of objects of amusement would become fallible. In fact, one can imagine conditions that would assimilate amusement completely to depression so that amusement would sometimes not even have an object, although the person might think it has. Let me say a few words about this contingency, for it seems to suppose the thesis of the identity of object and cause.

We are to imagine that amusement at objects can be produced by drugs, and that these drugs work in such a way that people become amused even if they would not otherwise have done so. Pears says that we would not accept the person's object report because we know the cause lies elsewhere, which suggests that if the object really were the remark, it would also be the cause.

In the first place, we must suppose that amusement does not appear differently to the person. For example, it does not appear to him that he simply starts laughing when a remark is made; it appears to him that he is laughing at the remark. Besides, the remark is still a necessary condition of amusement even if we do not call it the object: the drug works only when the remark is made. Finally, it is not clear that we would not call the remark the object. We might say that people are amused at certain things for reasons that are unusual or unknown to the person. But even if we say that the remark is neither object nor cause, our reason, I think, is that psychological conditions play no role in the explanation of the amusement. In other words, the choice of a remark by the drug-giver to trigger amusement is independent of psychological traits of the person. Hence, a dramatic change in the explanation of amusement is being supposed to take place. The remark does become less important to the amusement. Any remark would do if we had the right drug.

Thus, it is not that we are less inclined to think of the remark as object because we are less inclined to think of it as cause. It is rather that we suppose that if I am amused *at* the remark, it must be that certain *features* of the remark have an effect, so to speak, on my psyche. Thus, the normal object of amusement does not provide an important starting point for the explanation of amusement. So we should rather say that we are less inclined to think of the remark as object because we are less inclined to think of its *features* as cause. This seems closer to the truth and is in line with the general view I advocate.

THROUGHOUT THIS discussion, I have avoided the numerous claims that take the form: "The relation between X and Y is not really causal." We have been concerned with whether or not causal propositions are to be understood as the generality theory says. Thus, we must consider all clear cases of causation. We have considered some (reasons-action) that are debatable as cases of causal relations. The issues cannot always be kept distinct, for one sometimes hears the argument that a relation is not really causal, because it violates the generality theory.[73]

But we have examined sufficient examples and kinds of examples to convince ourselves either of the truth of the generality theory or of the necessity to consider it true for our purposes.

We conclude that a definition of determinism in terms of the concept of law is the only feasible one, a conclusion based on all our considerations thus far in this book.

[73] See, for example, Stuart Hampshire, *Freedom of the Individual* (New York: Harper & Row, 1965), p. 100.

PART 2

A DEFINITION OF DETERMINISM

V. THE STRUCTURE OF A DEFINITION

WE KNOW NOW THAT determinism should be defined in terms of the concept of law. Let us temporarily put aside the many questions about this concept and ask what the definition will look like. We may see the problems if we begin with the simple statement: All events are governed by law.

First of all, the scope of the definition put this way would be too narrow. All events involve the presence of some change. But determinists want to say that states in which no changes occur are as determined as states in which changes do operate. For example, the position of a hypothetical body at rest which has no forces acting upon it is clearly determined. It would be absurd to cite this case as a difficulty for determinism, yet it is in fact cited by those who interpret determinism as a thesis about events. If determinism is about events, and hence about changes, it is reasonable to say that whatever is determined has a cause—but if our hypothetical body is at rest with no forces acting upon it, no cause is involved, unless one wants to recognize negative causes. If, on the other hand, the body is moving uniformly—with no forces acting upon it—there will be an event having no apparent cause. Both types of case are easily handled by a determinist, for each body is in a state subject to deterministic laws. If only events are determined, a body at rest presents a difficulty for a determinist. If causes or determining factors are necessary, a body at rest or in uniform motion is a problem. But these are difficulties that can be avoided by not using the concept of event in the definition of determinism.

Workman has argued that certain events are neither determined nor undetermined.[1] He takes the position that determination requires a cause. One cannot, however, assign a cause to the behavior of the hypothetical particles described by Newton's first axiom ("Every body continues in its state of rest or of uniform motion in a straight line, except in so far as it is compelled by forces to change that state."), since this axiom describes the way particles normally behave, and causal explanation is appropriate only when deviations from normality are found. The behavior of these particles is "adetermined."

Even if Workman is right about the appropriateness of causal explanations, one need not view the behavior of such particles as "adetermined." The existence of such particles—if it were possible—would be confirmation of determinism rather than a refutation or limitation of it. One way to cover these cases is to drop the demand that only events be determined. In that case, the body at rest is included, and one will not necessarily be looking for a cause for genuine events. (This is not to say that a body in uniform motion is uncaused in the sense that there are no laws which, together with information about the body's mechanical state, enable deduction of its path to be made. For there are. But we do not think of the antecedent mechanical state as "cause." What I am suggesting is that even if we do not use the term "cause," it is irrelevant to determinism. The path of the body is determined because there are the appropriate laws and antecedent states.)

Another problem connected with our proposed definition of determinism is that many would say that achievements, for example, are not events. Smith crossed the line at a certain time; but his winning the race is atemporal. I am not sure this is correct, for his crossing the line may be identical

[1] Rollin W. Workman, "Two Extralogical Uses of the Principle of Induction," *Philosophical Studies*, XIII (January, 1962), 28.

under certain conditions with his winning the race. Of course, it does not follow from the fact that he crossed the line ahead of everyone else that he won, for he may be disqualified. But the identity of events does not demand deducibility relations among the various descriptions of the event. Smith's raising his arm is identical with his raising his arm one foot above his head; but the former description does not entail the latter. Moreover, one can ask: "When did he win the race?"

If, however, there are good arguments to show that achievements are not events, then these are also good arguments to show that determinism is not a thesis about events. For achievements are surely the sorts of things determinists would say are determined.

Finally, an objection to the definition as it stands that is conclusive in itself is implicit in the fact that event identity is extensional. Smith's having lunch is identical with Smith's eating a ham sandwich; but "Smith has lunch" is logically independent of "Smith eats a ham sandwich." Now, although it may be determined that Smith ate lunch at a certain time, it may be undetermined whether he ate a ham sandwich at that time. Hence, it is not events *simpliciter* that are determined, but rather events under a description. Or we may prefer to say that facts are determined, since the fact that Jones eats lunch is a different one from the fact that Jones eats a ham sandwich.

But this raises the question: For which facts or for which descriptions of events must a determinist say there exists the appropriate law? For example, take the event of Smith's throwing a baseball; some other descriptions of that event might be:

1. The shortest man in Wyoming throws a ball.
2. Smith throws a beautiful ball.
3. Smith manifests his disposition to play ball.
4. Smith throws a four-year-old baseball.

5. Smith throws a ball or the moon is made out of green cheese.

Obviously, no simple answer can be given. We must examine these and other descriptions and formulate a position accordingly. But what we will actually be doing is examining sentences, classifying them, and passing on them as regards the necessity for a determinist to require that laws govern what is described by these sentences. But, if we have to do this anyway, it may be advisable to shift the definition of determinism to the metalanguage, i.e., to formulate it as a thesis about sentences.

We may thus avoid decisions concerning the semantical interpretation of deterministic accounts. Are they about facts or events under descriptions? What are facts or events under descriptions? These are legitimate questions; but a determinist *qua* determinist need not be concerned with them. He need not make ontological commitments that some would consider dubious (e.g., facts).

It may be replied that there are ontological issues on the metalinguistic level, too: What are sentences? Can we restrict ourselves to inscriptions and utterances or must we think of sentences as types? Or ought we to shift entirely to the language of propositions? But we have these problems anyway, for we must provide an ontological interpretation for laws. Are they inscriptions, sentence types, or propositions? We have insisted that the notion of law appear in the definition and, so, we have this question. There is, therefore, no point in burdening ourselves with additional semantical and ontological problems.

Another advantage in formulating our definition of determinism as a thesis about sentences is that the notion of being governed by a law is explicable only in terms of relations between sentences or propositions. To say that an event under a description is governed by some law is to say that the sentence that specifies the description under which the event is taken is entailed by laws together with other sentences. Hence, we cannot avoid reference to the sentences for which deterministic accounts are provided anyway.

Finally, it seems to me that one understands completely which facts a determinist must demand a deterministic account for only if one knows which sentences he must demand a deterministic account for. Look at the list of alternative descriptions of the event of Smith's throwing a baseball. We do not have a clear concept of "fact (or event under description) for which a deterministic account may be demanded" unless we do the job of sentence classification. And if we think in terms of sentences, we are more aware of the complexity of our task. We recognize many different types of sentence, but make much grosser distinctions on the extra-linguistic level (e.g., general, negative, singular, disjunctive facts). There is, therefore, heuristic value in a metalinguistic definition.

We shall, therefore, try to formulate determinism as a thesis about sentences. The first question we face is: For which sentences would there have to be deterministic accounts if determinism were true? I cannot hope here even to approach a complete answer to this question. But I shall try to give some idea of the scope of this class of sentences by an eliminative procedure. We shall suppose that all sentences are in the class unless ruled out. What follows below are candidates for omission. But often candidacy is rejected and they remain in.

It will be helpful, in this examination, to make a distinction in the class of admitted sentences between primary and secondary sentences. A primary sentence is a sentence whose admission will be justified on the ground that the traditional doctrine of determinism supposed it necessary to include this sentence. Now, I see no objection to construing a deterministic account of some sentence as a deterministic account of each logical consequence of that sentence, and this proposal

133

will, therefore, be adopted for the sake of simplicity. Any sentence whose inclusion can be justified in this way will be called a secondary sentence. Although all primary sentences are also secondary (the simplest of several reasons being that a sentence is its own logical consequence), some secondary sentences will not be primary.

This does introduce an indefinite amount of artificiality. If "P" and "Q" are admissible, then so are "$P \equiv Q$," "$P \vee Q$," "P or the moon is made out of green chese," etcetera. Also, "P" may have nothing to do with "Q." But artificiality alone is not a high price to pay for theoretical simplicity:

1. False sentences.

2. Logically necessary sentences and sentences of the form "$Px_1, x_2, \ldots, x_n$" where this is a logical truth if the designated objects exist.

3. Non-singular sentences.

4. Sentences that do not specify a time at or during which the predicate applies to the individual(s).

5. Sentences with evaluative predicates.

6. Sentences with negative predicates.

7. Sentences with numerical predicates.

8. Sentences with temporal predicates.

9. Sentences with philosophical predicates.

10. Sentences with psychological predicates.

11. Sentences with novelty predicates.

12. Sentences with observational, dispositional, or theoretical predicates.

13. Sentences with causal predicates.

False Sentences: These are ruled out, since determinism applies only to the actual world.

Logically necessary sentences and sentences of the form "$Px_1, x_2, \ldots, x_n$" where this is a logical truth if the designated objects exist: These are ruled out for obvious reasons as primary although *all* will be included as secondary since

134

they will be logical consequences of primary sentences. (An example of the second kind is "John is tall or not tall." It is not strictly a logical truth for John may not exist. But evidently we wish to rule it out.)

Non-singular sentences: We want to rule out general (universal and existential) sentences as primary although many will be included as secondary. We do not, however, rule out a sentence whose predicate has more than one place (is relational).

Since the sentences are true, the singular term designates a real individual. Ought there, however, to be restrictions on the way individuals are designated? No. Suppose John is a tall mathematician. It is determined, let us suppose, that John is tall and that he is a mathematician; but there is no law connecting these two characteristics of John. If we demand a deterministic account of "John is a mathematician," ought we also to demand a deterministic account of "That tall person (or the tall person who is married to the second daughter of the President of General Motors) is a mathematician," if John is the designated tall person? I see no reason for not making this demand, once we acknowledge, as we shall, that the account may be given by deducing from laws and certain conditions one sentence, and then substituting any individual constant in that sentence for any other that designates the same individual. We may then also demand a deterministic account of "That P is a Q" where "P" is a predicate that we shall later reject as inadmissible *qua* predicate of the sentence. For there will be an innocuous way of referring to that P (say, "that R") and if we can provide a deterministic account of "That R is a Q," we can also provide, in accordance with the stipulation just mentioned, a deterministic account of "That P is a Q."

Ought there, then, to be some restrictions on the kinds of things that can be individuals? No. It is not necessary for a determinist *qua* determinist to get embroiled in these meta-

135

physical issues. For example, consider the sense data/physical object discussion. Some say that sense data are genuine individuals; others reject the entire language of sense data. Evidently, the question whether or not the language should contain names for individual sense data depends on the resolution of this dispute. To get into this dispute, however, would take us far afield. It should be mentioned, however, that the translatability position (physical object sentences are translatable into sense data sentences, nation sentences are translatable into individual person sentences, person sentences are translatable into bodily or mental event sentences, etc.) allows for names on both levels. For if, say, nation sentences are translatable into individual person sentences, then there is a mutual deducibility relation and nation sentences will thereby be included as secondary. The names of nations are, therefore, admissible. If, however, the translatability thesis fails, then we shall *still* need names on both levels if sentences on both levels are true. For example, it is not implausible to say that translatability of physical object sentences into sense data sentences fails because sense data language is confused or because there are no such things as sense data. If so, then we ought not to have the "names" of sense data in our language for there are no true sentences about sense data. But it would be difficult to maintain that the failure (if it is a failure) to translate nation sentences into individual person sentences is due to the fact that nation language is confused or that there are no nations. If translatability fails, therefore, we shall need names for both nations and individual persons. There will be true sentences on both levels and the levels are logically independent of each other.

We ought, therefore, to be liberal about name types, for the inclusion of two types does not prejudge the issue of reducibility; but it does prejudge the issue of clarity or existence. That is, if, say, we have names of sense data, we ought to have a clear idea of what it is we have names of, and there ought to be some candidates. Evidently, there is nothing more a *determinist* can say about this matter.

Suppose we substitute for "John" in "John is a mathematician" the expression "That man whose becoming a mathematician was undetermined." This is ruled out by the second restriction. But what about "That man who made an undetermined decision"? That is, if the resultant sentence is true, then determinism is false. Although a determinist believes that there are no (true) sentences like this, I see no reason to place a priori restrictions on their inclusion. If we find that they are included, then, if the truth of determinism is our sole interest (it is not), our inquiry ends.

There is one weak restriction demanded by the next point, viz., that individuals be part of the temporal order. That is, the predicates that apply to individuals apply at certain times, and the individuals are of a sort that can acquire and lose properties during the course of time. Hence, we will not allow names of abstract individuals like propositions and properties. Nor will we allow metalinguistic names since sentences and terms are not part of the temporal order. We will, of course, allow names of inscriptions and utterances.

Sentences that do not specify a time at or during which the predicate applies to the individual(s): It is determined that the body be at that position *at a certain time.* Hence, we want sentences that specify date.

We thus admit only true, contingent, singular, and temporal sentences as primary. But many sentences that meet these formal criteria contain inadmissible predicates.

Evaluative predicates: Traditionally, determinists did not have evaluative predicates in mind. They did not think of a painting's being beautiful as determined, but rather its having certain colors, shapes, textures, etc., and the viewer as having certain reactions. I think tradition can be maintained.

Surely evaluative predicates are automatically excluded if

137

the non-cognitivists are right, for they say that sentences that contain them are neither true nor false. But if "That painting is beautiful" is neither true nor false, it is excluded by our first restriction.

Nor will naturalists be slighted if evaluative predicates are excluded, for their view is that there exists a purely descriptive equivalent for each evaluative predicate. Hence, no content is lost if evaluative predicates are dropped. In fact, though, evaluative predicates are included as secondary if naturalism is true.

But what about non-naturalists? For them, evaluative predicates are also descriptive. But if we decide to drop evaluative predicates, do we not reject *a priori* the claim of the non-naturalist, to wit, that some of these terms designate objective characteristics of the objects to which they are applied that are not designated by any other descriptive predicate?

Suppose the non-naturalists are right about the term "good." Now it is impossible to suppose that all characteristics of good objects are determined, except their goodness, for goodness is necessarily connected to a subset of these other characteristics. It is absurd to suppose that a man who is honest, conscientious, considerate, loyal, generous, and so on, just happens also to be good. Another way of demonstrating this point is by a *reductio ad absurdum*. If goodness is contingently connected to other characteristics, it is possible to suppose that two objects or persons are identical in all respects save goodness. But this is absurd: to say that one object is good and another bad is to imply that they differ in at least one other respect, the respect that constitutes the reason for the distinct evaluations. Now, whether or not these other characteristics are determined, goodness is determined by them. Similar conclusions follow for other evaluative predicates. So if we do not include evaluative predicates, a non-naturalist may add them and we know *a priori* that the designated characteristics are determined.

138

I prefer not to include evaluative predicates on the slim chance that the non-naturalists are right. In this way, we also avoid evaluative (moral, aesthetic) laws. These laws would specify the conditions under which some object necessarily has some evaluative property. It is evidently preferable not to have to countenance these sentences.

Unfortunately, it is very difficult to define the class we have just eliminated. Philosophers like to distinguish sentences that describe from sentences that perform other jobs, e.g., evaluate, request, command, promise, and so on, but they disagree as to how to define these differences. A discussion of this issue is relevant to determinism since determinists are interested in descriptive sentences only. But I consider the issue a major one to which I cannot address myself in this work.

Negative predicates: Whether or not a predicate is negative is clearly a syntactical affair if we restrict ourselves to a form like "non-*P*." But if we wish to include predicates like "other than blue," semantic information is required. In either case, I see no good reason to exclude negative predicates. If "negative" is a syntactical predicate, it is always possible to rewrite some sentence by using an equivalent expression like "other than." If, on the other hand, "negative" is a semantic predicate, then its domain of application is unclear. Which is the negative predicate: "odd" or "even"? We can imagine a language that has only "odd" and "non-odd," and one that only has "even" and "non-even." If the decision is a conventional affair, this seems even more reason to impose no restrictions. Finally, if we restrict ourselves to natural languages, a determinist surely wants a deterministic account of someone's *not* making a certain decision (as opposed to his making a decision not to choose between two alternatives).

Many bizarre sentences are admitted if we impose no restrictions. We shall have to have a deterministic account of

139

"Jones is not now falling from the Empire State Building in a blue serge suit."

These sentences may be handled in two ways. First, some are logical consequences of sentences that are easier to handle, e.g., "Jones is now walking." Second, we may be able to specify the laws governing "falling" or "falling from the Empire State Building" and formulate a law like "(x) (If x falls [from the Empire State Building], then Ax or Bx or Cx or . . .)." The initial conditions for Jones are: $-Aj$, $-Bj$, $-Cj$, etc. We shall have occasion to make use of such laws again when we consider temporal predicates.

Thus, negative predicates are not ruled out.

Numerical predicates. We surely want to allow for the use of predicates that contain numerical (and other mathematical) expressions, e.g., "owns three cars," "is moving at sixty miles per hour," "is twice as large as." A deterministic account may, therefore, have to include sentences from the formal sciences that are required to effect a deduction.

In reflecting on some numerical predicates, e.g., "is twice as tall as," it seems clear that it may first be necessary to provide deterministic accounts of "X is ten feet tall" and "Y is twenty feet tall" and then conjoin these accounts with the appropriate formal and linguistic truths to create a deterministic account of "Y is twice as tall as X."

Numerical predicates are not ruled out.

Temporal predicates: Besides the temporal designation required by all predicates, some predicates are intrinsically temporal, e.g., "old," "is one week prior to his marriage." Consider, for example, "Smith is 40 years old at t." The sentence follows from "Smith was born at $t - 40$" and "Smith is alive at t." If these two are sentences we want deterministic accounts of, then "Smith is 40 years old at t" is included as secondary.

We surely want a deterministic account of "Smith was born at $t - 40$." But some have maintained that we do not give causal or deterministic accounts of sentences like "Jones is alive," "the bridge is standing," "the regular United States government is in power," etc. Causal accounts are given for the unexpected or abnormal or for changes in some state rather than for the continuation of the state.

As far as I can see, there is little theoretical importance in the fact that people do not normally *request* explanations for such facts. If, then, we allow sentences like "Smith is alive at t," we must also allow "Smith is alive at $t - n$," where "n" is a very small number. But are there any laws which, together with "Smith is alive at $t - n$," enable deduction of "Smith is alive at t"? The view we reject points out here that the laws we have are those concerning death since we look for the causes of death. (We do not have many such laws yet; but these are the laws we are looking for.) Hence, the attempt at construction of some law governing life will contain a clause like "and no cause of death exists." Besides being an odd clause, it converts the "law" into something like a logical truth.

We may deal with this problem in one of two ways. On the one hand, one may look forward to a clearer characterization of the human body as a living system whose normal functioning is more clearly specified. Then, given normal functioning at one time, there will be laws that specify the way this development continues and its normality sustained, just as in the case of simple physical systems. Death or disease would be regarded as an interference with the system and one could also have laws that specify how such interferences work. On the other hand, even if one has only laws governing death, one can deduce that Jones is alive at t from the fact that he is alive at $t - n$ if one can say that Jones is an instance of no death-governing law. The envisaged deduction looks atypical for a determinist, since one is apparently not deducing from laws and initial conditions. But it is really not atypical. One simply needs more information than normally is required. One has to know all the laws governing death. Then, one puts these laws into one generalization of the form "(x) (If x dies, then Ax or Bx or Cx or . . .)." The initial conditions for Jones (j) are: $\sim Aj$, $\sim Bj$, $\sim Cj$, etc. Then one deduces that Jones is alive and, if one has the appropriate temporal information, that he is alive at t.

Thus I see no reason to rule out sentences like "Smith is forty years old at t."

What about sentences like "Jones is one week prior to his marriage at $t-7$"? We surely want "Jones is married at t." But the sentence in question (and all others like it) is a logical consequence of "Jones is married at t." Why may we not think of the deterministic account of "Jones is married at t" as a deterministic account of "Jones is one week prior to his marriage at $t-7$" as well?

How does this liberal attitude toward temporal predicates relate to the general problem of positional predicates, i.e., predicates which contain, perhaps tacitly, a temporal or spatial reference? The problem is that philosophers generally agree that positional predicates do not belong in scientific laws, but disagree as to the definition of "positionality," and, therefore, disagree as to the way to get rid of such predicates.

We will later take up the question of legitimacy as regards terms in laws. It is or should be evident that our concern here is different. If "grue" and "bleen" are in our language at all, then the fact that they cannot occur in laws does not preclude the possibility of giving a deterministic account of "That leaf is grue at t." One can give a deterministic account of "That leaf is green at t" that will also be the deterministic account of "That leaf is grue at t." Obviously, there are many ordinary terms that cannot appear in scientific laws; but we can give deterministic accounts of sentences that contain them.

I conclude that positional predicates in general or temporal predicates in particular are not ruled out.

Philosophical predicates: These are predicates that philosophers have taken an interest in. Some examples are: "is an observation term," "is an action," "is about *P*," "has free will," "knows that *P*." Some of these are ruled out since they are metalinguistic, and we do not allow the names of linguistic entities (e.g., "is an observation term").[2] But many are not. Ought we to consider them a distinct class that can be dealt with in one way?

First of all, one must distinguish philosophical pronouncements concerning these terms or concepts from sentences containing them. Since " '*S* knows that *P*' means ' . . . ' " is metalinguistic, it is excluded. But the following are not excluded: (1) "Dewey utters (or writes) '*S*.' " (2) "Dewey's deliberations take course *C*." (3) Moreover, common appeals by philosophers in support of their positions refer to facts that are admissible, e.g., "Scientists say (or believe) that *P*," or "I intuit that causes cannot go out of existence before their effects come into existence."

What about "Dewey decides in favor of *S*."? This sentence is admissible, as we shall soon see. But one problem that arises here may be more easily seen if we turn to other sentences that contain philosophically interesting terms, e.g., "Smith knows that *P*."

Some say that if *P* is true, Smith believes *P*, and he has adequate evidence for it, then Smith knows that *P*. If, for purposes of discussion, we suppose that deterministic accounts are given for "Smith believes *P*" and "Smith has adequate evidence for *P*," then if *P* is true, why not say that his knowing is determined?

But some reject the above analysis of "Smith knows that *P*" on the ground that this sentence does not express a proposition, i.e., is neither true nor false. A similar claim has been made about sentences like "Dewey decides in favor

[2] If it is claimed that these philosophical analyses are about concepts rather than terms, we do not allow names of concepts either for they are not part of the temporal order.

of *S*." If these philosophers are right, then deterministic accounts cannot be provided for these sentences.

The particular kind of disagreement that so often crops up in philosophical cases concerns the proper role of the sentence. Determinists are interested only in sentences that simply describe the world. But the distinction between descriptive sentences and sentences that perform other tasks, e.g., evaluatives, performatives, and so on, represents a fundamental philosophical question. As noted earlier, we have to make do with an unanalyzed notion of a descriptive sentence. The issues in this analysis are too deep and complex to deal with here. I conclude that no class of predicates to which we have alluded deserves a new restrictive ruling.

Psychological predicates. There are psychological predicates like "believes" and "desires" which raise problems that are not due to their psychological character. For example, we shall want next to deal with the traditional trichotomy of predicates, viz., observational, dispositional, and theoretical, in order to see what the attitude of a determinist must be toward this trichotomy. But many of the questions about psychological predicates concern their location in this trichotomy. Thus we shall want to deal with psychological (or any other) predicates *qua* dispositional or *qua* theoretical.

The other class of psychological predicates that raises problems is the class of action terms, i.e., predicates that designate actions of persons. It has been argued that sentences containing these predicates are such that deterministic accounts cannot be provided.

Again, no restrictions are imposed.

Novelty predicates: Some criticisms of determinism are based on the (logical) impossibility of predicting events like the birth of the first human being or the discovery of some scientific law. One reason for rejecting definitions of determinism in terms of foreknowledge or predictability is to avoid these criticisms. The adoption of a definition in terms of law does avoid them, for an event may be law-governed although no one knows or uses the law to make a prediction. Novelty predicates, whose exclusion would raise an objection to determinism, need not, therefore, be ruled out. (The exclusion of evaluative sentences is obviously not an objection to determinism.)

Observational, Dispositional, and Theoretical predicates: An observational predicate is one whose applicability can be determined merely by observing the object to which the predicate purportedly applies, e.g., "is red," "moves," "dissolves." Some predicates that fail this test, e.g., "is soluble," may, however, be defined in terms of a conditional proposition or a set of conditional propositions containing only observational predicates. For example, "X is soluble in water" means "X would *dissolve in water* if it were *placed in water*." (The phrases italicized are supposed to be observational predicates.) A normal descriptive predicate that fails to be either observational or dispositional is theoretical. A theoretical term, therefore, "goes beyond" all actual and possible observations. Since its link to observation is not definitional, the possibility emerges that it is only statistical. That is, since the applicability of some theoretical term T does not follow from the applicability of any set of observational or dispositional terms, it *may* be that there are only statistical laws of the form "If O_1a, O_2a, O_3a, then *probably* Ta" where "O_1," "O_2," and "O_3" are observational terms. The term "theoretical" is used to characterize these terms because scientific theories are the best source of them. In fact, presence in some theory is often taken as a defining characteristic of theoretical terms. Some suggested examples are "electron," "mass," "gravitional field," "gene," and "unconscious."

This extremely brief and oversimplified account does not point up the many difficulties that defenders of this trichotomy have had in upholding its clarity and applicability. Some maintain, for example, that the observational-theoretical distinction is a bogus one.[3] Critics say that a clear definition that divides terms into distinct classes cannot be provided. They normally add that the traditional motivation behind the insistence upon a distinction is misguided. What is the traditional motivation?

Briefly, the motivation is empiricistic. Since terms whose applicability is determined by simple observation are models of clarity, expressions that cannot be defined ultimately in terms of observational predicates are suspect. So we set aside a class of theoretical terms and worry about what to do with them. If they are not legitimate terms, then sentences that contain them are not meaningful and are not, therefore, true or false.

But, say the critics, there is nothing to worry about anyway. The sentences chosen as theoretical are as true or false as the sentences that only contain predicates like "is red." There is neither a clear way to distinguish two classes of terms nor is there any reason to be concerned about the cognitive status of some subset of scientific sentences.

Since a determinist believes that there are deterministic accounts of true sentences only, he has a stake here. For example, suppose we temporarily accept the dichotomy of terms into observational and theoretical in order to construct this case: We have a law that is formulated in strictly observational terms: $(x)(O_1x \supset O_2x)$. An indeterminist comes along and postulates the existence of a theoretical state T_1 relative to which there are but two laws (to make matters simple): $(x)(O_1x \supset$ the probability that T_1x is .7) and $(x)(T_1x \supset O_2x)$. The indeterminist claims that determinism has been shown to be false because T_1-states are undetermined.

The case cannot be constructed if an observational term

[3] See, for example, Grover Maxwell, "The Ontological Status of Theoretical Entities," *Minnesota Studies in the Philosophy of Science,* ed. Herbert Feigl and Grover Maxwell (Minneapolis: University of Minnesota Press, 1962), III, pp. 3-27.

146

"O_3" replaces "T_1" for one can hope to *discover* laws governing O_3-states. But theoretical terms are "introduced" and if they are introduced in a sufficiently minimal way, as in our example, a *prima facie* problem for determinists is created.

Our first reaction to this argument is to reject it on the grounds that one has no right to concoct or create theoretical states by such sleight of hand. Surely, some canons of scientific procedure have been violated. This is so. Let us suppose that we can formulate these canons. Suppose in fact that we are blessed with an omniscient philosopher of science who selects for us a set of sufficient conditions of scientific adequacy from considerations like evidential adequacy, simplicity, comprehensiveness, predictive power, suggestiveness, and the like. The next question, then, is: if T_1 belongs to one of these scientifically acceptable theories (SAT), and if it is the ultimate theory, what is a determinist to say?

The problem is not that T_1-states are undetermined. If that were all, then determinism would be false and that would be the end of it. The problem is that there are deterministic laws that connect all the observational predicates of the theory. There is a strong inclination to say that this is all we really require. One form that this inclination takes is the rejection of truth values for sentences containing theoretical terms, i.e., for scientific theories. But if SAT is neither true nor false, it poses no problem for a determinist. There would have to be deterministic accounts only for sentences containing observational predicates.

It may be helpful at this point to distinguish various views. There are some who consider that the observational-theoretical distinction is a bogus one. Normally, this view accompanies a realistic attitude toward scientific theories, i.e., they are true or false. This view holds, then, that SAT is incompatible with determinism.

Others, conversely, would say that the observational-theoretical distinction is legitimate and scientific theories are true or false. Again, *SAT* is incompatible with determinism. Finally, still others would say that the distinction is legitimate; but scientific theories are neither true nor false. Scheffler calls this view "fictionalism" and he distinguishes two varieties.[4]

Instrumentalism: Scientific theories are not the proper objects of cognitive attitudes; they are tools for the making of predictions rather than propositions we may or may not assent to. (Notice again how the issue before us turns on the question of whether or not a sentence functions in a descriptive way.) This position is difficult to defend. It would be completely untenable if the empiricistic assumption upon which it rests, viz., that observational terms are the only models of meaningful, non-logical terms, were undercut.

Eliminative Fictionalism: The theoretical portions of science must be eliminated. It does not suffice to create a new role for them as the instrumentalist does. One must at least show how they can be eliminated even if they are retained in practice. This program is far from the achievement of its goal. No eliminative technique has proved adequate, at least in the eyes of most philosophers.

Hence, although fictionalism would enable us to eliminate sentences containing theoretical terms and would, therefore, eliminate *SAT* as a threat to determinism, fictionalism is not that tenable a position. It looks as if we must say that scientific theories are true or false and that *SAT* is incompatible with determinism. Are we forced, therefore, to ignore the feeling that determinism is sufficiently established if it is established for all observational predicates?

We note first of all that the feeling that determination of theoretical states is only instrumentally important has two sources: (a) Theoretical states are not quite real. They are

[4] Israel Scheffler, *The Anatomy of Inquiry* (New York: Alfred Knopf, 1963), pp. 178-222.

"introduced" only to organize experiential data and the latter are the real components of the world. But this is fictionalism, a view that is difficult to embrace. (b) Theoretical states are simply not important in themselves. If there are deterministic laws governing the onset of depression, and if the theory that accounts for depression contains the notion of a superego, it matters little that some indeterminism for the superego reigns. But this source is general and extends beyond the area of theory. There are observational states that are unimportant on any reasonable criterion: if it is determined that Jones drinks six ounces of Beefeater gin each day, it does not matter whether or not the gin touches his lower right wisdom tooth as it goes down. It *may* be important; but anything may be important.

Thus, we shall have to deal with this question of importance generally, and I prefer to see the issue of theoretical states as a special case of this general issue.

We shall not here impose any restrictions on sentences containing theoretical predicates.

This liberal attitude creates a problem that at first sight seems quite serious. We are here trying to define a class of sentences for which there must be deterministic accounts if determinism is true. The assumption that has been tacit is that the existence of deterministic accounts for all the sentences is a sufficient condition of the truth of determinism. But if we admit theoretical terms, this assumption turns out to be false.

When mathematical techniques are introduced to distinguish theoretical states, it is assumed that there is a distinct state for each real number. For example, the series of possible velocity states is mathematically continuous. Moreover, the number of *actual* states of, say, position assumed by a moving particle is identical with the number of real numbers. If, therefore, each actual state in the world can be described, we require a language whose sentences equal in number the real numbers. But no language is like that. At most, the number of sentences of any actual language is denumerably infinite. It follows that there are not enough sentences for all actual states: the world is too rich for our language. Hence, the truth of determinism does not follow from the existence of a deterministic account for each sentence since the states that are not described may be undetermined.

One recourse is reversion to the language of propositions for, I suppose, the numerical limitations on sentences are absent for propositions. But it is not necessary to shift to the language of propositions.

If there exist deterministic accounts for all sentences in the class we eventually define, then determinism is true if there is some way to guarantee that the undescribed states are also determined. This guarantee is provided by the truth of the law that governs the phenomenon in question. The general form of a law guarantees that the states for which there are no sentences are instances of the law just as much as the states that are described by some sentence.

For example, Galileo's law is: For any body falling under a constant force from rest (at position zero), its position $Z = \frac{1}{2}g \cdot t^2$ (where g is a constant). If Galileo's law is a law, i.e., true, then all states of position of any body subsumed by it are in accordance with the equation. It follows that all states of position for which there are no sentences are in accordance with the equation. Notice as well that the law does not commit itself to states of position as *entities*. Bodies are the entities that *have* positions. There may be problems about the number of properties objects may have; but these problems are not ours. All we require to solve the problem at hand is the existence of laws like Galileo's.

We must, therefore, add this stipulation: Let S represent any sentence in the class we are defining that contains a determinable term (e.g., position, velocity, weight, size) whose determinate terms (e.g., position 1, velocity 2.63, weight $\frac{2}{3}$, size π) admit as values any or almost any real number. (Restrictions are, of course, possible, and the most obvious is a restriction on all negative numbers. But no restrictions that eliminate a true sentence are allowed.)

Determinism demands that there exist laws that appear in deterministic accounts for each S. We further demand that each account include a law essential to the deduction of S and containing an equation whose values for the determinable in S may take values from any or almost any member of the set of real numbers. (As above, restrictions are possible.)

Let us call this stipulation the "continuity-requirement."

One motive for defining determinism in terms of sentences rather than events, facts, or states is that we avoid unnecessary ontological burdens. It is to be noted that the continuity requirement does not commit us to one of these ontologies rather than another. We have managed to remain on the linguistic level.

What about dispositional terms? Although there are problems in the analysis of sentences containing dispositional predicates (dispositional sentences), that is hardly a sufficient reason to exclude them. We do not exclude laws although the problems in their analysis are at least as serious. Furthermore, dispositions do not fail on temporal grounds, for an object may gain or lose flexibility just as it may flex at certain times and not at others. Finally, one can deduce from laws and initial conditions that an object will acquire a disposition, just as one can deduce from laws and initial conditions that some event occurs.

The sole objection in this context is the feeling that dispositional states are not *bona fide* states. Strictly speaking, it is said, "solubility in water" does not designate a real state of sugar: the real state is whatever structural feature we discover to account for the fact that sugar dissolves when placed in water. Moreover, it is this structural trait that is really acquired or lost when it is said that the object acquires or loses a dispositional property. Hence, the "opponent" of dispositional predicates will not mind their inclusion so long as we regard this inclusion as provisional. Once we discover the associated non-dispositional term, we are obliged to replace the dispositional term with it.

I must admit to a certain sympathy with this metaphysical complaint. I think that it can be buttressed from a determinist's point of view by considering what a dispositional predicate is.

One objection to the elimination of dispositional predicates is a very practical one, viz., we shall have to give a careful characterization of them. Surely, syntax is no guide—they don't all end in "able" or "ible." Moreover, one and the same term may be considered dispositional or not, depending on how we interpret it. For example, "sharp" may refer to the power to cut or a combination of traits like thinness and hardness, etc.

I think, then, that a term is dispositional only if it is defined in terms of a law.[5] "Sharp" is dispositional if it is defined as "would cut such and such under certain conditions." Thus, dispositional predicates are applied to objects in virtue of the fact that these objects are instances of some law.[6]

But a determinist pictures the world in a divided way. It is a collection of facts or states that are governed by laws. He thus considers it improper to *add* to the world whose laws he seeks the fact that it exemplifies some law. The trouble with dispositional terms is that they violate this breach. Since objects are instances of laws, dispositional terms are perfectly good, and the sentences in which they appear may certainly be true. But for the determinist they

[5] But not any law.
[6] Or some expression that is already instantiated from a law. "Weighs 20 pounds" applies to *a* because "If *a* is placed on *this scale,* the pointer reads 20."

are superfluous. If one has all the non-dispositional facts and then one has all the laws, there are no new (dispositional) facts to be discovered.

But if dispositional terms are eliminated, then are not almost all terms eliminated? For one can almost always construe a term as dispositional: "is red" can be defined as "appears red under normal conditions."

This is a conventional matter, I think. If one wishes to define "is red" this way, then it would be dispositional. But one may not be interested in the predicate "appears red" and it may then suffice to take "is red" as primitive. Of course, for a determinist, there has to be a deterministic account of "appears red." In the theory in which *this* account appears, "is red" may be eliminable. But we do not have to eliminate "is red" if the theory in which it appears as primitive provides deterministic accounts.

Hence, any proposal to eliminate dispositional terms must be construed as a proposal to eliminate a class of tokens that is given a certain definition—in a certain theory, perhaps.

If we could be sure that all dispositional terms will or can be replaced by non-dispositional terms, then we may accept them on the provisional basis agreed to by the critic. But not only can we not be sure; we can be sure that there will always be a dispositional term or that it will be easy to construct one. For there must always be some underived, fundamental law in any domain, and a dispositional term can be defined in terms of this law. If a structural trait replaces the dispositional one, then the laws governing this structural trait are now considered fundamental, and a new dispositional term may be introduced as a summary form of the law.

This fact supports the intuitively-based rejection of dispositional predicates, for the disposition associated with a basic law (a basic disposition) cannot be determined. For example, if "Any object at rest will remain at rest unless acted upon by an outside force" is a basic law, and if this law means "All objects are inertial," then there is no deterministic account of "Object *a* is inertial," for the existence of such a deterministic account is incompatible with the premise that the law is basic. If there is a deterministic account, however, then the new basic law has an associated basic disposition for which again no deterministic accounts exist.

But we surely reject this argument against determinism, for it does not show that any non-dispositional trait (e.g., position) is undetermined. We do not feel that it is necessary to provide a deterministic account of basic dispositions since it is impossible.

If we are not perturbed by the failure to provide deterministic accounts of basic dispositions, what is our reaction when the failure applies to non-basic dispositions?

Suppose there are no deterministic accounts of "solubility in water" for any kind of substance may sometimes dissolve when placed in water. In this case, though, there is also no deterministic account of "dissolves." Sometimes substances dissolve and sometimes they do not. So our concern about the absence of a deterministic account of "solubility" seems to be based on a concern about the absence of a deterministic account of a non-dispositional property.

Are there cases other than those involving basic dispositions in which we can give a deterministic account of some non-dispositional property, but not the corresponding dispositional one? Consider the following:

Sugar is soluble for no reason. There is no structural trait of sugar or combination structural-relational trait that accounts for its solubility. But we do have the law "Sugar is soluble." Do we provide a deterministic account of "This piece of sugar dissolves" by referring to the law plus "This piece of sugar is placed in water"?

If we say, as we have, that the solubility is undetermined, we ought also to say that the dissolving is undetermined. If "being sugar" is not a deterministic account of "being soluble," then I cannot see how "being sugar and being placed in water" becomes a deterministic account of "dissolving."

But we may think of the solubility as determined. For one can produce it by growing sugar. That is, there is a sufficient condition of solubility although there is no structural trait that replaces it. To take another example, we believe that habits (a subclass of dispositions) are determined by certain behavior and experience. We also believe that the reference to habits is replaceable by some reference to the nervous system. But these beliefs are independent. If we reject the latter belief, we may still believe that habits are determined. But if so, we would also believe that the instances of habits are determined. By hypothesis, this is not a case in which any dispositional trait is thought of as undetermined.

Hence, if the dissolving is thought of as determined, then the solubility is too. Or we may come to think of the law "Sugar is soluble" as a kind of basic law which enables us to provide deterministic accounts of dissolving; but no account of solubility is necessary. Evidently the law is far from basic, and so we do suppose laws from which it can be derived.

The conclusion is that we are never concerned about determinism for dispositional traits unless the concern derives from one that applies to non-dispositional traits. If determinism is true for all non-dispositional traits, we are satisfied. Moreover, it may be false for some dispositions (the basic ones); but this does not affect the truth of determinism.

The only reason left for the inclusion of dispositional predicates is that one may have to refer to some disposition in the deterministic account of some non-dispositional sentence. That is, the relevant law has as one of its antecedent conditions a dispositional sentence. It seems unfair to allow dispositional states as antecedent conditions, but eliminate them from those that determinists have to provide deterministic accounts of.

(Notice again that to say that deterministic accounts are unnecessary is not to say that they cannot be given. So the critic of dispositional predicates is not saying that one cannot give deterministic accounts of sentences that have to be referred to in a deterministic account. Nonetheless, one may feel that deterministic accounts should be required for at least those dispositions that function as antecedent conditions.)

Again, the critic of dispositional predicates does not mind references to dispositions as antecedent conditions just so long as the reference is regarded as theoretically eliminable. Although it may be possible to imagine a case in which the reference is theoretically uneliminable, I doubt that such a case actually exists. It does not matter that I cannot prove that there are no such cases, for we shall not rule out dispositional predicates thus: (a) We have not really defined the class of dispositional predicates for we have not specified the restrictions on laws that are used to define these terms. (I do not think any law will do.) In fact, I do not believe there really is a clear class of dispositional predicates in which case any definition would be somewhat arbitrary. (b) A determinist believes that accounts can be given for dispositional sentences since they can be given for all non-dispositional ones. The alleged superfluity of dispositions works two ways—one may reject them or, if there are reasons, one may allow them. (c) It may be practically useful to include dispositional terms for, although we may have excellent reason to believe that replacements exist, none may be available at the moment. (This is not a strong reason since, even if we do not require deterministic accounts for dispositions, they can still be given.) (d) The determinist's beliefs about dispositions can be advanced even if dispositional terms are not eliminated.

If we allow dispositional predicates, we must rule out basic dispositional predicates. We stipulate, therefore, that any sentence of the form "Bx," where "B" is a basic dispositional predicate or any logical consequence of "Bx," is ruled out.

A predicate "B" is a basic dispositional predicate if and only if "Bx" is logically equivalent to a sentence that is a basic law. A basic law is one that *can* appear as axiomatic in a reconstruction of the laws in the domain in question. The word "can" is essential because different formulations of a scientific theory can take different laws as basic. So "basic" is to some extent a syntactic matter.

We have taken dispositional terms to be those that are defined in terms of certain kinds of laws. But the great majority of terms that pass as "dispositional" are given much looser definitions. No one can specify *actual* laws for terms like "irritable," "friendly," "brittle," and so on. Given this large class of terms, analyses may be classified under headings such as (1) actual laws; (2) vaguely specified laws; (3) statistical laws; (4) capacities, i.e., sentences of the form "There exist conditions under which . . . " There is no problem in requiring deterministic accounts for all sentences containing these terms for, given any term T_1 that is analyzed à la (2), (3), or (4), there either is a term T_2 that is analyzed à la (1) so that sentences containing T_1 are logical consequences of sentences containing T_2, or there is a deterministic account of sentences containing T_1 directly. As to the first alternative, if by "brittle" we mean some actual law, then the deterministic account of sentences containing "brittle" will serve as the account of sentences like "This glass will usually break when struck" or "This glass can break." As to the second alternative, the deterministic account of "brittle" will do for the weaker claims even if we do not have "brittle" in the language.

The only restriction we impose is that basic dispositional sentences and their logical consequences are ruled out.

Causal predicates: A causal predicate is any relational predicate that is logically equivalent to "causes," "is a contributory condition of," "is a necessary condition of," or "is a sufficient condition of."

Although determinists do not demand that deterministic

accounts of laws be given, we can very often provide an account of some law that looks just like a deterministic account except that the account is of a law rather than a singular sentence. For example, Kepler's laws can be deduced from Newton's plus facts about the solar system just as the location of planets can be deduced from Kepler's laws plus facts about the solar system. But we speak of Kepler's laws as being explained or reduced rather than determined.

From the law "$(x)(Px \supset Qx)$" and "Pa" we can deduce both "Qa" and "Pa is a sufficient condition of Qa." Hence an explanation of "$(x)(Px \supset Qx)$" that looks like a deterministic account would also look like a deterministic account of "Pa is a sufficient condition of Qa" if "Pa" is added to it. In fact, "$(x)(Px \supset Qx)$," itself, plus "Pa," looks like a deterministic account of "Pa is a sufficient condition of Qa."

But a determinist simply does not see these accounts as deterministic because causal sentences do not really refer to singular facts. Given the generality theory, they are in fact incipient deterministic accounts, and we do not demand deterministic accounts of deterministic accounts.

We rule out causal sentences, therefore.

Should causal sentences also be ruled out of the class of antecedent conditions? If "Pa is a sufficient condition of Qa," can this sentence plus some laws be part of a deterministic account of some sentence?

Sometimes a reference to "Pa is a sufficient condition of Qa" is only apparently necessary. If I cite the fact that Smith's taking aspirin relieved his headache in an account of the fact that Green's headache was relieved, where Green took Anacin, a product that is basically aspirin, the reference to Smith is really evidence for the law that is being (tacitly) invoked rather than a reference to a condition of Green's relief.

More difficult cases are provided by learning experiments

in which animals respond to earlier reinforcements of correct behavior. Here, improvement must refer to the fact that correct behavior was rewarded by, say, a pellet of food.

But if the animal is responding to the food's *following* his performance, we need not refer to the fact that his performance *induced* the reward to account deterministically for his improvement. Thus, he would have improved had the appearance of food accidentally followed his responses. It would be incredible to learn that an animal who improves when the experimenter rewards him fails to improve when, say, the food pellets just happen to appear when he presses the correct buzzer. Now, there are actually two cases that must be distinguished. The animal's behavior may not cause the appearance of food, although it would be reasonable to expect its presence once the correct behavior has been performed. For example, there happens to be food at the end of a maze. In this case the animal is not responding to any causal fact. And if he believes that his arrival at the end of the maze produces the food and he would not improve without this belief, it is the *belief* in a causal connection, not a causal connection itself, that is causally relevant. In the buzzer pressing case, where the pressing causes a pellet to drop down, the pellets may have been randomly arranged so that no reliable inferences can be drawn. If it should turn out that the first few pellets that drop down happen all to be on the right side, it would be incredible to discover that the animal does not then form the disposition to press the buzzer on the right. Explanations in terms of inability, emotional upset, previous learning may be provided. Should these fail, we might be forced to resort again to the animal's belief that no causal relation exists. Here again, though, a causal relation *per se* is not a condition of some occurrence.

According to the view of laws we shall develop, the difference between an instance "$Pa \cdot Qa$" of a law and "$Pb \cdot Qb$," where the latter is not an instance of any law, does not consist in the presence of a special connection between Pa and Qa, e.g., a necessary connection. Thus, in our view, an apparent effect of "Pa is the cause of Qa" that cannot be understood as really the effect of "$Pa \cdot Qa$" or "A believes that Pa caused Qa" or, perhaps, some other noncausal condition, would constitute a serious difficulty.

We, therefore, suppose that causal sentences may not be antecedent condition-sentences and will formulate subsequent definitions accordingly.

This completes our discussion of restrictions on predicates. It is interesting that only three restrictions are required, viz., restrictions on non-descriptive, basic dispositional, and causal predicates. The traditional conception of determinism as an all-embracing theory is thereby maintained.

Notice, finally, that we allow vague predicates. For example, "Jones is stupid" follows from the more specific characterization "Jones's I.Q. is 70." We require a deterministic account of the latter. We require, therefore, a deterministic account of the vaguer sentence, and it is provided by the account of the more specific sentence.

(Strictly speaking, the above discussion is unnecessary for we said originally that all sentences are in unless excluded. But clarity is fostered by making points explicit.)

We now have a class of sentences, primary and secondary, for which there must be deterministic accounts if determinism is true. Let us call this the class of "Required sentences" or "R-sentences."

STATE DESCRIPTIONS

A deterministic account of the position of some particle includes both laws of motion and sentences describing the prior position and velocity of the particle. Generally, it is necessary to supplement laws with what are called initial conditions, antecedent conditions, or state descriptions. We choose the third expression. Given some R-sentence of the form "Pa_t," what may or may not be included in the state description? Obviously, science will tell us what the state description *is*. We have to determine the *a priori* constraints.

For convenience sake, we shall broaden the ordinary notion of a state description to include everything other than laws that is required to deduce "Pa_t." This includes the following:

1. Mathematical, logical, and linguistic truths. The third is very important for it enables us to go from a scientific description to a description in more ordinary language.

2. All true sentences of the form "$x = a$." The reader will recall that we allow, within specified limits, almost any alternative name for "a."[7] But, then, in order to deduce "Pa_t," we may need "$x = a$" for the law may be formulated in terms of "x."

The remainder of the sentences are what we normally think of as the state description, which is comprised of sentences selected from the class of *R*-sentences. There are only two revisions that are suggested here:

1. Sentences containing basic dispositional predicates are allowed.

2. Sentences containing positional predicates in general and temporal predicates in particular are ruled out. Although it is harmless to provide a deterministic account of "This grass is grue," we do not want to say that grueness or being forty years old determines anything. We shall have a good deal more to say about this when we talk about laws.

There are two additional restrictions on state descriptions: independent specifiability and temporal constraints.

Independent Specifiability: A state description for "Pa_t" must be logically independent of "Pa_t." Moreover, there must be a set of conditions constituting the criterion for the truth of the state description and logically independent of the truth conditions of "Pa_t." I take this as evident.

[7] See above, p. 135.

161

Temporal Constraints: We stipulate that no sentence refers to a time period subsequent to *t*. Although it seems evident that the future cannot determine the past, there are complications we shall raise in another context.[8]

A state of some system is often defined by selecting a set of predicates applicable to each member of the system or each member of a selected part of the system. These predicates represent determinables, and the set composed of one determinate of each determinable characterizes the state of one member of the system (or subsystem) at a particular time. The state of the system at a particular time is defined as the state of each member of the system (or subsystem) at that time. The characterization of the state may or may not be mathematical, depending upon whether or not the determinables are numerical magnitudes. If D_i is one of these determinables, then the system is ordinarily considered deterministic relative to D_i if there are laws which, when conjoined with a description of the state of the system at a particular time, entail sentences which specify the determinates of D_i for all the members of the system at any other time.

Since this account of the notion of a state of a system has been abstracted for the most part from examples in physics, emendations are necessary in order to generalize the account. Notice, for example, that D_i must be predicable of the members of the system at any time if the system is deterministic relative to D_i. This condition is satisfied by the determinables of physics: mass, velocity, position, density, and so on. In psychology, however, which is of especial interest to us, many of the predicates employed are not applicable to human beings at all times. Human beings are not always deciding, for example, and we certainly want to allow for the possibility that some decisions are determined. This difficulty might be resolved in an artificial way by taking "deciding" and "not deciding" as the determinants of a determin-

---

[8] See chap. VIII.

able. But there is a second difficulty. In Hull's learning theory, the reaction of an organism depends primarily, but not solely, upon its reaction potential. But the reaction potential is determined not by factors which include previous values of the reaction potential, but rather by factors such as drive and habit strength. Hence, the reaction of an organism is predicted on the basis of a knowledge of the values of variables which are distinct from the variables that are used to describe the reaction.[9] We must, therefore, reformulate the conception of a deterministic system.

Again, we define a system as deterministic relative to a determinable D_i. A finite set of predicates (no evaluative or positional ones) which represent determinables is selected. These predicates must apply at some time to some members of the system. They may or may not include D_i. The state of the system is defined as the state of each member of the system. The state of a member of the system is defined as a set of determinates of some—perhaps all—of the determinables. The determinate-predicates are true of this member (or, if they are relational predicates, of a group of members) either at a single instant, at different times, or during some temporal interval.[10] Moreover, there are no "simultaneity-restrictions" on the states of the various members of the system. Finally, there is a set of laws which, when conjoined with a description of the state of the system, entails sentences which tell us when D_i will be instantiated, the members of the system to which the determinates of D_i apply, and the determinates of D_i at each instantiation.

It is important to notice, first of all, that the state of a system is a relative notion in that it varies depending upon the determinable relative to which the system is deterministic. Thus, if the system has a state relative to D_i, it follows that the system is deterministic relative to D_i.

[9] Ernest R. Hilgard, *Theories of Learning* (2nd ed.; New York: Appleton-Century-Crofts, 1948), pp. 132-52.
[10] These distinctions are taken from Nagel's discussion of alternative ways of characterizing states. See pp. 287-93.

163

Secondly, we have liberalized the temporal restrictions on the notion of a state since it may not be possible to formulate laws which enable predictions to be made if the state must be specified at a single instant. This is especially important for psychology since predictions about the subsequent behavior of a person are conditioned on the occurrence of certain environmental situations. For example, "He will refuse a job if he is offered one." Thus, if the system is expanded to include features of the environment, the relevant laws may have to refer to elements which occur at different times. Also, if the person is thought of as a single member of the system, one may have to know about aspects of the person at different times. Even if one assumes the superiority of an instantaneous state description, there is no reason to reject other types of state descriptions from the point of view of an explication of determinism. It is still the case that "the past determines the future," that "only one future is possible given the past," and similarly. In other words, the unicity requirement is satisfied. Thus, so-called historical laws are not necessarily precluded.

ONTOLOGICAL QUESTIONS

Is determinism to be formulated in terms of sentences or propositions? If the former, do we mean sentence type (hereinafter just called "sentence") or inscription-or-utterance (hereinafter just called "inscription")?

The advantage of inscriptions is that they are concrete entities. We therefore avoid a commitment to the existence of abstract entities. Moreover, there is no unique problem of defining the conditions under which the relation "is the same inscription as" applies. For since inscriptions are physical objects—or, if utterances, events—the problem is the general one of identity for physical objects and events. And the solution to this problem does not require the introduction of notions that some deem obscure, viz., intensional notions like

164

synonymy. Let us call a person who advocates a definition of determinism in terms of inscriptions an "inscriptionalist."

But it is not possible to define determinism in terms of inscriptions and yet retain the view that, even if determinism is true, a deterministic account of *all* R-sentences will not be produced, a view no sane person can avoid. Consider the following definition:

$$(x)[x \text{ is } R\text{-inscription} \supset (\exists y)(\exists z)(y \text{ is a state}$$
$$\text{description-inscription} \cdot z \text{ is a law-inscription} \cdot$$
$$\dashv(y \cdot z) \supset x)]$$

Here we require an actual (not necessarily present) deterministic account for each R-inscription. Moreover, the definition covers only R-inscriptions and, therefore, does not demand a deterministic account for R-sentences never written or uttered. A determinist would accept neither aspect and would, therefore, reject this definiton.

More sophisticated attempts to retain inscriptionalism will also fail.

If, for example, we have a correct linguistic description of English, then we may write these principles down. If we do not, then we may construe the principles as dispositions of speakers of English. There are problems inherent in the latter proposal: we must choose speakers carefully to avoid deviant cases; one must be able to isolate the dispositions that are the rules of English from all the other dispositions associated with language; linguistic performance is compatible with an indefinite number of possible sets of rules, only one set of which is labeled "the rules of English." We shall waive these problems.

Hence, "There exists a collection of rules for English" may be read so as not to make any commitments to abstract entities.

We may suppose also that we possess a dictionary for English and a finite number of English inscriptions. According to the present interpretation of rules as inscriptions or dispositions of persons, to say that there exist English sentences that are never inscribed or uttered is to say that the rules of English have an infinite number of properties. For example, if "Jones is tall" (J) is a non-inscribed sentence of English (which it is not), then the rules of English have the property "legitimize-J" A few words are in order about this predicate.

The predicate is not relational: we are not asserting a relation of legitimization between rules and sentences. For we would then have to commit ourselves to the existence of non-inscribed sentences. I am taking Quine's suggestion here[11] and construing "legitimize" as an operator that operates on inscriptions to form predicates. Once formed, the predicate must be treated as a unit, i.e., as single-placed rather than relational.

The above interpretation of "legitimize" does not require an infinite number of dictionary entries since we are not adding to the list of English words. The fact that we can generate an infinite number of predicates out of a finite number of words should be no more disturbing than the fact that we can generate an infinite number of sentences out of those words. And the fact that the "legitimize-S" predicates are single-placed does not mean that a separate entry is called for. "Is tall" is single-placed; but all we need are entries for "is" and "tall."

Nor do we commit ourselves to an infinite number of properties, for we commit ourselves to no properties. We need no predicate variables.

But the problems that remain are insuperable.

In the first place, we cannot be sure that the rules of English will ever be formulated. But, then, "legitimize-J" will have to be thought of as applying to dispositions. This will

[11] Willard Van Orman Quine, *Word and Object* (New York: John Wiley, 1960), p. 216.

require us to talk about dispositions and dispositions are abstract entities. Before, we thought we might be able to talk just about persons that have dispositions.

One can avoid this difficulty by construing "legitimize-*J*" as a predicate that is true of persons. That is, if Smith has a certain disposition or collection of dispositions that is recognized as legitimizing-*J*, we say rather that Smith legitimizes-*J*.

Furthermore, assuming that we have formulated the rules of English and can construe them as inscriptions to which "legitimizing-*S*" predicates apply, there is still no way to formulate determinism without introducing abstract entities. For determinism says that for any sentence of a certain kind, there exists a sentence of a certain kind that entails it. But we cannot formulate this just as a thesis about rules. We would have to say something like:

$$(x)(x \text{ is the collection of rules of English} \cdot$$
$$x \text{ legitimizes all } R\text{-sentences} \supset \ldots)$$

So we would have to quantify over sentences. We would also have to do this if the categorical assertion that the rules legitimize all *R*-sentences were made.

Another alternative is to list all the "legitimize-*S*" predicates or all those in which "*S*" is identical to some *R*-sentence. But since there is an infinite number of them, determinism would require an infinite number of sentences for its formulation. If we *could* produce an infinite number of sentences, there would be no problem of unexpressed sentences, and we might just as well forget about this whole machinery.

Also, since determinism claims an entailment relation to hold between sentences, the relation would have to be reduced in some way to a relation between rules.

Finally, the "legitimize-*S*" predicates that truly apply to rules are determined in part by the vocabulary of English specified by the dictionary. But the formulation of an adequate scientific theory may (it always has in the past) require the introduction of new terms. It may even be necessary to scrap English altogether in order to formulate new conceptual insights. But then we cannot deal with the entire class of non-inscribed sentences by thinking of them all as properties of rules, for rules are limited by vocabulary whereas what the determinist has in mind is not.

Let us hereby record the "demise of determinism without abstract entities." I see no way out of these dilemmas for one who is inclined both to determinism and this brand of nominalism.

I say "this brand of nominalism" for some philosophers are called "nominalists" even though they accept abstract entities like sentences and classes. These nominalists are disturbed not by the abstract nature of certain alleged entities, but rather by the unclear character of the criteria of identity. For example, sentences are deemed legitimate because it is a fairly straightforward question as to whether or not two token sentences are of the same type. But, it is said, propositions are not legitimate because two sentences express the same proposition if and only if they are synonymous, and synonymy is not a clear notion. Can we at least satisfy these nominalists? Can we formulate determinism in terms of sentences?

We can see that the last problem of the previous proposal applies to the new suggestion. We there pointed out that, in order to allow for vocabulary expansion, sentences cannot be exhaustively determined by the present rules and dictionary of some language. For us, "English sentence" means "sequence of words that is in accordance with certain rules of English," where "word" means "an actual or possible dictionary entry." We require possible entries in case the English language dies out too soon. But what is a possible dictionary entry? Almost any sequence of letters can be given a definition and placed in an English dictionary. We cannot call them words, however, for "oxlyop" is not an English word. Moreover, it may never become an English word. But if we restrict ourselves to actual words (including all past and future ones) determinism is falsified if a Frenchman introduces a new term for the ultimate scientific theory after English dies out.

Suppose we shift our conception to "sentence in *some* natural language." But what if the world blows up tomorrow and no language has an adequate vocabulary for the ultimate scientific theory? Nor will it help to shift to "sentence in some *possible* natural language." For even if we have the ultimate theory of language, i.e., the principles in terms of which all natural languages are organized, we do not understand what class of objects sentences are until we have a vocabulary and we may not have any adequate vocabulary.

At this point or earlier, many would be content to relativize the definition, i.e., to define "determinism in English," or "determinism in 1966 English." But, then, few determinists would be able to locate a thesis to which they subscribe, for few determinists want to say that determinism is falsified if it cannot be formulated in English. Another procedure is to define "determinism in 1966 English" and then indicate how future definitions can be constructed out of the features of this definition. Again, though, a determinist will not be able to locate the thesis to which he subscribes, for he allows that any actual future definition may fail although determinism is true. And to shift to a "possible future definition" is to revert to problems we are trying to solve. Some think that one ought only to talk of theories as deterministic or indeterministic and forget about determinism as a thesis at all. All these objections and alternatives to a general definition of determinism will have to be taken seriously if we fail to offer a general definition. But our first commitment is to a general definition.

If the objections to a definition in terms of sentences are taken seriously, one will reject any linguistic characterization of determinism. For the general objection to a linguistic account is that the truth of determinism requires the existence of language users. But objections based upon the possibility that natural languages will never in fact achieve sufficient richness evidently have the same source. The general idea is that the truth or falsity of determinism has nothing to do with linguistic habits.

It is tempting at this point to turn to the language of propositions. For, since propositions are not linguistic entities, they are not bound by the restrictions we have been talking about.

But there are objections to propositions. The first of which is that they are abstract entities. We have seen that if this objection is accepted, then determinism cannot be defined at all. We shall not, therefore, consider it seriously. Secondly, the criteria of identity are unclear. This is perhaps the case if the strong requirement of sentence synonymy is adopted. That is, a proposition is that which is expressed by any of the members of a set of synonymous sentences. If, on the other hand, we define propositional identity in terms of logical equivalence rather than synonymy, fewer persons would object to propositions. There are, it is true, problems concerning the clarity of the notion of logical equivalence. But we require this notion anyway. For example, a deterministic account is a deductive argument. But "logical equivalence" means "mutual deducibility." So if we require "deducibility" or "logical entailment," we cannot consistently object to "logical equivalence."

The objection to logical equivalence as the criterion of propositional identity may be illustrated by belief contexts. If Smith assents to "Either the Packers or the Colts will win the championship" (E), but rejects "It is false that neither the Packers nor the Colts will win the championship" (F), we may think he is highly unintelligent. But it does appear that Smith believes that E and does not believe that F, although E is logically equivalent to F. Now if logical equivalence determines propositional identity, then E expresses the same proposition as F. And if deterministic accounts are about propositions, then a deterministic account of "Smith believes that E" would also be a deterministic account of "Smith believes that F." But this is absurd if the first is true and the second false.

The above argument contains a false premise. Even if deterministic accounts are about propositions, it does not follow that a deterministic account of "Smith believes that E" is a deterministic account of "Smith believes that F." A missing premise is that these two express the same proposition. But from the fact that E and F express the same propositions, it does not follow that "Smith believes that E" expresses the same proposition as "Smith believes that F." It does not, for the two are not logically equivalent. They cannot be logically equivalent for one is true and the other false.

The false assumption underlying the argument under examination is that propositions are the objects of belief. (It is false if "Smith believes that E" does not entail "Smith believes that F.") But a definition of determinism in terms of propositions is compatible with the rejection of propositions as objects of belief. One may try to dispense with objects of belief altogether. In any case, one need not think of "Smith believes that E" and "Smith believes that F" as expressing the same proposition.

So there is no serious objection to the proposal to analyze propositional identity in terms of logical equivalence of sentences. And since logical equivalence is a notion we already have made use of, we may as well conceive of propositions in this way.

A third objection to propositions asks how extensive the class of propositions is. We may certainly include everything that is expressed by a sentence in any past, present, or future natural language. And we may think of "sentence" as "any possible sentence," i.e., "any type in accordance with the rules of some natural language." But propositions are helpful to us only if we can go beyond this point since we can make do with "sentence (type) in some natural language." We must, therefore, countenance propositions that no sentence expresses (timelessly). Since propositions are not themselves linguistic entities, there is no objection on this score. But one can surely ask for an explanation of this concept of a proposition. And if we understand the term "proposition" as "that which is expressed by all sentences that are logically equivalent to one another," we are faced with the same problems we had when we considered a definition in terms of sentences. For, in trying to define "sentence" in this definition, we will again see that the meanings are either inadequate or unintelligible. There are alternative renderings of "proposition," however. "The meaning of a sentence" will not do for similar reasons. "That which is true or false" does avoid the word "sentence." But I shall concede that one does perhaps understand the general term "sentence," and, therefore, the term "proposition," even though there are doubts concerning the intelligibility of the attempt to extend the latter's extension.

The point is that the appeal to propositions is no more intelligible than the appeal to sentences. The difficulty with sentences is that they belong to languages none of which may be adequate. The advocate of propositions tells us not to be concerned, for there are entities that are expressed by no sentences which will do the job required of them. By hypothesis, we can produce no samples. But it is not evident to me that "proposition expressed by no actual sentence" is clearer than "sentence in some possible language." A proposition is like heaven—what looks only possible down here is said to be actual somewhere else. And so it may be. But my understanding does not increase when I am told there is an entity that meets my requirements.

I am not, therefore, denying here the existence of propositions (expressed by no sentence). Nor do I believe that these remarks regarding the intelligibility of the concept establish the unacceptability of a definition in terms of propositions. But if this notion is not superior to the notion of a sentence in a possible language, perhaps we ought to try to clarify the latter notion. If we are successful, we may ignore propositions. *A fortiori,* propositions may be ignored if we can actually replace the notion of a possible language with the notion of a suitably expanded *actual* language. This latter idea is the most tempting one to develop from an ontological point of view. Given as well the remarks at the beginning of this chapter regarding the superiority of a definition of determinism on the linguistic level, we shall succumb to this temptation. In the light of some of the difficulties we are facing, however, let us first reconsider the possibility that determinism should be defined as a thesis that is directly about the world.

We know that events *simpliciter* are no good because we may possess a deterministic account of e and e is the same event as f, but there may be no deterministic account of f.

We are left with events under descriptions or facts. But the former is clearly no superior to sentences. This becomes evident as soon as one inquires into "descriptions." For "event under description" is "event as given by some sentence."

Facts are very much like true propositions: they are both abstract entities whose identity may be thought of as determined by the logical equivalence of sentences. To discover a fact is to discover that some proposition is true. We may not accept the converse, for we may not wish to identify certain propositions, e.g., necessary and universal ones, with facts. But all this means is that facts are very much like *some* true propositions. If, however, propositions are not superior to sentences, can facts be superior to sentences?

If we think so, it is because we think of facts as in some way less dependent on language than propositions. We feel

173

strange about propositions that are tied down to no language; but we do not feel so strange about facts that no language reports. Facts are there to be discovered or not; propositions have a manmade quality to them. So any facts may be asserted intelligibly to exist. For example, we all recognize as a fact that there are entities that no language has a name for.

Some objections to facts have no force. Objections on the grounds either that facts are abstract or that criteria of identity are unclear are out of order for the same reasons they were considered out of order for propositions.

The above argument against the objections to the use of facts is not quite correct. We allowed logical equivalence as the criterion of identity for propositions in part because we already had logical entailment in the definition of determinism. But if we adopt facts, we no longer need logical entailment since we no longer need laws. That is, a determinist would assert that for any fact of a certain kind, there exist other facts that have a certain relation to it, viz., necessitation or determination. Even if a determinist introduces general facts, it makes no sense to talk of facts entailing other facts. (This represents one difference between facts and propositions—although some would insist that only sentences can be related by entailment.) So we need logical entailment and/or equivalence whether or not we adopt facts, but for different reasons. We need these concepts for the identity of facts and propositions or for the relation between linguistic entities.

We concluded earlier that only a careful examination of sentences really tells us which facts a determinist must believe there is a deterministic account for. But an advocate of facts may accept this conclusion and simply rewrite our discussion of R-sentences in terms of the language of facts. A determinist would be one who believes that for any fact of a type that can be represented by an R-sentence, there exist other facts of a similar type that determine it.

But I am not really sure that facts are any clearer than propositions. The feeling that they are may be illusory. We began above to explain facts in terms of sentences, and this road may lead to the same dead end we encountered with propositions. In any case, an attempt to formulate a definition of determinism in terms of sentences will be made.

We allow variables that range over the denumerably infinite number of sentences (types) of some natural language, say English. But the class of sentences will be thought of as embracing entities beyond those that are legitimately constructible out of actual (past, present, future) vocabulary and rules. These entities are defined in the following way.

We add to our English dictionary a very large number of uninterpreted constants and classify them as individual constants (names), predicate constants, and the like. In fact, there will be a large number for each distinct part of speech. Since each constant is relegated to a definite grammatical status, whether or not any sequence of uninterpreted constants (or combination of uninterpreted and interpreted constants) is, from a syntactical point of view, a sentence, can be determined. Any sentence that contains an uninterpreted constant does not possess a complete semantic interpretation and cannot, therefore, be called true or false. We shall call these "uninterpreted sentences."

Since no uninterpreted sentence is true, none can be an R-sentence. The R-sentences within the class of interpreted sentences will be called "IR-sentences" (interpreted R-sentences).

We now specify a set of procedures for semantic interpretation, e.g., producing a definition of an uninterpreted predicate in terms of interpreted ones, or specifying some conditions for the application of a new primitive predicate. These semantic rules, like syntactical ones, will appear as interpreted sentences.

The sentences that actually interpret uninterpreted sentences in accordance with semantic rules are called "I-sen-

175

tences" (interpreting sentences). (Names for each uninterpreted constant are, therefore, needed.) *I*-sentences are obviously interpreted sentences since we can not understand how a sentence is interpreted if the *I*-sentence contains an uninterpreted constant. (*I*-sentences contain names of uninterpreted constants. But these names are obviously interpreted.)

I-sentences are of two types, basic and nonbasic. A basic *I*-sentence contains only interpreted constants and the names of interpreted constants, i.e., words (and the names of words) that at some time or another are *actually* interpreted, either because they are interpreted in the original dictionary, or because they are interpreted later, or because they are being interpreted by the *I*-sentence itself. For example, if I introduce "gloob" by the *I*-sentence " 'All apples are gloob' means 'All apples are red'," then this *I*-sentence is basic. Suppose I then introduce "plom" by " 'All apples are plom' means 'All apples are gloob or green'." This too is a basic *I*-sentence because "gloob" has an interpretation, and "plom" is being given one. By convention it is basic even if "gloob" is interpreted *after* "plom."

We are more concerned with nonbasic *I*-sentences, since basic *I*-sentences do not enable us to expand the class of sentences beyond past, present, and future types.

An uninterpreted sentence is a sentence that *never* receives a complete semantic interpretation. Any uninterpreted sentence can be paired with any member of an infinitely large class of nonbasic *I*-sentences. For example, if "gloob" is never actually interpreted, then "This apple is gloob" is uninterpreted. It may be paired with a nonbasic *I*-sentence from the following class: (1) " 'This apple is gloob' means 'This apple is red' "; (2) " 'This apple is gloob' means 'This apple is green' "; (3) " 'This apple is gloob' means 'This apple is sticky' "; etc. It may be that 'This apple is gloob' is paired with " 'This apple is gloob' means 'This apple is plom,' " where "plom" is never given an interpretation. In such a case, we add to this nonbasic *I*-sentence other nonbasic *I*-sentences until a link to basic *I*-sentences is established, thereby providing a unique interpretation in terms of interpreted constants. Thus, for each uninterpreted sentence, we have an infinite number of initial nonbasic *I*-sentences. Corresponding to *each* of these, there is an indefinitely long chain of *I*-sentences (0 to ∞), the length depending on content. Each chain constitutes a unique semantic interpretation.

We now add to the interpreted sentences of English pairs each of which is composed of an uninterpreted sentence and a unique semantic interpretation. These pairs are also called sentences. They are clearly no less obscure than original sentences, for they are created out of original sentences and uninterpreted sentences. The chain of *I*-sentences is simply a conjunction of original sentences. (Remember that they contain names of constants, not the uninterpreted constants themselves.) And the uninterpreted sentences are defined by *actual* vocabulary (including all uninterpreted constants) and the syntactic rules that define *any* sentence, interpreted or uninterpreted. Hence, no one can object to our expansion. These new sentences are called "*A*-sentences" (additional sentences).

It is an easy matter to locate the *R*-sentences among the *A*-sentences. Most of the restrictions on *R*-sentences are at least partly semantic (true, contingent, descriptive, etc.) and, therefore, require an examination of the semantic interpretation. Others (singular) are syntactic and require only an examination of the uninterpreted sentence.

We are now in a position to define determinism:

$$(x)[x \text{ is an } R\text{-sentence} \supset (\exists_y)(\exists_z)(y \text{ is a state}$$
$$\text{description-sentence} \cdot z \text{ is a law-sentence} \cdot$$
$$\dashv(y \cdot z) \supset x)]$$

This definition does not suffer from the deficiencies of our

177

previous attempt (see above, p. 165): (a) noninscribed sentences are included among both the sentences for which there have to be deterministic accounts and the sentences that provide the accounts; (b) sentences that *might* be added to English are also included under both categories. This result has been achieved with a very modest ontology. We consider briefly some objections.

Suppose English were to die out soon and some other language take its place. But as long as English existed at some time, it might be possible to translate the ultimate scientific theory into our expanded conception of English.

Suppose future conceptual revolutions are not so translatable. For example, it may be necessary to revise radically the semantic rules of English. If we possess the true theory of language, we may have universal semantic rules which permit us to give semantic interpretations to English sentences that are not permitted by the peculiarities of English semantics. But there are obviously problems in trying to squeeze such sentences into the class of English sentences. I prefer to say simply that I cannot formulate a thesis to take care of the envisaged contingency. "Determinists" of that era will have to formulate their own thesis. If one is really concerned about this, one may drop any definition of determinism and convert (3) into a schemata.

Or one may retain a definition in terms of facts. There is no crushing objection to this, and it has the merit of not requiring a language for the truth of determinism. I can only say that the reservations previously mentioned lead me to reject it. We shall think of determinism as: $(x)[x$ is an R-sentence $\supset (\exists y)(\exists z)(y$ is a state-description sentence $\cdot z$ is a law-sentence $\cdot -\!|(y \cdot z) \supset x)]$.

VI. THE REGULARITY THEORY: TRANSLATABILITY*

THE ISSUES SURROUNDING the question of the nature of laws are so large that only some can be dealt with here. I shall ignore some problems entirely and take stands on issues without adequate warrant. But I shall say something about matters that appear to be crucial for an understanding of determinism and its implications.

One central issue, the debate between necessitarians and regularity theorists, is entirely pertinent. If necessitarians are right, then laws are necessary truths. And if laws are necessary truths and determinism is true, it seems to follow that everything that happens happens necessarily—including human actions and decisions. No human action or decision, therefore, can be different from what it is, and no human being is ever morally responsible for this reason. Moreover, the reconciliationists, i.e., those who see no incompatibility between determinism and freedom, are wrong. Here is an issue, then, that requires our serious attention.

Chisholm makes a point in another context that might be used against the above argument. He says that it is fallacious to conclude that Socrates is necessarily rational because Socrates is human and is also necessarily rational-if-human.[1] One might argue analogously that it is fallacious to conclude

---

* The major portion of this chapter was first published, in a somewhat different form, in *Nous,* III (November, 1968). Copyright © 1968 by Wayne State University Press, reprinted with permission.

[1] R. M. Chisholm, "Query on Substitutivity," *Boston Studies in the Philosophy of Science,* ed. Robert S. Cohen and Marx W. Wartofsky (New York: Humanities Press, 1965) II, p. 276.

179

that some human action A is necessary because a condition C is present and "$C \supset A$" is necessary.

The standard systems of causal modality construe causal necessity on the analogue of logical necessity in regard to this question of distribution. Thus one can go from "$\boxed{C}(P \supset Q) \cdot \boxed{C}P$" to "$\boxed{C}Q$," but not from "$\boxed{C}(P \supset Q) \cdot P$" to "$\boxed{C}Q$." Thus, even if determinism is true, and P, therefore, is determined, we will not have the right to add "$\boxed{C}P$" for the same reason we do not have the right to say "$\boxed{C}Q$," namely, the premises "O" and "$\boxed{C}(O \supset P)$" are not sufficient for "$\boxed{C}P$." Only if the world began necessarily, e.g., emanated necessarily from the divine essence, will we be entitled to say that anything, actually everything, happens necessarily even though every event is governed by a necessary law.

So much the worse for standard construals. In the case of logical necessity, we evidently require such a restriction. Without it, all true propositions are logically necessary for, in the case of any true proposition Q, there is some other true proposition P such that $\Box(P \supset Q)$. Also, Q's being logically necessary is not an attribute that hinges on the relation between Q and other propositions.

Neither of these reasons has an analogue for causal necessity. If Q is true, there is not always another proposition P such that P causally implies Q—unless determinism is true, and if it is true, we are prepared to say that all R-sentences are causally necessary if laws are. And whether or not some event is necessary is dependent upon the occurrence of some other event. We may be tempted here to distinguish unconditional from conditional causal necessity and construe Q as conditionally (on P) causally necessary. But all cases of causal necessity are equally conditional. "$\boxed{C}(P \supset Q)$" is contingent, I would argue, on many other sentences—especially in light of the truth of the generality theory.

It seems to me that we do allow the inference from

180

"$\boxed{\text{C}}(P \supset Q) \cdot P$" to "$\boxed{\text{C}}Q$." If we use the language of causal necessity, we suppose that the cause makes it necessary for the effect to happen. From the point of view of human freedom, therefore, the question as to whether or not laws are necessary seems to be relevant.

A regularity theorist rejects the premise that laws are necessary. If this theory can be defended, the argument that concludes that there is no freedom may be rejected, and its conclusion will have to be defended in other ways by those who wish to do so.

Regularity theorists face two obstacles. They reject the sentential connective *"ni"* (nomic implication) as unnecessary or mistaken for the formulation of laws. They attempt, therefore, to formulate laws and theories in a language whose connectives are all truth-functional. Thus, laws are sentences of the form "$(x)(Px \supset Qx)$." But not all true sentences of that form are laws. There are many substitution instances that record so-called "accidental generalizations," e.g., "All U.S. Presidents from Missouri who serve during the first half of the twentieth century order atomic bombs to be dropped on Japan." Also, all substitution instances with empty antecedents, e.g., "All 200-year-old men are vegetarians," are true. The regularity theorist is then faced with the problem of formulating a set of conditions that rules out non-laws. Evidently, he cannot introduce modal operators in the statement of these conditions. A successful completion of this task will have certain characteristics as well.

First, all clear cases of laws are not ruled out and all clear cases of non-laws are. We might also hope that the borderline character of the borderline cases is accounted for by the set of conditions.

Second, allowing clear cases of laws but ruling out clear cases of non-laws is easy to achieve. We simply draw up a list of laws and a list of non-laws (assuming, contrary to fact, that we know all of the laws). Or we formulate a disjunctive property $L_1 \vee L_2 \vee L_3 \ldots \vee L_n$, where each L is a law, and define the class of laws as that class each of whose members has this property. Evidently, even if we had the knowledge to do this, it would not count as a successful defense of the regularity theory. The conditions, then, cannot be *ad hoc*. They must be selected in accordance with criteria actually used by scientists and laymen. (This is, of course, not to say that people have ever formulated or even been consciously aware of these principles.) Hopefully we may then apply this information in an effort to account for border-line cases.

By the "Thesis of Translatability," I mean the view that this program can be carried out. This chapter is an examination of the tenability of that thesis.

There are, however, some who reject the regularity theory independently of the thesis of translatability. They maintain that "must" statements are evidently not adequately captured by any set of "is" statements. Or they argue that certain facts cannot be adequately accounted for by the regularity analysis. Suppose, for example, that we distinguish laws from non-laws in terms of principles each of which is acknowledged to have some role in our recognition of the difference between the two classes. The thesis of translatability is thereby established. A regularity theorist must still defend a second thesis to the effect that these criticisms that are not touched by the translatability thesis are mistaken. We call this the "Thesis of Adequacy" and discuss it in the next chapter.

There are actually two varieties of necessitarianism. Some believe that laws are logically necessary, whereas others believe that laws are necessary in a different sense. We shall use the term "nomic" to characterize this second, distinctive kind of necessity although other terms have been used, e.g., "causal," "etiological," and "physical." I am not interested in the view that laws are *logically* necessary for I think it is untenable and I can add nothing to a critique such as

Nagel's.[2] Hence, the connective "*ni*," is not to be read as "logically implies."

Also, we countenance as a necessitarian position the view that not all laws are necessary, although those that are not are based upon or explained by laws that are necessary. This view is, in part, motivated by the same considerations which lead some to distinguish mere empirical generalizations which have little or no explanatory power from higher-order theoretical statements possessing a great deal of explanatory power. Since the theoretical relationships explain the empirically observed ones, it may be thought that the empirical generalization's status as a law depends upon the possibility of providing some theoretical account, even if the one we provisionally accept turns out, ultimately, to be unacceptable. This weaker brand of necessitarianism fares no better, however, if "*ni*" is completely unnecessary. And if the theses of translatability and adequacy are accepted, "*ni*" is ruled out completely.

We shall suppose in the discussion that follows that "is a law" is true of sentences in virtue of facts that are independent of the attitudes and/or beliefs of persons relative to the sentences, including beliefs regarding evidence and the truth of related generalizations. Attempts to define "is a law" in the "non-objective" way we are rejecting have been made.[3] But we shall take an "objective" approach unless we find reason to reject it. There would obviously be problems for determinists if a non-objective approach proved more feasible. The non-objective approach is invariably advanced by those who are sympathetic with the regularity theory. For example, if it looks as if objective factors are insufficient to

---

[2] Nagel, *Structure*, pp. 52-56.
[3] See, for example, A. J. Ayer, "What is a Law of Nature?" in *The Concept of a Person and Other Essays* (London, 1963), pp. 209-34. A position of this type was also espoused by R. B. Braithwaite at one time; but he surrendered it in *Scientific Explanation* (Cambridge, 1953).

define the difference between laws and non-laws, some take the path of the necessitarian while others turn to subjective considerations.

A built-in limitation to a philosophical investigation into the nature of laws may be illustrated by relativity theory. The equations of motion of general relativity theory are invariant under transformations to arbitrary reference frames. The invariance of the classical equations of motion, however, is limited to transformations to reference frames moving with uniform velocity relative to one another.

It has been argued that Einstein believed that the limitations of the classical equations are such as to render the sentences in which they appear *non-lawlike*. (We use the term "lawlike" to mean "if true, a law.") In other words, even if the sentences in which the equations occur are true and confirmed as such, they cannot be considered laws because they are simply not the right type. Regardless of the historical question as to whether or not Einstein did believe this, and regardless of the merits of the view itself, we must concede that there may be conditions of lawlikeness for individual sciences over and above certain general conditions with which philosophers have been primarily interested. The expression "lawlike in physics" may mean more than "lawlike and belonging to the science of physics."

Philosophers would be unwise to impose *a priori* limits on the kinds of conditions of lawlikeness that individual sciences may legitimately impose. Of course, some conditions may be acceptable because of a general philosophical requirement. An example might be: The laws of astronomy may contain no reference to desires. This condition of lawlikeness is bound up with the purported requirement that laws be explanatory—or, perhaps, counterfactual sustaining. We shall later discuss these requirements. Suffice it to note here that a complete explication of the distinction between laws and non-laws may not be possible if some principles

184

of lawlikeness for individual sciences cannot be construed as consequences of general philosophical principles. The task we face, therefore, may be called the definition of "philosophical lawlikeness."

There are several purported requirements on laws; let us examine them to discover those we shall accept. Moreover, we shall consider whether or not the acceptance of a certain requirement commits us to nomic necessity in those cases in which there is *prima facie* reason to think that it may.

Formal requirements: Although laws do not have to take the canonical form "$(x)(Px \supset Qx)$," for any sentence that is a law, there is a logically equivalent sentence that has this form (or the form of a biconditional) or a slightly more complicated form in which there are quantifiers following the universal quantifier. Any remarks about laws should be taken as applying to this form. Of course, any sentence can be put into this form. So we know nothing if we know of S that it has some logically equivalent version of this form. But it is natural to think of laws in this form and remarks about laws often depend upon their being expressed this way.

Truth: Laws are true sentences. The adoption of this requirement poses problems for a determinist.[4] But we shall consider these problems when we talk about the truth-status of determinism.[5]

Logical contingence: We find no warrant for the view that laws are logically necessary.[6]

Philosophical legitimacy of predicates: We acknowledge that certain predicates are ruled out of certain sciences on the basis of principles peculiar to those sciences. But there are, I would argue, three types of predicates that are *a priori* inadmissible into any scientific law.

Those of the first type are self-contradictory predicates. Clearly, no predicate in a law should be self-contradictory.

[4] See above, pp. 37–38.   [5] See Part III.
[6] See above, p. 182.

(This does not preclude psychological predicates like "believes that p and not-p." If it can be shown that this whole predicate is self-contradictory, then it is illegitimate, and the psychological facts would have to be redescribed. But the stipulation against self-contradictory predicates does not in itself rule it out.)

Predicates that are not open-ended are the second type. A predicate "P" is not open-ended if and only if "Px" entails "There are a finite number of individuals which satisfy 'Px.'" (The definition is essentially similar if "P" is relational.)

The acceptance of this requirement captures in part the idea that scientific laws are open-ended. Thus, although there is a finite number of planets in the solar system, this fact is not deducible from Kepler's laws.[7] Generally, if L is a scientific law, there is no logically equivalent version "(x) $(Px \supset Qx)$," such that one can deduce from this version that there are a finite number of P's.

The term "individual" is important in the formulation of the definition. We do not wish to rule out as laws sentences that restrict the number of kinds (e.g., elements) in the universe.

Positional predicates are the last type. This restriction would have been accepted prior to Goodman's famous critique of definitions of positionality,[8] when he pointed out that positionality is syntactically relative in that it is a function of our choice of primitive terms. Thus, if "green" and "blue" are primitive, then "grue" (which applies to green things before t and blue things thereafter) and "bleen" (which applies to blue things before t and green things thereafter) are positional.[9] But if "grue" and "bleen" are primitive, then "green"

---

[7] See Nagel, p. 59.

[8] Nelson Goodman, *Fact, Fiction and Forecast,* 2nd Ed. (New York, 1965), pp. 77-81.

[9] Strictly "grue" applies to all things examined before t just in case they are green and all other things (examined or not) just in case they are blue.

and "blue" will receive definitions that make them positional. If we wish to eliminate "grue" and "bleen," therefore, we cannot merely say that they are positional, for we can choose a language in which they are primitive.

It is important, moreover, to eliminate "grue" and "bleen" for purposes of confirmation theory, because, if we accept some form of the generalization principle according to which sentences like "$Pa \cdot Qa \cdot Pb \cdot Qb \cdot Pc \cdot Qc$" confirm "$(x)$ $(Px \supset Qx)$," we shall run into this difficulty: suppose that "grue" and "bleen" are primitive and that "green" means "grue before t, bleen thereafter." If all emeralds observed until t have been grue (green), the generalization principle entitles us to infer that the others—to be examined after t—are also grue (blue). But this is absurd, for we shall be taking the fact that all emeralds so far observed have been green as grounds for believing that the rest are blue. Clearly, we must get rid of these objectionable predicates.

Goodman suggests that these predicates may be eliminated through the elimination of hypotheses in which they occur, by, basically, formulating alternatives to the objectionable hypothesis. What constitutes an alternative is given by two rules. In all cases, the alternative must contain a predicate that is much better entrenched than the corresponding predicate (antecedent or consequent) of the objectionable hypothesis. The degree of entrenchment of a predicate is determined by the frequency with which that predicate (or any coextensive with it) has appeared in hypotheses that have actually been adopted. There is much more in the rules; but entrenchment is the key idea.

Thus, we predict that the first emerald to be examined after t is green, not blue, because "green" is much better entrenched than "grue."

It is important to examine Goodman's proposals in some detail because he sees little hope in attempts to define positionality. Thus, his proposals form an alternative to that enterprise. Moreover, when worked out, they constitute the outlines of a general definition of confirmation, i.e., a theory as to which hypotheses are confirmed by a class of evidence sentences at a given time. Since susceptibility to confirmation is a mark of lawlike (as opposed to accidental) hypotheses, then success here amounts to completion of the major task of defining "is a law." Goodman admits that there may be serious problems in specifying the steps which entitle one to go from "is projectible (legitimately adoptable) at t" to "is a law"; but he obviously feels that his analysis of the former is a major contribution toward the elucidation of the latter. We must look at his work, therefore, not only because it contains suggestions for the elimination of undesirable predicates, but also because it contains views on the general problem before us.

We have seen that a projectible hypothesis must pass two tests. In each case, one must fail to find an alternative hypothesis that satisfies certain conditions, one condition of which is the presence of a predicate that is much better entrenched than the corresponding predicate of the original hypothesis. It is not difficult to show—Goodman himself provides examples—that many non-lawlike hypotheses pass these tests.

Suppose there are three men in room A and (quite accidentally) they are all bald. We have examined two. Although "All the men in room A are bald" is true, we do not want to take our two instances as confirming this generalization. The first rule finds the fault in the consequent predicate. But I doubt if one can find an alternative hypothesis that satisfies the requisite conditions and has a consequent that is much better entrenched than "bald." The other rule requires that the reference hypothesis have the same consequent and a much better entrenched antecedent. If we suppose that we know that scalp condition P is the cause of baldness, we might suggest "All men with condition P are bald" as a candidate. But for reasons we need not go into, Goodman requires that the antecedent of the reference hypothesis not apply to some things that the antecedent of the original hypothesis does, i.e., some of the men in room A must fail to have condition P. This might work if there were several causes of baldness and the baldness of the unexamined man was due to a condition different from P. But even if luck is on Goodman's side, we must also suppose that "men with condition P" is much better entrenched than "men in room A" and it may not be. We may have only recently considered it as a plausible hypothesis.

Now a predicate "Q" with negligible entrenchment may inherit some from parents in this way: if there is a predicate "P" that applies only to classes, and one of these classes is the extension of "Q," and "P" is highly entrenched, then "Q" inherits this entrenchment and may use it to eliminate another predicate that is about equal to "Q" in earned entrenchment, but inferior in ancestry. Hence, we may be able to eliminate our troublesome hypothesis by considering the parents of "men with condition P."

Suppose, to make matters simple, we notice that the presence and amount of hair in all animals is a function of the presence of any of a class of nutrients N. We have a great deal of evidence for the hypothesis "All animals who are deficient in nutrient N are either bald or have little hair." Suppose then that scalp condition P is the absence of a particular nutrient in this class.

Although one might think that this procedure is typical for the accrual of entrenchment, it is not. For "animal deficient in nutrient N" is *not* a parent of "man with scalp condition P": the parent applies to *classes,* not individuals. But "animal deficient in nutrient N" is not like Goodman's examples ("army division," "bagful in stack S") in that it is an individual predicate. (Even if it is allowed that an animal is a class of parts, the class of men with scalp condition P

189

is not one of the classes "animal deficient in nutrient N" applies to because the latter predicate does not classify animals.) Once this is seen, one will recognize that it is next to impossible to find a parent predicate of "men with condition P" that has *any* entrenchment. It must be a predicate that applies to this *class* and others.

For similar reasons, the entrenchment of "men in room A" will not be increased. But the point is that the present attempt to eliminate "All the men in room A are bald" fails on the supposition (not unlikely) that "men with condition P" has about the same entrenchment as "men in room A."

As Goodman points out, this sort of failure is not so very serious, because we may be able to show that the *degree* of projectibility of unacceptable hypotheses is so low as to render them virtually unprojectible. That is, hypotheses that pass the two tests are called "presumptively projectible" and are then ranked on a scale of projectibility. Perhaps, then, all obviously illegitimate hypotheses will appear on the lower end. Before considering this possibility, it is worth repeating that many accidental generalizations that contain no queer predicates will turn out to be presumptively projectible.

With respect to degree of projectibility, an initial index is provided by ranking hypotheses according to the relative entrenchment of their predicates. On prior suppositions, therefore, "All men with condition P are bald" receives the same ranking as "All men in room A are bald." We may suppose that many non-lawlike hypotheses will fare as well as lawlike ones. There is now but one way to affect this initial ranking. The degree of projectibility of some hypothesis H may be increased through the confirmation of a presumptively projectible hypothesis I that is related to H as a "positive over-hypothesis." I is a positive overhypothesis of H if and only if the antecedent of I is a parent of the antecedent of H and the consequent of I is a parent of the consequent of H. Or, if I is a negative overhypothesis of H, i.e., the antecedent of I is a parent of the antecedent of H, but the consequent of I is complementary to a parent of the consequent of H, then its confirmation *decreases* the degree of projectibility of H (provided again I is presumptively projectible).

But we are then faced with the same severe limitation that we discussed earlier, to wit, that we are not free to confer (more) lawlikeness on some hypothesis by bringing to bear more general hypotheses in the typical way this is done. "All metals conduct electricity" is not a positive overhypothesis of "All copper conducts electricity." "All animals are mortal" is not a positive overhypothesis of "All men are mortal." Newton's laws of motion do not comprise a positive overhypothesis of Kepler's. We must rather look for class predicates in the overhypothesis. It is no accident that Goodman's examples concern bags and stacks of marbles.

Consider "All metals conduct electricity." Could we not change the antecedent to "classes of metals" and allow the consequent to be the same as the consequent of "All copper conducts electricity" as a degenerate case of parenthood? This might be all right if "conducts electricity" is a class predicate; but it is not. Nor may we substitute "uniform in the conductivity of electricity" for this predicate is compatible with the conductivity's being zero. We may introduce "class each member of which conducts electricity"; but its entrenchment is nil. We do not usually talk about classes when we can as easily talk about the members. Finally, even if one can defend the view that a class is the sum of its members, thereby enabling "class of objects that x" to receive the entrenchment that accrues to "x," it will not be possible to construe any term T whose extension includes the extension of U as the parent of U. For T must apply to classes, i.e., T must at least classify the objects in its extension, and the extension of U must be one of these classes.

The conclusion is that even if Goodman's approach is

tenable, it is seriously limited. Moreover, one wants to extend it to the same area, viz., higher-order generalizations. A natural question is whether or not Goodman can simply liberalize his conception of an overhypothesis.

Within the extensionalistic limitations Goodman imposes upon himself, the only admissible liberalization that might help would allow a parent to apply to all the individuals its child applies to. A parent would then simply be a predicate that applies to more individuals than its child applies to. But this would be an impossible step for Goodman to take.

On the one hand, it would be virtually impossible to rule out any hypotheses with bizarre predicates, since it would not be difficult for these predicates to inherit entrenchment. "Mu" which applies to men before time t and gnus thereafter would receive a great deal of entrenchment from the parent "animal." Our friend "grue" would likewise inherit entrenchment from "color." And if physical predicates apply to everything, their entrenchment confers entrenchment on all other predicates. Thus, Goodman's central idea would be lost.

On the other hand, just as positive overhypotheses strengthen some hypothesis H_1, so negative overhypotheses can weaken H_1. A necessary condition for the weakening of H_1 by a negative overhypothesis H_2 is that both be presumptively projectible, which implies that both are supported and unviolated. Under the suggested liberalization, however, it is impossible for both to be supported and unviolated. The confirming instances of H_1 violate H_2. Hence, if H_1 is supported, H_2 is violated. This conclusion follows from the fact that the consequent of the overhypothesis affirms that each member in the extension of its antecedent is outside the class determined by the consequent of H_1. But the antecedent of H_1 designates a subclass of the extension of the antecedent of H_2. For example, a confirming instance of "All copper conducts electricity" violates "All metals fail to conduct electricity." Goodman does not have this problem, for one can have evidence for both "All the marbles in bag B are red" and "All the bagfuls in S are nonuniform in color" without violating either. Clearly, the fact that the predicates of the overhypotheses are class predicates makes this possible.

Hence, Goodman cannot accept the suggested liberalization without radically altering his approach to allow for the effect of negative overhypotheses.

We are thus drawn again to the same conclusion, viz., that although Goodman's restrictions may be tenable, they are not sufficient. Moreover, if we feel, as I do, that higher-order generalizations do play a key role here, we must look to ways of introducing them that go beyond the limited approach under discussion.

Goodman may be quite right about positional predicates. That is, there may be no clearly defined class of this kind and elimination has to be effected via the basic idea of relative entrenchment. I certainly have nothing superior to offer in this connection.

It is interesting to note that Goodman's approach may fare a little better if one is interested, as we are, in a definition of "law." For, although we may be forced against our wishes to accept a hypothesis as lawlike e.g., "All men in room A are bald," eventually it will probably be eliminable in favor of "All men with condition P are bald," for the antecedent predicate of the latter will be entrenched if it is not now entrenched. So if we take Goodman's suggestion (he calls it a "first approximation") and define a law as a sentence that is projectible immediately before its last positive case is established, we may suppose that at that time, "men with condition P" is nicely entrenched.[10] One serious problem is that, on prior assumptions, "All men in room A are bald" could be considered a law much earlier, for we examined two men and there was only one remaining in room A. But we might be able to work out criteria to eliminate

[10] Goodman, p. 107.

it later after "men with condition P" becomes entrenched and the other conditions for laws are satisfied by "All men with condition P are bald."

But I would again insist that we are in a better position to make these decisions earlier if we know how to make use of higher-order generalizations. I shall explore this direction later in this chapter.

As to positionality, I shall leave the matter open. We shall say that positional predicates are ruled out, although the best way to deal with them may perhaps be in terms of entrenchment (in which case the concept of positionality is dropped).

Hence, a predicate must be non-self-contradictory, open-ended, and non-positional in order to appear in a law. Such predicates are called "philosophically legitimate."

Purely qualitative predicates: A predicate is purely qualitative if and only if its analysis contains no reference to a particular object. Thus, "lunar" is not purely qualitative; but "red" presumably is. Of course, it is not always clear whether or not some expression is purely qualitative since there may be disagreement over its analysis. Also, some versions of the resemblance theory of universals entail that there are no purely qualitative predicates since all predicates are analyzed in terms of resemblance to paradigm cases.

The reason for the belief that laws contain only qualitative predicates is simple. If we believe that "Smith gets angry when you call him a Communist" and "The moon revolves around the earth" are or point to laws, we also believe that some feature of Smith or the moon is what is responsible. Hence, the "real" law will contain the expression that describes this feature. Clearly the feature in question is not "being Smith" or "being the moon"; it is a feature that conceivably might belong to other objects, i.e., a feature describable by a qualitative predicate.

The main objection to the adoption of this stipulation is the existence of clear cases of laws that violate the stipulation, e.g., Kepler's first law. It has been suggested in rebuttal that these examples are laws only because they follow from laws that contain only qualitative predicates.

One cannot, however, deduce Kepler's first law ("All the planets revolve around the sun in elliptical orbits") from the axioms of Newtonian mechanics alone. The premises that must be added (e.g., "The gravitational attraction of the planets is negligible"), moreover, refer to particular objects.[11]

We can, however, derive the following generalization from the axioms of mechanics: All planets of any star whose masses are small in comparison with the mass of the star will revolve around that star in elliptical orbits. Again, to derive Kepler's first law, we require the information that our solar system satisfies the antecedent of the generalization, information which concerns particular objects. There is, nonetheless, the feeling that laws like Kepler's cannot stand alone in the sense that they are considered laws because we believe that there are other laws with only qualitative predicates that ground the laws like Kepler's. We would be disturbed to discover that no general property of our solar system explained Kepler's first law. We would tend under those conditions to think of the fact about the planetary orbit as an interesting cosmic fact.

Moreover, if we do not impose this restriction, many accidental generalizations become laws. For if "All A is B" is an accidental generalization, then if there is a law governing B-type occurrences, say "All and only C is B," then we shall be able to deduce "All A is B" from the law together with the possibly non-qualitative information that all A is C. And there may be no good reason to reject "All A is B" as a law if we are willing to accept Kepler's first law as a genuine law.

What then is the difference between Kepler's first law and

[11] See Nagel, p. 58.

195

"All men in room A are bald"? In each case a law with qualitative predicates only explains the generalization; deduction from that law requires non-qualitative information. One obvious difference is that location in room A is known to be irrelevant to baldness whereas no extraneous predicate appears in Kepler's law. Now it is true that whenever a law is *subsumed* under a higher-order law, a predicate of the lower-order law is thereby shown to be irrelevant. What distinguishes copper from other metals is irrelevant to the conductivity of electricity. "Copper conducts electricity," however, is still considered a law. But subsumption here requires no non-qualitative premise since all copper is metal. If scalp condition P is the cause of baldness, on the other hand, we have to add "All men in room A have scalp condition P" to deduce "All men in room A are bald." So "men in room A" suffers on two counts: (1) location in room A is known to be irrelevant to baldness; (2) the relevant causal predicate does not appear in an analysis of "men in room A." The predicate contains too much and not enough.

A possible objection to this account is that it implies by presupposition a sharp distinction between the analysis of a predicate and facts about its extension, i.e., between analytic and synthetic propositions. But this presupposition is not made. No sharp distinction between accidental generalizations and lower-order laws exists for the very reason that no sharp distinction between analytic and synthetic propositions can be made. "All pygmies are short" is one of many examples that does not fall clearly under either heading.

Regardless of the way we distinguish accidental generalizations from laws that contain non-qualitative predicates, a determinist would not be satisfied by an account that contains laws with non-qualitative predicates. Since he believes that there are laws containing only qualitative predicates governing all phenomena, the simplest procedure is to stipulate that non-qualitative predicates be ruled out from laws. We shall have to make more restrictions to define the kind of laws that may appear in deterministic accounts. A sense of the term "law" that is more than usually restrictive seems advisable, therefore, and subsequent clarifications of the term will be rendered accordingly.

But if we adopt the suggested procedure, we eliminate laws that seem to satisfy the requirement of "generality" that Kepler's laws lack. For if we define an inertial system as one that is not accelerated relative to the fixed stars, then, since "the fixed stars" denotes a particular, laws about inertial systems will have to be eliminated. I propose the adoption of this procedure with a change in the definition of "qualitative predicate" to "predicate that can logically apply to an indefinite number of entities." Hence, "lunar" is still non-qualitative; but "is an inertial system" is not.

Exhaustion of instances: Some distinguished philosophers of science have suggested that the predictive function of laws is not merely a contingent characteristic of these propositions. Goodman, for example, asserts: "Rather than a sentence being used for prediction because it is a law, it is called a law because it is used for prediction."[12] Nagel says, "If the observed cases were believed to exhaust the scope of application of the conditional, it is more likely that the statement would be classified as a historical report."[13] The rationale for this requirement, according to Nagel, is the predictive use to which laws are put. He, therefore, agrees with Goodman that "to call a statement a law is to assign a certain function to it."[14]

Suppose a libertarian were to employ one or both of the following arguments.

Since the claim that some type of human action is determined entails the existence of a law governing that type, and since a law is a sentence which is used to make predictions, no human action is determined unless there is a law *which*

[12] P. 26.   [13] P. 63.   [14] Ibid.

is actually used to predict actions of that type. Hence, almost all human actions are *known to be* undetermined.

With respect to that class of human actions which are determined or which will "become determined," the judgment that they are so is only temporary since, "at the end of time," the sentences which were laws will no longer be laws because they will no longer be used to make predictions. This conclusion can easily be generalized to embrace all events. Judgments of freedom, too, are time-bound. Actions which were unfree may become free when the relevant laws are no longer used for predictive purposes.

Since determinists and libertarians do not view their debate along these lines, we must see whether or not it is possible to eliminate pragmatic considerations from the definition of "law" without eliminating the possibility of a significant explication of determinism.

Consider the following propositions on the assumption that the evidence for them is known to exhaust their scope of predication:

1) All men who are the first to see a living human retina contribute to the establishment of the principle of conservation of energy.[15]

2) All Presidents of the United States from Missouri order an atomic bomb attack on Hiroshima.

3) All copper conducts electricity.

Proposition (1) is special in that the evidence for it *must* be known to exhaust its scope of predication. It is not a law for several reasons, one of which is its violation of the requirement that all predicates in a law be qualitative.

The evidence for (2) can be known to exhaust its scope of predication only if supplementary information is provided. For example, if the United States becomes a monarchy in 1972, then there will have been only one President from Missouri. We will show later how (2) can be eliminated.

[15] This is Nagel's example, p. 64.

If we learn that all the copper in the world has been destroyed and there is no way of replenishing the supply, then we know that the evidence for (3) exhausts its scope of predication (except for the possibility of historical postdictions). We may then view (3) as a historical report rather than as a law. But if we had been thinking of it as a law for a long time, I do not see why we might not continue to do so. It will no longer be an *important* law (although the system in which it apears may still be important); but we can continue to think of it as sustaining counterfactuals, and so on.

We still have the problem (that is our present concern) of explicating the distinction between an historically true generalization and a law. We shall see, however, that the distinction can be made without supposing that some evidence for laws is missing.

As philosophers of science, Nagel and Goodman are concerned to point out features common to the sentences which are distinguished as laws. One of these features—use for predictive purposes—if it were made a condition of lawlikeness, would radically alter the nature of the determinism-libertarianism debate. But I shall try to show that the distinction between law and non-law can be preserved even if we ignore this feature.

Counterfactual sustaining: It is noteworthy that the propositions which meet all preceding requirements, but which are not considered laws, are those that do not sustain their counterfactuals. "All men in any room with olive green walls and 600 square feet of window space are bald" may satisfy whatever requirements we have accepted, but it is not true that John would be bald if he were in such a room. The necessitarian explains this fact by noting that there is no necessary connection between the antecedent and consequent properties of the generalization.

A satisfactory analysis of laws will not resolve many issues regarding counterfactuals. Any serious analysis of counterfactuals, for example, must take account of the role assumptions play in the assertion of counterfactuals.

Broad has argued that the very fact that laws entail counterfactuals is incompatible with the regularity theory.[16] On the regularity view, he argues, these counterfactuals are either false or trivially true. They are false if the law is interpreted to hold only for cases in which the antecedent is satisfied. But this interpretation of laws is clearly unacceptable, since we do regard these counterfactuals as true. If, on the other hand, the law does apply to cases in which the instance of the antecedent is false, then the counterfactual is trivially (truthfunctionally) true.

If "$(x)(Px \supset Qx)$" is a law, then "$Pa \supset Qa$" is trivially true if $-Pa$. But the truth of "$Pa \supset Qa$" derives rather from the non-trivial fact that "$(x)(Px \supset Qx)$" is a law.

Perhaps Broad is saying that it is inconceivable how the law can apply to a, a non-confirming instance, if laws simply state regularities. He is concerned about either the meaning of the counterfactual or its confirmation. If the former, it is true that some reference to laws or their existence must enter into the analysis to preserve nontriviality. The details are controversial and I shall say no more about it. If Broad is concerned about confirmation, on the other hand, he must be saying that "$(x)(Px \supset Qx)$" is never confirmed directly by its instances. For this generalization does apply to a even though $-Pa$. He evidently wants to say that "$(x)(Px \supset Qx)$" is indirectly confirmed via the confirmation of "(x) $(Px \ ni \ Qx)$." But then this simply amounts to a statement of rather than an argument for necessitarianism.

He may point out that generalizations from a finite sample cannot be warranted unless the appropriate necessary con-

[16] C. D. Broad, "Mechanical and Teleological Causation," *Proceedings of the Aristotelian Society: Supplementary Volumes* (1935), XIV.

nections are postulated. This is, of course, the problem of the justification of induction, a problem whose examination has often been the occasion for the introduction of the concept of necessity. But unless a necessitarian is prepared to say that the relation of necessity is actually observed in the instances of some law, the inference to a necessary law creates the problem of induction just as easily.

Hence, laws sustain counterfactuals, and we shall shortly try to account for this fact without postulating necessitarianism.

Explanation: Ewing has presented a number of arguments to show that certain kinds of facts, e.g., perception, memory, and rationality, cannot be explained without postulating nomically necessary connections. He also presents reasons to believe that all psychological explanations postulate nomically necessary connections. Since these arguments are directed against the thesis of adequacy, they will be discussed later.

We earlier rejected definitions of determinism formulated in terms of the concept of explanation, but conceded that the concept of explanation might enter the picture in the analysis of laws. We are not interested in a general discussion of explanation (for example, we have nothing to say about explanations that might be achieved with statistical laws or no laws at all), but rather with the question of how laws, as we have defined them, achieve explanatory power. Can explanation be achieved, for instance, without supposing that laws are necessary?

For discussion purposes we call a sentence L a "law" if it meets all requirements so far adopted, viz., it is a true, logically contingent universal conditional with legitimate and qualitative predicates that sustains its corresponding counterfactual. Since an explanation using L may be rejected on the grounds that there is insufficient reason to believe L, suppose in addition that L is highly confirmed. Finally, suppose that L subsumes an event e in the sense that L together with an instance of its antecedent entails "e." Under what conditions would we say that L fails to explain e?

Notice, first of all, that the fact that L sustains its counterfactual is extremely important in this context. Smith's being in a room with mauve walls does not explain his baldness because "All the men in a room with mauve walls," although true, does not sustain its counterfactual. Hence an explanation of the counterfactual-sustaining property of laws becomes even more important.

Second, all sorts of contextual considerations might be involved in the failure. For example, the law might not be sufficiently specific to satisfy me. "Heat, oxygen, and a combustible material" does not distinguish arson from spontaneous combustion. Or I may really want an explanation of L rather than e. Again, however, *our* context is crucial. We are seeking a definition of law for the purpose of defining determinism. To that end, there is only one kind of subsumption that might fail to explain *and also* fail to provide a deterministic account: I am thinking of sufficient-condition laws that are not deterministic.[17] The law of the pendulum tells you a sufficient condition of some pendulum's altitude, but neither explains nor provides a deterministic account of it. Laws that connect the effects of a common cause, e.g., "All readers of the *National Review* vote Republican," have the same status. We shall deal with this problem later.

A most difficult question that we now turn to is: Given that some sentence L is a true, logically contingent, universal conditional with legitimate and qualitative predicates, can we account for its power to sustain its counterfactual without supposing that L is necessary? If we can, we shall also be able to satisfy the thesis of translatability, for we shall be able to eliminate accidental generalizations.

[17] See above, pp. 32, 40.

The approach I shall take is not new. Most regularity the-orists have acknowledged that a proposition that meets all our requirements plus perhaps others will fail to meet the counterfactual requirement because it lacks a crucial rela-tionship or link to a certain body of propositions. But no one, to the best of my knowledge, has adequately defined this relationship.[18] The most promising of these approaches, by far, is Nagel's. I should like to present my position as an extension of his.

After examining various ways, all of which we have dis-cussed, in which a proposition can be rejected as a non-law, Nagel says that "there is often a strong disinclination to call a universal conditional L a 'law of nature,' . . . if the only available evidence for L is direct evidence."[19] But it would be too strong, he says, to call this a requirement.

There are two senses of "indirect evidence": "L is jointly derivable with other laws L_1, L_2, etc., from some more gen-eral law (or laws) M, so that the direct evidence for these other laws counts as (indirect) evidence for L";[20] (2) "L can be combined with a variety of special assumptions to yield other laws each possessing a distinctive scope of predi-cation, so that the direct evidence for these derivative laws counts as 'indirect' evidence for L."[21]

In this discussion, Nagel is more concerned with the analy-sis of predicates like "has (sufficient) reason to call L a law" than he is with the predicate "is a law." If we wish to sup-pose, as we do, that a proposition can be a law without there being anyone in possession of evidence that it is a law, we

[18] In *Determinism*, (Ph.D. Dissertation, Columbia University, 1963), I examined the defense of the regularity theory by the following: Braithwaite in *Scientific Explanation*, Nagel in *The Struc-ture of Science*, and Arthur Pap in *An Introduction to the Philosophy of Science* (Glencoe, Illinois, 1962).

[19] Nagel, p. 66.

[20] Ibid., pp. 64-65.

[21] Ibid., p. 65.

shall have to be careful in the way we use Nagel's conception of indirect evidence.

Consider the first sense of indirect evidence. One must take steps to avoid its being trivially satisfied. For example, "All men with physiological condition P are bald" is, let us suppose, a law; and "All the men in room A are bald" is, let us suppose, true. But the fact that they are both derivable from "All men who have physiological condition P or are in room A are bald" lends no credence to the claim that the direct evidence for "All men with physiological condition P are bald" is indirect evidence for "All the men in room A are bald."

In fact, however, Nagel rules this case out on the grounds that the higher-order generalization is not more general than the deduced generalizations. Now Nagel's analysis of "degree of generality" drops the "seemingly plausible requirement"[22] that logically equivalent statements are equally general, and for certain purposes, it may be desirable to drop this requirement. But I would like to define this notion so that we can eliminate objectionable cases, and its applicability is invariant to formulation.

I am only prepared to present a rigorous definition for the simple class of cases in which "All R is S" follows from a single generalization "All P is Q." The account would have to be extended to include, for example, generalizations containing an existential quantifier as well as the great majority of scientific examples. One cannot deduce one Keplerian law from one Newtonian law. Nor can one deduce from Snell's law what the ratio $\frac{\sin i}{\sin r}$ is for any substance since the law only tells you that it is constant.

For the simple class of cases the definition is this: "All P is Q" is "higher on the scale of deductive systematization" than "All R is S" if and only if:

[22] Ibid., p. 39.

1. "All P is Q" entails but is not entailed by "All R is S";

2. There is a sentence "All T is U" which is logically equivalent to "All P is Q" and there is a sentence "All T is V" which is logically equivalent to "All R is S" such that

    a) "Ux" entails "Vx" in one step in accordance with the Rule of Addition or

    b) "Ux" entails "Vx" in two steps, the first of which is in accordance with the Rule of Simplification and the second of which is in accordance with the Rule of Addition;

3. "Vx" is a disjunction each disjunct of which must be one of the following: $Px, Qx, Rx, Sx, -Px, -Qx, -Rx, -Sx$.

4. (x) (If x is a sentence and x entails "All R is S" and is entailed by but does not entail "All P is Q," then the three preceding conditions apply to the relation between "All P is Q" and x and this relation is not infinitely generative in the following sense.

One type of case we wish to rule out is: "$P \supset (Q \cdot R)$," $\therefore$ "$P \supset Q$." We can find appropriate sentences that satisfy (2) and (3):

    (a) $-(P \supset (Q \cdot R)) \supset ((P \supset (Q \cdot R)) \cdot (-P$
$$\vee Q))$$

    (b) $-(P \supset (Q \cdot R)) \supset ((-P \vee Q) \vee Q)$

There is an x that satisfies the antecedent of (4): "$-(P \supset (Q \cdot R)) \supset (-P \vee Q)$." X is related to (a) in terms of logical form in the same way "$P \supset Q$" is related to "$P \supset (Q \cdot R)$." Since this logical form is ruled out by (2), the conversion of this pair, x and (a), would generate analogues to (b) and (a), and a new x that, were it and the (a)-analogue to be converted, would generate a new x, ad infinitum. This sort of situation is ruled out by the stipulation that the relation not be infinitely generative.

205

This definition eliminates, as modes of deductive systematization, the following:

(1) $\quad\quad\quad\quad\quad\quad (P \lor Q) \supset R$
$\quad\quad P \supset R \quad\quad\quad\quad\quad\quad\quad\quad\quad\quad Q \supset R$

(2) $\quad\quad\quad\quad\quad\quad (P \lor Q) \supset R$
$\quad\quad (P \cdot S) \supset R \quad\quad\quad\quad\quad\quad\quad (Q \cdot T) \supset R$

(3) $\quad\quad\quad\quad\quad\quad P \supset (Q \cdot R)$
$\quad\quad P \supset Q \quad\quad\quad\quad\quad\quad\quad\quad\quad\quad P \supset R$

(4) $\quad\quad\quad\quad\quad\quad (P \lor R) \supset (Q \cdot S)$
$\quad\quad P \supset Q \quad\quad\quad\quad\quad\quad\quad\quad\quad\quad R \supset S$

(Note: I have used the sentential calculus for simplicity. Also, (3) is merely a formulational variant of (1).)

Notice that degree of deductive systematization (DDS) is relative to certain definitions. Thus, if "human being" means "man or woman or child," then the following fail to have this relation:

A. $\quad\quad\quad\quad$ "All human beings are mortal";
B. $\quad\quad\quad\quad\quad$ "All women are mortal."

Our belief that (*A*) is higher on the scale of deductive systematization than (*B*) is contingent upon our tacitly providing an alternative definition of "human being."

(Hence, laws must be relativized to definitions or whatever devices are employed to give the terms in laws meaning, e.g., theories. But this consequence is not more debatable than the claim that laws are sentences: obviously a sentence that is a law can be changed to a non-law by changing the meanings of some constituent terms.[23])

To put the matter informally, the exhibition that one sentence is higher on the scale of deductive systematization than another amounts to a demonstration that some characteristic is superfluous relative to another characteristic. (One would have to modify this informal account to rule out characteris-

[23] John O'Connor pointed out to me the necessity for relativization.

tics which are shown to be superfluous via the demonstration that their negations are sufficient. In the example immediately above, A shows that "being a man or child" also refers to a sufficient condition of mortality and, therefore, shows that "being neither a man nor a child" is superfluous relative to mortality.)

We must now expand the definition to include a large class of important cases, viz., those involving a determinable-determinate relation. For example, "All colored objects emit a wavelength" will not be higher on the scale of deductive systematization than "All red objects emit a wavelength" according to the definition because "red" cannot be analyzed as a conjunction of "colored" and some other term.

Generally, D_1 is a determinate of the determinable D if and only if "D_1x" entails but is not entailed by "Dx," "D_1" cannot be defined in terms of a conjunction of "D" and an independent predicate, and "D" cannot be defined as a disjunction of "D_1" and some other predicates. "P" is independent of "Q" if and only if "Px" is logically independent of "Qx."

We can preserve the original definition of DDS by allowing ourselves artificial definitions of the form " 'red' means 'colored and red.' " But the definition will also suffer from narrowness. We consider as a legitimate case of systematization one in which generalization from one determinate to several but not all determinates of one determinable is effected. For example, we may prove that a property applies to all objects that fall within a certain temperature range or velocity range. But if the range is defined disjunctively, as it might well be (ignoring the fact that in actuality the range is often a mathematically continuous one), "All slowly moving objects are P" will not be higher than "All objects moving at 1 mph are P." I propose then that we add the following disjunct to the definition:

5. or clause 1 applies and there is a sentence "All T

is U" which is logically equivalent to "All P is Q" and there is a sentence "All T' is V" which is logically equivalent to "All R is S" such that

a) T' is a determinate of the determinable T

or

b) T is a (disjunctive) set of determinates of the

same determinable of which T_1 is a determinate.

Assuming there are no serious problems in the extension of the defiinition of DDS to more complicated cases, we can go on to embrace both of Nagel's senses of indirect evidence: L_1 is deductively systematized if and only if there exists a sentence L_2 which meets all the requirements we have imposed on laws (but no reference to the counterfactual requirement is made), and L_2 is either higher or lower on the scale of deductive systematization than L_1.

Nagel's second sense of indirect evidence does introduce the notion of scope of predication. We shall say something about this notion shortly.

Should we impose as a requirement on laws that they be deductively systematized? First of all, it would clearly be far too strong to demand for some candidate L_1 that two sentences be produced, one higher and the other lower on the scale of deductive systematization than L_1. This would fail for the most general laws (the axioms) and for the least general laws. Secondly, there is no harm in making this a requirement for *it eliminates no sentences*. Given any true sentence of the form "All P is Q," there will always be some predicate which is true of all or some P's, say "R," and "All PR is Q" is deducible, thereby satisfying the definition of deductive systematization. Moreover, in the same way, an indefinite number of sentences can be derived from "All P is Q." From "All the men in room A are bald," for example, one can deduce both "All the short men in room A are bald" and "All the tall men in room A are bald."

Thus, this requirement eliminates only an objectionable way of deductively systematizing sentences. It forces systematizations into a mold to which other criteria may be applied.

I conclude that in order for a sentence to be a law, it must be deductively systematized. (I shall call this the "*DS*-requirement," and by a *"DS"* shall mean a set of sentences each member of which is deductively systematized by some other member. Moreover, in order to avoid the arbitrary concatenation of axioms, an axiom is eliminated if the only sentences it systematizes would still be systematized if that axiom were the sole axiom of the system. This restriction applies, of course, only to systems with more than one axiom.)

Let us turn now to another possible requirement which we shall call the "scope of predication-requirement" (*SP*).

Again, our definition will be somewhat different from Nagel's and, again, we shall not be able to define this notion with complete rigor. Nagel's definition is simpler because it is not formulationally invariant.

"All *P* is *Q*" has a distinctive scope of predication from "All *R* is *S*" if and only if: There exists a true confirming instance of "All *P* is *Q*," say "*Pa · Qa*," such that the following is true: There are no predicates which are true of *a* such that one can deduce from the information that these predicates are true of *a* a confirming instance of "All *R* is *S*," i.e., a sentence of the form "*Rx · Sx*."

Conversely, what is true of "All *P* is *Q*" relative to "All *R* is *S*" is true of "All *R* is *S*" relative to "All *P* is *Q*."

The *SP*-requirement is: The deductive systematization of *L* must include at least three sentences, two of which are entailed by the other. Moreover, the two entailed sentences must have distinctive scopes of predication. (*L*, of course, may be either the higher sentence or one of the lower ones.)

The *SP*-requirement does eliminate one sort of case. Let

us call a predicate a uniqueness-predicate (*U*-predicate) if and only if it is a contingent fact that it is true of one and only one object. It is always possible to take any object *x*, find a predicate "*P*" which is true of it, and then find three *U*-predicates for *x*. We then construct the following *DS*:

$$U_1 \supset P$$

$$(U_1 \cdot U_2) \supset P \qquad\qquad (U_1 \cdot U_3) \supset P$$

This fails to satisfy the *SP*-requirement for the only true confirming instance of "$(U_1 \cdot U_2) \supset P$" refers to an object *x* which is also referred to by the only confirming instance of "$(U_1 \cdot U_3) \supset P$." Since examples like these are objectionable, the *SP*-requirement performs a valuable service.

Pap would object to this requirement on the grounds that it implies that there must be some evidence for laws.[24] (The requirement does not imply the existence of *direct* evidence for laws, and this fact is important for there are vacuous laws.) Moreover, he used the word "evidence" in such a way that evidence can exist without anyone knowing it. Thus, Pap is *not* arguing for the very plausible position that a sentence may be a law although no one has any reason to think so. He is rather arguing for the view that a sentence may be a law—and, therefore, true—even though there are no facts in the world which could even constitute indirect evidence for the sentence.

A necessitarian might buttress Pap's position by claiming that certain relationships may hold even though certain facts about the world prevent our discovering them. For example, we may know that "$(P \cdot Q) \supset R$" is a law, but not be able to test "$P \supset R$" for all *P* is *Q*. The *SP*-requirement would presumably rule out "$P \supset R$" since any lower-order sentences of the form "$(P \cdot X) \supset R$" do not have scopes of predication

[24] Arthur Pap, "Reduction Sentences and Disposition Concepts," in *The Philosophy of Rudolf Carnap*, P. A. Schilpp, ed. (La Salle, Illinois, 1963), pp. 559-97.

distinct from "$(P \cdot Q) \supset R$." Since all P is Q, any object that confirms "$(P \cdot X) \supset R$" also confirms "$(P \cdot Q) \supset R$." But might not "$P \supset R$" be a law? Might not "If a were P and not Q, it would still be R" be true? The regularity theorist is forced to say that there are conditions under which this counterfactual is false or truth-valueless. (I shall let the Russellians and Strawsonians battle this one out.)

That the regularity theorist is right can be brought out by introducing two predicates "tigephanteon" and "laviar." The former means "having the face of a tiger, the body of an elephant, and the color changes of a chameleon." The latter means "having lettuce and salmon caviar as one's natural diet." Harry is neither a tigephanteon nor a laviar. But a necessitarian would have to argue that the sentence "If Harry were a tigephanteon, he would be a laviar" may be true. It is conceivable that a biologist *would* be able to tell us its truth-value. But I am supposing that *all* the past, present, and future biological facts are completely neutral. What can it possibly mean to say that it might be true except that there might have been facts which would have made it true? In this sense, propositions known to be false might be true. The necessitarian wants to say that the supposition that it is true does not require the supposition that any facts are different from what they are. Or take the same question in a Carnapian-type world of two objects, a and b, of which *only* the predicates "red" and "square" apply. The necessitarian is committed to a strange version of realism if he insists that the truth-value of the sentence is there, waiting to be, but not, known. I conclude that there are conditions under which "If a were P and not Q, it would be R"—if this is a counterfactual which is supposed to be sustained by a law "All P is R"—is truth-valueless or false.

Unactualized potentials, unrealized dispositions, and the like are realities, however, so I cannot impose too strong restrictions on laws. Moreover, the type of example initially mentioned (in which we do not know if a would be R if it were P but not Q) is not nearly as bizarre as "all tigephanteons are laviars." In fact, however, the SP-requirement is so weak that, in that original type of example, "$P \supset R$" *would always satisfy it* and, therefore, be considered a law unless other stipulations are made.

If "All P is Q" and "All P and Q are R," it follows that all P are Q and R. If "$P \supset (Q \cdot R)$" is a law, it follows that "$P \supset R$" is a law. But "$P \supset (Q \cdot R)$" satisfies the SP-requirement. If this requirement is sufficient, therefore, we shall have to conclude that "$P \supset R$" is a law. "$P \supset (Q \cdot R)$" satisfies the SP-requirement if there is more than one object that is P. Then, one simply divides the class of objects that are P into, say, the two classes "$P \cdot X$" and "$P \cdot -X$." "$(P \cdot X) \supset (Q \cdot R)$" and "$(P \cdot -X) \supset (Q \cdot R)$" both follow from "$P \supset (Q \cdot R)$" and have distinctive scopes of predication.

Another objection to the SP-requirement is that it begs certain questions regarding the notion of confirming instance. If "All P is Q" is logically equivalent to "All $-Q$ is $-P$," why cannot sentences of the form "$-Qx \cdot -Px$" represent confirming instances of "All P is Q"?[25]

Even if the notion of confirming instance is liberalized in the suggested manner, the objectionable DS (originally conceived to be confirmed by only one object) still does not meet the SP-requirement. The expanded sets of confirming instances of the lower-order sentences are still co-extensive.

$$\{U_1 \cdot U_2 \cdot P, -(U_1 \cdot U_2) \cdot -P\} = \{U_1 \cdot U_3 \cdot P, -(U_1 \cdot U_3) \cdot -P\}.$$

Also

$$\{U_1 \cdot U_2 \cdot P, -(U_1 \cdot U_2) \cdot -P, -(U_1 \cdot U_2) \cdot P\} = \{U_1 \cdot U_3 \cdot P, -(U_1 \cdot U_3) \cdot -P, -(U_1 \cdot U_3) \cdot P.\}$$

Unfortunately, however, *no* laws meet the SP-requirement if we completely liberalize the notion of a confirming instance to admit as confirming all that is not disconfirming. For then,

---

[25] I am, of course, alluding to Hempel's paradox; see "Studies in the Logic of Confirmation," *Mind*, LIV, Nos. 213 and 214 (January and April, 1945).

everything will confirm all laws. That is, any true confirming instance will confirm any law. If we accept the *SP*-requirement, therefore, we must commit ourselves to a theory of confirmation more in accord with common sense. Perhaps an approach in terms of selective confirmation will prove most feasible in this direction.[26]

But we shall not adopt the *SP*-requirement, because the kind of case it eliminates is easily ruled out by the next requirement and because we may thereby remain uncommitted on controversial matters regarding confirmation.

The most important requirement is a comprehensiveness-requirement (*C*-requirement). To define this requirement, we must first define a set of sentences we shall call the set accounted for by a *DS:* that subset of *R*-sentences each member of which is entailed by the *DS* plus all sentences belonging to a legitimate state description. The term "legitimate" here refers to the restrictions on state descriptions specified in the previous chapter, including the temporal restriction. Thus, this set might be thought of as determining all the facts the theory *can* account for.

An additional stipulation is necessitated by the fact that, as it now stands, an accidental generalization accounts for the negation of its antecedent when the negation of its consequent is a legitimate state description. Hence, "All men in room *A* are bald" can account for "*x* is not a man in room *A*" or "*x* is a man not in room *A*." The absurdity of the supposition that sentences of this form (*S*) are accounted for in terms of *x*'s having hair derives from the fact that the sentences whose predicates determine subsets of the predicate of *S* are invariably accounted for in other ways.[27] Hence, the objects whose specific locations are accounted for by

[26] See Israel Scheffler, *The Anatomy of Inquiry* (New York, 1963), pp. 289-95.

[27] Of course, many of these cases violate the restriction that the event to be explained must not precede the occurrence of the antecedent condition. But some cannot be dealt with in this way. So let us suppose that *x* remains in room *A* until he acquires hair.

some DS are not uniform with respect to baldness. We must, therefore, restrict the set accounted for by a DS thus: If DS_1 plus all legitimate state descriptions SD_1 that are instantiations of the same sentential function entail all the members of a set of sentences A, but all or almost all sentences more specific than the members of A are accounted for by DS's whose SD's are independent of SD_1, then DS_1 does not account for the members of A or any logical consequences of these members.

Since the sentences in A are the ascriptions of a property to one or more objects at a certain time, then a sentence B is more specific than one A_1 in A if B ascribes a more specific property to the same object(s) at the same time. Hence, the predicate of B is more specific than the predicate of A_1, and this relation holds if and only if, for any legitimate predicate "P," "All A_1 is P" is higher on the scale of deductive systematization than "All B is P."

SD_1 is independent of SD_2 if and only if some members of SD_1 (a set of legitimate state descriptions) refer to objects that have properties incompatible with the property ascribed by SD_2 (exclusive of the temporal references required by all state descriptions).

The predicates of the R-sentences in the set accounted for by a DS can often be construed as the determinates of various determinables. A theory of motion, for example, will account for many facts that represent determinates of position. Corresponding to any DS, therefore, there will be a set of determinables the instantiation of some determinates of which are accounted for by that DS.

The C-requirement says: L is a law only if it appears in a DS which accounts for each sentence of a set S_1 (perhaps only a subset of the entire set accounted for by that DS) each member of which entails some sentence of the form "Px" (or "Pxy," etc.) such that there is no other DS that accounts for the members of S_1 plus other sentences entailing sentences of the form "Px." (If "P" is a determinable predicate, it might itself appear as a predicate function whose value is determined by the particular application of DS_1, e.g., "has x number of hairs on his head.")

"All men in room A are bald" is rejected in favor of "All men with scalp condition P are bald" for the latter accounts for all the bald cases in room A plus others.

The importance of the DS-requirement, which, in itself, eliminates nothing, is now apparent. If, for example, we had a uniqueness-predicate for each bald person, U_{bn}, we could, were it not for the DS-requirement, create a comprehensive theory of baldness by concocting the following axiom:

$$(x)(U_{b1}x \lor U_{b2}x \lor U_{b3}x \lor \ldots U_{bn}x \supset x \text{ is bald})$$

Suppose, however, there are two independent causes of baldness, scalp condition P and scalp condition Q, and some men in room A have one condition and the rest have the other condition. Notice first that the two genuine laws governing baldness will be certified by our rules. Hence, it is natural to suggest as an additional requirement that a sentence L be ruled out if the only facts its DS accounts for are accounted for by other laws belonging to DS's (or a DS) different from L's. (If the laws appeared in L's DS, L would have to be a law. "Copper conducts electricity" is not ruled out as a non-law when it is deduced from "Metals conduct electricity.") A DS containing L may be ruled out by this requirement, although L may eventually turn out to be a law because it belongs to some DS that passes this and all other requirements.

An objection to this requirement, however, is that it rules out symptomatic laws, i.e., laws that record the independent effects of a common cause. (If the effects are not independent, we are dealing with a causal chain, and each law will be certified in the regular way. For example, if drinking alcohol causes both a neurological condition and insulting behavior, and if the neurological condition can also be thought of as the cause of the insulting behavior, then the latter connection will be certified as lawful by the use of our adopted rules.)

For our purposes, however, the rejection of symptomatic laws is desirable because these laws are not deterministic. But ought we not to deal with the distinction between symptomatic laws and accidental generalizations? We can do this very easily. Let us adopt the suggested Superfluity or S-requirement, thereby ruling out symptomatic laws. We then define a symptomatic law as a sentence that meets all requirements on laws specified prior to this section (i.e., excluding the DS-, C-, and S-requirements), fails the S-requirement, and is a conclusion of an argument that takes one of the following forms (where all premises are laws):

$$\frac{\begin{array}{l} P \equiv Q \\ P \supset R \end{array}}{Q \supset R} \qquad \frac{\begin{array}{l} (P \cdot S) \equiv Q \\ P \supset R \end{array}}{Q \supset R} \qquad \frac{\begin{array}{l} P \equiv Q \\ P \equiv R \end{array}}{Q \equiv R}$$

A sentence that meets all requirements on laws specified prior to this section, but is not a symptomatic law, is an accidental generalization or some sentence, like a developmental law, that is neither accidental nor symptomatic, but not, for one reason or another, a law in *our* required sense.

Another objection to the S-requirement is that it seems to rule out some non-symptomatic laws. For example, if a gas is heated in a container whose volume is constant, its temperature and pressure will increase. We might want to say that the relationships among pressure, volume, and temperature as formulated in Boyle's law are neither causal *nor* symptomatic. But according to our view, Boyle's law is *not* symptomatic because it accounts for facts involving these determinables that are not accounted for by the law that specifies the results of heating the gas, e.g., results that accrue from increasing the pressure of the gas. So Boyle's law is genuine even if it is non-causal. (The further distinction between causal or deterministic law and non-causal law is a concern of a later chapter.)

The famous "hooter" example must be dealt with: "Whenever the hooter of factory a hoots in London, the workers of factory a go to lunch" and "Whenever the hooter of factory b in Manchester hoots, the workers of factory b go to lunch" are laws; but because the hooters always hoot simultaneously, "Whenever the hooter of factory a hoots in London, the workers of factory b go to lunch" (H) is true. The former two are laws because they belong to a comprehensive psychological theory (DSp) whose key axiom can only roughly be characterized: Whenever the members of a group agree to respond in a certain way to a pre-arranged stimulus, then, when the stimulus is perceived, other things being equal, the members will respond in that way. This DS explains many determinates of the determinable "respond in a prearranged way" other than "leaves factory x." Hence, the C-requirement eliminates the accidental generalization H. But a new problem arises. If we add the fact that certain hooters hoot simultaneously (HS) to DSp $(DSph)$, we will be able to account for all the facts DSp accounts for alone as well as deduce H and many sentences like it. Is there any way to rule out $DSph$?

This problem is really the general one of showing that a genuine theory is better than that theory conjoined to some accidental generalizations under the apparently conflicting demand of comprehensiveness for genuine theories.

First of all, the DS-requirement places some restrictions that are relevant, viz., the restriction on generalizing by disjoining predicates, and the restriction on completely irrelevant axioms. But $DSph$ does not contain completely irrelevant axioms because H cannot be deduced without HS. Since the facts accounted for by H-type sentences are accounted for by DSp alone, however, the only additional facts $DSph$

accounts for are those *HS* accounts for by itself. Hence, it seems plausible to add an axiom economy requirement (*AE*): If *A* is the axiom set of a *DS* accounting for facts *F* and there exists a conjunction *B · C* such that: *B · C* is logically equivalent to *A*, *A* is not higher on the scale of deductive systematization than either *B* or *C*, and *B* and *C* each account for a distinct subset of *F*, then the *DS* of which *A* is the axiom set is eliminated. (Again, a sentence may be ruled out because it appears in an illegitimate *DS* and yet be a law because it also appears in a legitimate *DS*.) This requirement does not rule out "All metals conduct electricity" in favor of distinct *DS*'s for each distinct metal for the very reason that "metal" is *not* equivalent to "copper or zinc or lead or . . . " The point of adopting a theory to organize a set of laws is lost if we end up with something equivalent to that set—this is in effect the *DS*-requirement. Also, we are now in a position to eliminate the following objectionable *DS* if the *S*-requirement fails to do the job:

$$(P \vee Q \vee R \vee \ldots Y) \supset Z$$
$$((P \vee Q \vee R \vee \ldots Y) \cdot O) \supset Z$$

"All Presidents of the United States from Missouri order an atomic bomb attack on Hiroshima" is easily eliminated because there is a competing account in terms of beliefs and desires held by Truman that is far more comprehensive.

But are we not relying on the mere hope that these vague, commonsense theories (e.g., the one explaining Truman's decision and *DSp*) will turn out to be genuine scientific theories? First of all, I am trying to account for our belief that certain sentences are laws, while others are accidental generalizations. This belief hinges very often, I am arguing, on a belief that certain general theories are true. The fact that scientific evidence can overturn these beliefs proves only that claims of the form "*L* is a law" or "*L* is accidental" are empirical in part. I disagree, therefore, with those who say that "*L* is lawlike" is *a priori*. Empirical evidence bears on both truth and lawlikeness.

Secondly, it may turn out that the comprehensive theories we appeal to are not strictly deterministic. We have not, in fact, discussed the repercussions of the possible inclusion of statistical laws in *DS*'s. Although this omission is major, I see no reason to conclude that the basic idea presented here is untenable.

Another criticism is that the insistence upon systematization seems to rule out laws that do not belong to a comprehensive theory. This criticism is easy to rebut. First of all, any generalization can be trivially systematized by making it an axiom and deducing lower-order generalizations from it. Then we consider whether or not a more comprehensive theory is in the offing. If there is none, a generalization that looks relatively isolated will be a law on the present approach.

I contend that a true, logically contingent universal conditional with non-self contradictory, open-ended, nonpositional, and qualitative predicates sustains its counterfactuals and is, therefore, a law if and only if it meets the four outlined requirements (*DS, C, S, AE*). The thesis of translatability is sustained.

We are now in a position to reply to the criticism of the regularity theory which says: The predicates that appear in laws are often dispositional. Hence, even if the principal connective in a law is truth-functional, necessity might be implicit in the dispositional term because there might be a necessary connection between the conditions of the disposition and its manifestation.

This concern is without foundation. We consider first simple dispositions, i.e., those associated with a single test

219

condition. Let "D" be any simple disposition, "Q" its test condition, and "R" its test result.

"Dx_t" means "$(\exists P)(Px_t \cdot$ It is a law that $(y)(t)((Py_t$
$$\cdot\, Qy_t) \supset Ry_t))$"

Kaila, who proposed a definition very similar to the above, was criticized by Carnap on the ground that "Px" cannot be "$(x = a) \lor (x = b)$".[28] But since the universal conditional must be a law, "Px" cannot be "$(x = a) \lor (x = b)$" for the latter is not open-ended and, therefore, not philosophically lawlike. (In Kaila's context, where no analysis of law is provided, a stipulation that the conditional be a law would be question-begging.)

Wedberg pointed out that "$Qx \supset Rx$" cannot be admitted for "Px."[29] But since this instantiation would convert the universal conditional into a logically necessary truth rather than a law, we can rule it out.

Of course, "P" may be dispositional or a DS in which the law referred to in the analysis appears may contain other laws with dispositional terms. But I am not trying to eliminate all dispositional terms. I am only saying that, given one, it can be analyzed without recourse to necessitarian notions.

Multiple dispositions, like "being friendly" and "$x°C$ temperature," are associated, often vaguely, and often in an open-textured way, with a set of test conditions and corresponding results. For each member of the set, the above analysis applies.

[28] Kaila reports in *Der physikalische Realitätsbegriff* that Carnap pointed out this difficulty to him.

[29] Wedberg's criticism appears in "The Logical Construction of the World," *Theoria* (1944), Pt. III.

VII. THE REGULARITY THEORY:
ADEQUACY

GIVEN THE ESTABLISHMENT of the thesis of translatability, a necessitarian may still insist that certain facts require the supposition that laws are necessary truths.

The most interesting fact alleged to require a necessitarian interpretation is simply that a truth-functional interpretation of laws, no matter how complicated, evidently fails to capture at least part of what is meant by the claim that *B must* nomically follow *A*. There does not appear to be any contradiction in saying that "All *A* is *B*" satisfies all the conditions for laws stated in the previous chapter; but it is not the case that all *A* must be *B*.

This argument is occasionally expressed by saying that we all have the idea that there is more in the relation of cause and effect or the terms in a law than the regularity theorist acknowledges. (We have already seen that this version of the argument is sometimes used to support the activity theory of causation—the "more" we are supposed to acknowledge is activity or power.) Sometimes the point is driven home by examples. If causation consists simply in regularity, Ewing says, then a gun shot has no more intrinsic connection with death than tea-drinking has.[1] Although there are some important and relevant differences between a gunshot and tea-drinking (death often follows the former, but rarely the latter; there is a comprehensive theory that accounts for the connection between a gunshot and death), Ewing's point has force.

[1] *Idealism*, p. 153.

The necessitarian is claiming that the regularity theorist commits something like the naturalistic fallacy. Just as "good" cannot be identified with "pleasant" or "in accordance with my conscience," so "must" cannot be identified with "is."

A naturalistic rejoinder in the sphere of ethics is unfortunately not available to the regularity theorist. Some moral philosophers have said that the difference in meaning between ethical and non-ethical terms can be accounted for in terms of the fact that sentences containing ethical terms are typically used to evaluate rather than describe. Since evaluation is a different kind of linguistic act from description, sentences containing ethical terms are not synonymous with sentences that do not contain ethical terms. We are not, therefore, forced to suppose that the object being talked about possesses ethical properties over and above its non-ethical ones. In other words, although it is true that "good" does not mean "pleasant," etc., it does not follow that goodness is an objective and distinctive property of objects. To suppose that goodness is an additional property because "good" does not mean "pleasant," or "in accordance with my conscience," etc., is to commit the descriptivist fallacy, i.e., to suppose that sentences have but one job: to describe the world.

Whether or not the naturalistic rejoinder is tenable, the *prima facie* fact that evaluation is a different kind of activity from description has no obvious analogue that can be of service to the regularity theorist. What distinctive function is performed by "must" statements? Perhaps one can eventually show that the peculiar force of "must" can be accounted for in terms of a non-descriptive job done by "must" statements. But no one has to *show* that "x is good" is used to evaluate x.

Nor can the regularity theorist say that he is not concerned with the ordinary man's vague ideas about laws. If the regularity theorist is advancing his view as a "rational reconstruction," performed in accordance with certain criteria of adequacy of peculiarly philosophical interest (e.g., truth-functionality), we are left in the dark regarding the necessity of laws as we normally understand them. And we really want to know whether or not laws are necessary, not whether or not we can create a "purified" concept that will be serviceable to some extent. Imagine a man insisting that he is remaining in a certain spot voluntarily, even though a ton of bricks is on top of him, because he can provide a rational reconstruction of the concept of compulsion according to which we will not have to infer that his behavior is involuntary. Similarly, we want to understand the relation between deterministic accounts as normally understood and ascriptions of freedom.

What then is an alternative to an admission of defeat by the regularity theorist? We may seek an explanation of the use of "must" and allied concepts to express laws that will not require us to suppose that "*ni*" expresses a genuinely "objective" relation. This is a general approach of which the naturalistic rejoinder is a specific instance. And, of course, this was Hume's approach: the use of the concept of necessity, according to Hume, is an expression of our expectation that an event will occur given that we have experienced its usual concomitant. But we project this anticipation onto the objective situation and think of it as exemplifying a relation we call "necessity."

Hume's account is subject to certain difficulties if we take it as he intended, viz., as an account of the origin of the idea of necessity. For example, Hume never makes clear how an anticipation can give rise to the original idea of necessity. On his own view an idea is supposed to resemble the impression from which it is derived. But Hume's theory may be correct as an account of the conditions of application of the term "necessity" even if the source of the concept of neces-

223

sity lies elsewhere. Of course, if Hume's theory is not employed to explain the origin of the idea of necessity, a necessitarian may demand that a regularity theorist provide an account, since the latter denies that necessity is a relation in nature. I think, however, that Hume's theory can be revised both to explain in part the origin of the concept of necessity *and* to provide us with a statement of the conditions of application of the term "necessity" which does not require us to think of necessity as objective.

As an empiricist, Hume was disturbed by the fact that necessity is constantly attributed, but never observed. He concluded that this attribution takes place only after repeated experiences of the constant conjunction of pairs of events of the same kind as the pair alleged to be necessarily connected. Since the only relevant difference between the first and the last pair is the presence of a belief or expectation in the latter case, the idea of necessity must have its source in this subjective fact.

Hume would defend the use of "only" in the last sentence by arguing *independently* that necessity is not observed. The necessity of this argument derives from the possible rebuttal that repeated experience of pairs of events is required in order to come to see the objective necessity.

Paradoxically, I would like in one sense to bypass the issue of whether or not necessity is "observed." First of all, the issue is not at all clear. Are spatial or temporal relations observed? Secondly, even if Hume believed that the experience of a man before repeated conjunctions is the same as his experience after those conjunctions, the crucial question is whether or not necessity is ever observed in the *veridical* sense of "observed," and not whether or not a phenomenological difference can be found between those who believe and those who do not believe in the presence of some causal relation.

We must not forget that the regularity theory has two op-

224

ponents: believers in causal necessity and opters for causal activity. We must, therefore, show that causality in either sense is not veridically perceived. It might be mentioned here that the former seem to have a problem the latter may not have. The relation of causal necessity is one that holds only between a sufficient condition and its effect since a set of conditions cannot necessitate *e* if *e* might not occur in the presence of that set. But in all causal relations there are conditions in the sufficient condition that are not typically perceived when the situation is observed. A person who argues that causality is perceived in some of these situations is forced, therefore, to suppose that a relation is perceived where the first term of the relation (the sufficient condition) is not perceived. This difficulty might not be terribly serious, since part of the first term is perceived and we allow other relations to be considered perceivable when only parts of the terms are perceived. (I am not required to observe Smith's navel in order to see that Smith is to the left of Jones.) But this rebuttal is not satisfactory because I do observe Smith (or the book that I see to be on top of the desk, even if I do not observe every part of Smith (or the book), whereas I do not observe a sufficient condition if I perceive only some conditions in the sufficient condition. I do not perceive the sufficient condition of the ignition of a match because I do not perceive oxygen.

The necessitarian may reply that the relation can be perceived even if the first term is not wholly perceived because perceptual knowledge of the relation is virtually independent of knowledge of the terms of the relation. For example, if I come to learn that it was not Smith, but rather Green, who was to the left of Jones (or that it was *War and Peace* rather than *The Basic Works of Aristotle* that was on top of the desk), I still had observed that a person was to the left of another (or that a book was on the desk). Even if I learn that Green is a dummy (or that the book is a fake), I did

225

see that something was to the left of something else (or that something was on top of something else).

Regardless of the outcome of this debate, it would seem that this problem is not a problem for the advocate of causal activity because he presumably does not have to say that the entire sufficient condition acts on the effect. Another advantage of the activity theory is that the empirical evidence indicates that the causal impressions people seem to have are not impressions of necessity. Michotte, whose work we shall examine, maintains that we perceive not necessity, but certain specific forms of causal activity. He is also careful in distinguishing the general idea of activity from the various specific forms of causal activity. He fully supports the view expressed earlier (see p. 70) that human action or activity is not *per se* causal.

I shall, therefore, try first to show that causal activity is not observed and then apply the results of this investigation to the concept of causal necessity.[2]

A relation R between c and e in S is veridically observed by O, i.e., O perceives that cRe in S only if it is true that: If O understands and knows how to decide the presence or absence of "R" or its criteria, has the ability to tell whether or not cRe in the specific case S, and if the objective conditions of perception are standard or normal (e.g., lighting conditions if the perception is visual), then facts about S are empirically or logically sufficient for (1) it to appear to O that cRe in S or the belief that cRe in S and (2) cRe in S (the same facts about S for both (1) and (2)) (C).

(In C, facts about S must be empirically sufficient for it to appear that cRe in S *or* for the belief that cRe in S rather than simply for the belief that cRe in S because O may perceive that cRe in S even though he does not believe that cRe in S. I am thinking of cases in which a man rejects the tes-

<hr />

[2] I am grateful to John Cugini, one of my students, for his helpful comments on the material that follows.

timony of his own senses but happens to be wrong: "I see it; but I don't believe it." Thus, he perceives that cRe in S, it appears to him that cRe in S, but he does not believe that cRe in S. If a man prefers to think that O cannot perceive that cRe in S unless he believes that cRe in S, he may add the belief condition to C because C only constitutes a necessary condition of perception.)

Although several notions in C are not transparently clear, the notion of a fact about S cries out for clarification. The clarification proves quite difficult. For example, is it a fact about S that cRe in S? If so, then facts about S would always trivially be sufficient for the second condition, viz., cRe in S. If we insist that the facts about S be *empirically* sufficient for cRe in S, we beg the question against those who view causal activity as a simple, unanalyzable relation, for they would say that the appearance (belief) that cRe is caused simply by its being the case that cRe and the latter cannot be broken down further.

With regard to the plausibility of the claim that C is a necessary condition of veridical observation, the question whether or not cRe is a fact about S can be waived, as we shall see. The demand for general clarification of "fact about S" can also be waived in light of the fact that, however clarification is effected, we surely do not want to suppose that psychological and/or neurological facts about O are facts about S. This admission is, however, all we basically require to show that causal activity is not veridically observed.

Is C a plausible condition of veridical observation? If C is false, the appearance to O might depend on facts outside S that are distinct from facts regarding his perceptual and linguistic training. These facts determine the appearance that cRe in S whether or not cRe in S. Thus, if S satisfies certain necessary or contributory conditions, it will appear to O to be the case that cRe in S although it is not, and his ability and the conditions of perception are not to blame. (And since $-cRe$, the inclusion of cRe as a possible fact about S is irrelevant here.) If "cRe" is true, but C is false, it is still not the case that O perceives that cRe because, again, the appearance is still due to facts outside S. (This point can only be strengthened by the inclusion of cRe in the class of facts about S because, in this case, the appearance that cRe is not determined by the fact that cRe.) If, on the other hand, facts about S are sufficient for the appearance, but not cRe, then cRe can hardly be said to be perceived if O can come to learn that his "perception" was delusive without coming to learn that he or the conditions of perception were inadequate. (This sentence is still true if cRe is a possible fact about S because if cRe, the antecedent is false and if $-cRe$, the whole sentence is true.)

C is formulated to cover ordinary perceptual cases and those requiring specialized training, e.g., X-ray reading and wine tasting. Given the specialized training and good lighting, facts about the X-ray are sufficient for the beliefs that are created by examining the X-ray and their truth.

We may now concede the possibility that there exists a causal impression or a variety of types of causal impressions without having to conclude that causality is perceived. These impressions may be causal intermediaries between the determining facts and certain causal beliefs.

We now move on to show that causal activity is not veridically perceived because C is false where "R" refers to causal activity. My analysis may be charged with circularity on the grounds that the statement of the conditions of veridical observation uses the concept of causation (empirical sufficiency) and derivatively, therefore, on my analysis, the concept of law. But there is no circularity, because this statement about veridical observation is not part of the analysis of the concept of law. The laws involved in a case of veridical observation would receive the analysis of the preceding chapter, and any claim that instances of these laws are observed as causal would be repudiated by the application of this statement about veridical observation.

Although Hume's views about the psychology of causation may be wrong, his claim that the existence of causal beliefs (or appearances) depends on past experience may be supported by the evidence for the non-veridicality of causal observation. For if O's causal beliefs about S arise only when certain conditions P having nothing to do with S hold, these conditions must be psychological. (To avoid repetition, we shall ignore the obvious dependence of beliefs on linguistic and perceptual abilities which are themselves dependent on past experience.) And the most obvious candidate for P is O's past experience of constant conjunctions or O's general causal beliefs formed on the basis of his past experience. We may now distinguish three theses: (1) the *Illusion Thesis:* Causality is never veridically observed; (2) the *Inference Thesis₁:* The Illusion Thesis is true; causal beliefs about S always have certain conditions P outside S; P is comprised entirely of facts about the observer's past causal experiences or present beliefs about causation formed on the basis of past causal experiences; (3) the *Inference Thesis₂:* The Illusion Thesis is true; most causal beliefs are determined partly by conditions outside S that are constituted in the way stated by Inference Thesis₁. It follows that the few causal beliefs that are determined exclusively by conditions in S are beliefs whose truth is not determined in this way.

Although the stronger Inference Thesis₁ may be difficult to defend, Inference Thesis₂ can be established and will suffice for our purposes.

The Illusion Thesis is a consequence of the Generality Theory since the latter implies that a single veridical perception is not sufficient to establish the truth of any causal proposition. Hence, the extended defense of the Generality Theory provides strong support for the Illusion Thesis.

It would appear that the Generality Theory requires us

229

to suppose that "c causally activates e" is not a fact about S, for on any reasonable criterion of what constitutes a fact about the impact i of one billiard ball c on another e, we ought not to have to construe impacts involving other sorts of objects at different times and locations as facts about i. But since "c causally activates e" entails information regarding these other impact situations, it cannot be a fact about S.

Two problems connected with this may be mentioned. First, "A is red" entails that B is not the only red thing in the world although "A is red" is surely not about B. But the fact that B is not the only red thing in the world is obviously not just a fact about B, whereas the information about some impact other than i can be described so that it is just about the other impact situation. Second, many statements we make about situations can be analyzed into observable components and inferential components. For example, "Smith is running after Jones" has as one of its observational components "Smith is running behind Jones" and as one of its inferential components "Smith's intention to catch Jones is a causal condition of his running." Since the inferential component is causal, "Smith is running after Jones" cannot be about the observed behavior merely. There are numerous examples like this, many of which have inferential components that entail information about other situations not because the inferential component is causal. For example, "The car is blue" entails "The right side of the car is blue" and "The left side of the car is blue." The latter would be an inferential component for a man who sees the right side of the car only. Are we, therefore, forced to say that "Smith is running after Jones" and "The car is blue" are not facts about the individual situations?

The Generality Theory does *not* require us to say that "c causally activates e in S" is not a fact about S, or that "The car is blue in T" is not a fact about T. What it does require us to say is that *if* we construe "c causally activates e in S"

as a fact about S, it is not one of the facts that is included in the sufficient condition of O's belief (or appearance) that "c causally activates e in S." In other words, even if we allow other impact situations as facts about S, since these other situations are not causally relevant to O's belief that c causally activates e in S, the impact situations cannot be included in the sufficient condition of O's belief. Now, according to C, the same facts about S must determine both the truth of "c causally activates e in S" and the belief that c causally activates e in S. Hence, the facts about S that determine O's causal belief do not determine the truth of that belief (and the facts that determine truth do not determine the belief.) So the Generality Theory does imply the Illusion Thesis even if "c causally activates e in S" is a fact about S. We are, therefore, again saved from the necessity of explicating "fact about S."

Analogously, a man who forms the judgment that the car is blue on the basis of his observation of the right side of the car does not veridically observe that the car is blue even if we allow "The car is blue" as a fact about the situation. The car's being blue determines the truth of "The car is blue" but not his belief. (The car's being blue involves the causally irrelevant condition regarding the left side of the car.) And what determines his belief (the right side of the car is blue) does not determine the truth of "the car is blue" (for the car may be two-toned). We shall have more to say later about these partly observational, partly inferential statements.

Both parts of Inference Thesis$_2$ receive powerful support from the work of A. Michotte, even though he attempts to develop a thesis contrary to Inference Thesis$_2$ from his experimental data.[3]

Through various experimental designs involving the movement of discs and the projection of images, Michotte was

[3] *The Perception of Causality* (London: Methuen & Co., 1963).

able to reproduce a variety of apparently causal phenomena and record the observations of his subjects. The fact that every positive causal report was really false did not disturb Michotte, who feels that we can infer from the conditions of the causal report what conditions must hold in veridical situations for a causal perception. (I say "perception" rather than "belief" for Michotte considers that there are causal relations that are not perceived.) I think he would say that the false causal impression is analogous to the impression that a stick in water is bent. Just as we can see that the stick is straight when it is viewed under standard conditions, so we can see that *a* causes *b* under standard conditions.

Although looking at an object in water is not looking at it under standard conditions, it is not clear what makes the conditions of Michotte's experiments non-standard. The artificiality of the experimental situation would be irrelevant according to him because he concludes that the conditions of a causal report are found exclusively in structural features of the perceptual situation that are reproducible in everyday situations (the Structural Thesis). Also, the criticism "non-standard" cannot be made simply because the causal reports are false, for doing that would render *every* relation that is *inferred* from observed features of a situation veridically *observable*.

But even if Michotte can justify the label "non-standard" for his experimental situations, the Illusion Thesis can still be defended via a defense of an Inference approach in contrast to his Structural Thesis. (We shall *temporarily ignore* the distinction between Inference Theses 1 and 2 and speak just of the Inference Thesis.) For if causal beliefs, true or false, are formed on the basis of considerations outside the situation to which they are applied, causality is not veridically observed.

Although the facts are by no means conclusive, it seems to me that the Inference Thesis is far superior to Michotte's in its power to explain the data because: Michotte's Structural Thesis is extremely complicated, with many ill-defined distinctions; some of these distinctions are clearly *ad hoc,* i.e., introduced in a completely question-begging way just to save the theory; many experiments are easily accounted for by the Inference Thesis, whereas Michotte is forced to apply, tortuously and unnaturally in these cases, the Structural Thesis; the positive evidence against the Inference Thesis can be dealt with.

I shall say nothing about the first point, as Michotte himself virtually concedes it and anyone may easily verify it for himself. Two examples of the second point will suffice.

In the first place, for reasons we need not go into, Michotte's theory does not allow for the perception of causation where cause and effect are synonymous. But when a noise is produced at the same time one object strikes another, many observers report causation. Moreover, causal responses are clearer the closer the experimental situation approximates to real life. For example, the impact and the noise should appear to be truly simultaneous. Also, the responses are clearer if the second object moves forward after contact. These results clearly favor the Inference Thesis.

What is Michotte's response? He says that the noise must be a feature of the impact (a noisy impact) rather than an effect of it.[4] Even if this distinction can be rendered intelligible, Michotte presents no independent evidence that his interpretation is superior to a causal one.

Furthermore, Michotte is forced to admit that causation is sometimes "directly perceived" in cases where his theory cannot account for this fact. He also concedes that these cases can be accounted for by the Inference Thesis.[5] But if the Inference and Structural Theses exhaust the possible theories to explain Michotte's data, he makes his theory in-

[4] Ibid., p. 240.
[5] Ibid., pp. 367-68.

capable of falsification, for he imposes no restrictions on the recalcitrant data that have to be treated by the Inference Thesis. No data, therefore, need be taken as disconfirming the Structural Thesis. But, then, Michotte's "theory" really amounts to an existential claim, viz., there are experiments that the Inference Thesis cannot deal with.

We may productively consider here a few of the many examples that can be explained by the Inference Thesis far more simply than by the Structural Thesis.

First of all, experienced observers never perceive object A launch (set in motion) object B if B's speed is more than double that of A's. The laws of mechanics, too, set this speed limit on an object struck by another, no matter what the masses of the two bodies are. Michotte notes that "there seems to be a curious agreement between the laws of perception and that of the laws governing the physical world."[6] Michotte's explanation of this "curious agreement" is that A's initial priority, produced by the fact that it is acting at a time when B is not, is offset by the priority of B's speed, resulting in a complete or partial segregation of the two movements. If the segregation is partial, i.e., the speed of B is not much greater than that of A, the observer reports that A triggers rather than launches the motion of B. In other words, the observer acknowledges A's role in setting B in motion, but does not see a simple pushing of B by A. An advocate of the Inference Thesis would simply say that the experience of triggering is the consequence of our acquired belief that, in cases like these, A's movement caused some mechanism to be activated, resulting in a movement by B faster than simple mechanical action allows.

Furthermore, one of Michotte's fundamental theoretical principles is "ampliation of the movement." It is the continuation of the movement of an object A after the *object* has ceased to move. The movement of A appears in the displace-

[6] Ibid., p. 112.

ment of *B,* the object struck. Thus *B*'s movement really belongs to *A.* Confirmation of the applicability of this admittedly difficult concept is provided by an experiment in which a spot of light, moving in the direction of a circle, disappears well before it reaches the perimeter of the circle. *Sometimes* the subjects report "that the spot disappears while *its movement* continues right up to the circle, and then is lost 'behind' it."[7] But to say that the spot disappears is not to say that it no longer exists. A natural explanation of this report, one that appeals tacitly to past experience, is that the spot is believed to be moving behind some obstruction. I do not wish to deny that this report reflects a distinctive phenomenal experience. I wish only to point out how this experience or report depends on past experience or beliefs formed from past experience.

In addition, Michotte has to introduce his theoretical apparatus (e.g., ampliation) in order to explain the "traction effect," i.e., the impression that one object pulls or tows another. But this impression is produced when the experiments approximate closely the conditions of towing or pulling in everyday life.

Again, Michotte uses his theory to explain the fact that a causal impression of launching by expulsion (e.g., throwing a ball) cannot be produced when two objects *A* and *B* move side by side for a while, after which *A* stops while *B* continues to move. The Inference Thesis says simply that there is nothing, e.g., features of *A* or *B*, in the situation that resembles any familiar case of launching by expulsion. But what happens when the experiment is preceded by the entrainment of *B* by *A*, i.e., when *A* starts out first, joins *B*, and then moves alongside *B*? Michotte's remarks require no comment:

As expected, the causal impression of launching is now

[7] Ibid., p. 138.

quite clear; we see *A* launch *B* after entraining it for some distance. Moreover the length of this distance influences the result; when it is too large (and exceeds the radius of action) the causal impression disappears, as one might expect. It is scarcely necessary to say that the situation presented in the experiment is one which occurs in every-day life.[8]

Finally, further confirmation of the Inference Thesis is provided by the fact that a causal impression between objects that begin to move together is produced when the situation resembles a familiar causal one, e.g., a bow and arrow. Michotte not only requires "ampliation" here; he introduces "continuous ampliation" ("the extension of the 'movement' of the active object on to the passive object is *made afresh* at each moment in the operation"[9]) to overcome the failure of temporal priority. Moreover, he requires additional principles to explain the selection of one of the events (the bow) as cause. Whereas an advocate of the Inference Theory need only cite the fact that in everyday situations the bow is acknowledged to cause the arrow's movement, Michotte is forced to introduce ill-defined concepts like dominance and centers of reference. Of course, there is the general problem of how we distinguish cause from effect in cases where they are simultaneous (and perhaps where each is a sufficient condition of the other).[10] But Michotte certainly provides no general answer to that question.

As for Michotte's purported evidence against the Inference Theory, the "negative" cases, i.e., those that failed to elicit a causal response where this is expected according to the Inference Theory, embrace various sorts of phenomena.

Michotte could not reproduce a causal impression of braking, for example. But he cites Levelt's experiments in which

[8] Ibid., p. 167.
[9] Ibid., p. 175.
[10] See the next chapter.

the frequency of braking responses was a positive function of the degree to which the situation approximates to real cases of braking. (Michotte's experiments had not contained a number of these factors that made the cases look more like genuine braking phenomena.) Conceding the role of acquired knowledge, Michotte nevertheless attempts to invalidate the application of the Inference Theory by noting that the subjects "never made any mention of a direct or immediate impression of a causal influence."[11] He then explains this fact by hypothesizing that the causal responses were suggested to the subjects by the similarity between the situations and those in everyday life.

If Michotte's interpretation is correct, an advocate of the Inference Theory who insists that a causal *impression* is the product of past experience would be disturbed. But we have left open the question of the existence of this impression and have accordingly formulated the Inference Theory as a Theory of causal *belief*. Hence, Michotte only confirms the Inference Theory as we understand it.

He confirms the Inference Theory also by noting that the frequency of positive responses is a function of the frequency with which subjects have made positive responses in earlier braking experiments, and reports that this kind of dependence has often been noted. In fact, he says "that causal responses on the part of subjects can also be influenced by earlier experiments made in similar schematic situations."[12] For an objective phenomenon, the causal impression is a quite delicate thing.

It is unnecessary to consider other cases because, although I have to concede that I cannot plausibly explain some responses in terms of Inference Thesis$_1$, Inference Thesis$_2$ is still defensible. Inference Thesis$_2$ allows for this kind of failure, requiring only that the truth of causal beliefs that cannot

[11] Michotte, p. 361.
[12] Ibid., p. 309.

be explained in terms of past experience be determined by factors outside the situation. Two types of *prima facie* problematic cases exist for the Inference Thesis. First, we encounter causal responses that would be false if they were made about structurally similar situations in everyday life and which are not due to the factors mentioned by Inference Thesis₁. These responses are not troublesome for, since they are false, causality cannot be said to be veridically observed. Furthermore, there may be causal responses that would be true if they were made about structurally similar situations in everyday life and which are not due to the factors mentioned by Inference Thesis₁. The problem for Michotte is to show that there are cases of this second type, for an Inference Theorist can argue that the fact that the responses are of a sort that would be made about similar situations in everyday life is evidence for Inference Thesis₁.

Let us, however, concede to Michotte that there are some cases of the second sort. (As far as I can see, the evidence requires us to admit only a few types.) Inference Thesis₂ is still preserved because the Generality Theory saves the Illusion Thesis. In these cases, although the causal response is in fact true, the facts that determine its truth are not those that determine the response (or the belief). That is, the causal response is inferential although the inference turns out to be correct.

An objection to the Illusion Thesis might be made along the following lines. When we realize that terms applied to observed situations are partly inferential, e.g., "running after," we can isolate the two components and the observable component will be genuinely veridical, e.g., "running behind." Thus, although it may be true that "*c* causes *e*" cannot be veridically observed, cannot we isolate the observable component and regard it as a proper object of veridical observation?

In the first place, we would have to find a suitable observation term. "Causal activation" is no good for, as we now understand it, "c causally activates e" entails "c causes e." Nor do we want "c seems to causally activate e" because we do not want a psychological term (that would in effect constitute surrender by anti-Humeans). We shall have to invent a term, therefore, say "c semi-causes e."

But there are two powerful objections against the introduction of this notion. In the first place, Michotte concedes that there is not even a *prima facie* case for the perception of causal activity outside the general area of mechanical transactions. (All advocates of causal activity I am familiar with would agree.) We would, therefore, be forced to suppose either (a) that causation is ambiguous in that it sometimes does and sometimes does not imply semi-causation, or (b) that the "observable" relation of semi-causation is always present, but hidden in large classes of cases for reasons that would have to be specified. In the second place, in almost all cases, even semi-causation is not veridically observed. It will be recalled that Inference Thesis$_1$ works for almost all cases. In these cases, any sort of appearance of causality is determined not by the situation but by the past experience or present causal beliefs of the perceiver. I conclude that this notion of semi-causation that is logically independent of the notion of causation, that is required at best for a handful of cases, and that forces us to view causation as ambiguous is a dead end for an activity theorist.

Inference Thesis$_2$ can evidently be interpreted as applying to the idea of causal necessity. The facts about the influence of past experience and the non-veridicality of the causal impression are equally as decisive. Moreover, we shall reject in the next chapter the argument that activity or necessity must be a part of the analysis of causation in order to distinguish cause from effect in those cases in which necessary inferences can be made both from cause to effect and from effect to cause. We have, therefore, succeeded in providing at least a partial account of the origin of the idea of "causal activity" without having to suppose that causal activity exists in nature. For since the experience of a causal relation by a person who sees it as a case of agency is different from the experience of one who denies the causal relation, this experience may be part of the genesis of the concept of causal activity; and we may now say this without suggesting that causal activity is actually perceived. This view is simpler than Hume's, for we are not saying that the idea of causal activity arises from the anticipation; rather the anticipation gives rise to the experience as one of causal activity. So the idea of causal activity has its source partly in the experience of one thing acting on another.

I say, "source partly" because I do not want to prejudge the possibility that other factors have a role in the genesis of this concept.

As to causal necessity specifically, we have seen that there is no *prima facie* empirical evidence that it is perceived and any evidence that might be forthcoming can presumably be dealt with by a version of Inference Thesis$_2$ for causal necessity. There is, in addition, the problem created by the fact that this relation only holds between a sufficient condition and its effect. Of course, if there is no impression of causal necessity, we cannot account for the genesis of this concept in the way we suggested for causal activity. I do not know how to account for the genesis of this concept. Perhaps the possession of the concept of logical necessity is causally relevant. Nor do I even want to prejudge the possibility that certain noncausal facts are apprehended as necessary (in a non-logical sense). For example, we do sometimes seem to know and sometimes certainly believe that we cannot try harder. "I cannot try harder" entails "It is necessary that it is not the case that I try harder." If the fact referred to cannot be expressed without some modal concept, there may be objectively necessary facts a knowledge of which might serve to explain in part the attribution of necessity to causal relations. Finally, perhaps the causal relations that are (non-veridically) perceived are confused or associated with causal necessity once we have the idea of necessity from non-causal sources.

Although this discussion is speculative, I see no reason yet for supposing that causal necessity (or, of course, causal activity) is an objective relation, i.e., one that holds independently of human knowers and perceivers.

Some philosophers are impressed by the existence of "verbs of causation," e.g., "strike," "push," "collide," and "bend."[13] We can say that we *saw* Jones push Smith and, therefore, causation is sometimes observed, not inferred. But to whom are such remarks addressed? Does Louch really believe that a Humean denies the propriety of remarks like "I saw the collision"? Does he believe that a Humean commits himself to the view that a temporal process of inference takes place prior to the assertion? If not, he must believe that there is no point to the development of a position like Hume's. And this belief is a consequence of his failure to see that Humeans are asking a philosophical question. Remarks about ordinary usage are relevant but not decisive regarding these questions. A Humean wants to know whether or not causal activity (or necessity) is a relation which would exist in a world devoid of knowers. In defending the Humean answer to this question, I have tacitly accounted for the ordinary propriety of remarks like "I saw the collision." But I do not feel that philosophy *ends* by noting ordinary usage.

Similarly, there is no impropriety in saying that falling bodies must continue to fall. Statements of this sort pick out genuine facts about the world. My contention is that an analysis of such statements does not require the assumption that there is a relation of necessary connection between

[13] A. R. Louch, *Explanation and Human Action* (Berkeley: University of California, 1966), p. 41.

events or conditions. The intuition of a diver that he must fall into the water is, therefore, right. But we can interpret his belief as the belief that there is nothing he can do in the circumstances to prevent his fall. And the eventual reading of this will not use the concept of necessity.

There remain objections to the regularity theory based either on the belief that it fails for certain specific causal relationships or on the claim that certain facts cannot be accounted for by the theory.

Desires cause actions in a non-regularity sense: The conclusion of chapter IV was that the generality analysis applies to the relation between desire and action if the relation is causal. Any claim that a stronger connection is perceived may be rebutted either by arguments in that chapter or by considerations adduced subsequently to show that the experience this claim may be based upon is non-veridical.

There must be a difference between "The belief that p *is determined by the belief that* q" *and "P-beliefs follow q-beliefs" for only the former entails that the belief is reasonable if* q *is a good reason for* p. *But there is no difference according to the regularity theory:*[14] First of all, a regularity theorist can easily account for ascriptions of logicality or illogicality to people. Since complex propositions can be believed, a person is logical if he believes that p implies q, and p does in fact imply q.

Causality enters the picture only when we consider at least two logically distinct beliefs. Suppose Jones believes that q because he believes that p and that p implies q. (For discussion purposes, we suppose that a person may logically believe that r and not believe that s, even though r entails s.)

Now there are a number of factors pertinent to Jones's rationality that a regularity theorist can acknowledge. For example, when asked his reason for believing that q, Jones

[14] Ewing, p. 163.

will cite p and, perhaps, p implies q. By now it should be evident that mere *de facto* universality is not sufficient for a causal connection. More sophisticated considerations enter into decisions regarding the presence or absence of a causal connection.

But even if there is a genuine causal connection between the belief that p and that p implies q, and the belief that q, the latter belief may not be held reasonably. One can construct an example analogous to Chisholm's example about desires.[15] Suppose Smith believes that p and that p implies q, but does not see the validity of *modus ponens*. This belief for some reason causes him to visit an astrologer who tells him that the stars "say" that q, and so Smith believes that q.

Thus, believing for a reason, like acting out of a desire, requires more than just a causal connection. One condition that might be added is compatible with the regularity theory. On a clue from the case of acting out of a desire, it seems reasonable to add the fact that a person would reject q whenever he comes to reject p or p implies q if he believes that q on the basis of p and that p implies q. This condition fails to be met by Smith. It also serves as at least a partial reply to Ewing's contention that the regularity theory ignores the relevance of the content of a premise in an inference.

If we still feel that Jones's believing that q might be a lucky accident rather than an instance of rationality, we are perhaps forgetting that one of the background conditions of the belief that q is the training and education that have led Jones to form his beliefs in accordance with rules like *modus ponens*. A regularity theorist would not object to the stipulation that Jones's belief is reasonable only if Jones is using a rule of inference he correctly believes to be reliable or valid. Then, if Jones believes that p and that p implies q, uses *modus ponens* to derive q, and believes that *modus*

---

[15] *Freedom and Determinism,* pp. 29-30. We shall comment in detail about Chisholm's actual example in chap. XIII.

ponens is valid, he must *logically* believe that it *would be reasonable* to believe that *q*. If he does believe *q* as a result of this process, he is displaying the training and education that have led him to form his beliefs rationally. To speak of training and education is to emphasize the non-accidental, directed character of the process. Moreover, since a set of beliefs is not normally a sufficient condition of another belief, factors like a man's assessment of the relationships between beliefs, his desires, character, consideration of consequences, may play a role in the development of intellectual character habits. It is no accident that a man forms a belief, perhaps automatically, because he believes it would be reasonable to do so.

In perception, when the self is passive, we are aware of something acting on us in a sense other than that described by the regularity theory:[16] If the act of perception *per se* provides insight into a non-regularity causal relation, the terms of the relation must be specified. "I see a book," for example, must entail a proposition of the form "*A* causes (non-regularity) *B*." What might *B* be?

If *B* is a change in me, which change is it? I now see a book, whereas before I did not. But that simply means that a relational proposition has become true. Since there are relational propositions that are not causal, there must be some other change or some special fact about this change that leads us to believe that "I see a book" entails a causal proposition.

B cannot be neurological or physiological since I am not aware that something is acting on my optic nerve.

B must, therefore, be something like a sense datum, and *A* would then be the physical object, the book, itself. But even if the causal theory of perception is true and a book is causing a sense datum of the book, no one would want

---

[16] Ewing, p. 165.

to say that we are aware of a book, aware of a sense datum, and aware of the causal relation between them.

When I see a book, I have the impression that what I see is not under my voluntary control. But I have the same impression when I learn that I was hallucinating, in which case no causal relation between a book and a sense datum existed.

In order for the successive states and qualities of a substance to belong to that substance, the connection between and among the states and qualities must be necessary:[17] Ewing argues that the distinctive property of all the states and qualities of some substance cannot be the property of belonging to that substance for this "separates" a substance from all its states and qualities. If, on the other hand, the relationship between the successive states and qualities is simply lawful, there would be no notion of substantial identity. Hence, the connection must be necessary.

Ewing is confusing two relationships: the relationships between the states (successive or simultaneous) of some substance, and the relationship between the states and the identity of the substance. We may pick out certain states and relationships between states as criteria of substantial identity. Thus, the absence of the states or relationships entails the presence of a distinct substance. But it does not follow that these relationships between states cannot be explicated as lawful succession. Certain lawful successions, in other words, are picked out as criteria of substantial identity, and we do not thereby imply that the connection is now a necessary one. All we imply is that its absence requires us to deny substantial identity. *A fortiori,* there is no reason to view as necessary connections the lawful successions in some substance which are not used as criteria of substantial identity.

The use of the inductive principle presupposes a constancy in nature which cannot be proved if one assumes the regu-

[17] Ibid., pp. 165-66.

larity theory:[18] The necessitarian claims that an inference from "All observed *A*'s are *B*'s" (*O*) to "All *A*'s are *B*'s" (*U*) is justified only if *O* warrants "All *A*'s are necessarily *B*'s" (*N*). But the necessitarian must also show that *O* warrants *N*. For if he cannot, a regularity theorist can say that the inference from *O* to *U* is warranted if nature is uniform even though he cannot show that nature is uniform. Neither position would have the advantage.

But the inference from *O* to *N* is warranted only if laws are (sometimes) necessary, and we have presented extensive argumentation against that position. Hence, the use of this objection as an argument for necessitarianism is similar to the use of the point that the existence of God would be beneficial to man as an argument for His existence. But this objection may be used simply as an argument against the regularity theory. Under these circumstances, it is uninteresting, for the necessitarian cannot solve the problem of induction either. Moreover, many philosophers reject scepticism without resort to necessitarianism. Some adopt the view that, although guarantees of success for inductive rules cannot be provided, it can nonetheless be shown that, if the use of inductive rules fail, all other techniques of predicting the future (e.g., using crystal balls) must.[19] Others insist that inductive rules can be justified inductively without begging the question.[20] Still others question the legitimacy of raising the general question of the justification of induction and insist that the question is applicable only to particular inductive

[18] Ewing, pp. 156-61; and Morris R. Cohen, *The Meaning of Human History* (LaSalle, Ill.: Open Court, 1947). This criticism is one of many which can be found in chap. iv of the latter.

[19] Herbert Feigl, "De Principiis non Disputandum . . . ?" *Philosophical Analysis,* ed. Max Black (Ithaca, N.Y.: Cornell University Press, 1950), p. 137; and William Kneale, *Probability and Induction* (London: Oxford University Press, 1949), p. 235.

[20] Max Black, "Inductive Support of Inductive Rules," *Problems of Analysis:* Philosophical Essays, (Ithaca, N.Y.: Cornell University Press, 1954), pp. 191-208.

rules whose justification rests on the appeal to standards which are in use.[21] Other approaches and variants on these approaches can be found in the literature. A careful examination of all these alternatives is, of course, beyond the scope of this book. If one of them proves tenable, however, the regularity theory does not entail scepticism.

We often use the following argument in order to justify the acceptance of an inductively established law: If there is no law connecting C to E, it is highly improbable that E should follow C in the observed cases. It is probable, therefore, that there is such a law.

If the regularity theory were true, however, we should be able to substitute for "law connecting C to E" the expression "fact that E always follows C." The result is: If it is not the case that E always follows C, it is highly improbable that E should follow C in the observed cases. It is probable, therefore, that E always follows C.

The premise asserts, in effect, that unless E always follows C, it is highly improbable for E to follow C in the observed cases. This is absurd, however, since it is evidently much more improbable for E to follow C all the time than it is for E to follow C some of the time.[22]

It is simply not true that there can be no cases in which the only way to reduce the improbability of some observed sequence is by reference to an hypothesis that is more improbable than the sequence. For example, the probability that the throw of a die will result in an ace five times in succession is $1/7776$. Perhaps the only assumption which can render this sequence more probable is the assumption that the die is loaded. And one can describe conditions under which the probability of the latter assumption is less than $1/7776$.

Ewing has no reason to be concerned about the fact that "All C's are E's" may be advanced to explain "All observed

---

[21] Goodman, pp. 63-68.   [22] Ewing, pp. 169-70.

C's are E's" even though the latter is more probable than the former. Normally we know that an event has occurred before we explain it, in which case the explanation will almost always be less probable than the fact to be explained. (Of course we may not be certain that the explanation we proffer is correct.)

The explanation of "Some C's are E's" in terms of "All C's are E's" may convey the new information that the observed C-E pairs share a common feature and ought not, therefore, to be treated as separate cases. Necessitarianism is not implied by the explanation. If Ewing is making the point that we cannot have reason to believe that all C's are E's if the regularity theory is true, we have dealt with this argument above (see p. 246).

No inference from cause to effect is possible unless the sentence describing the cause entails the sentence describing the effect, for no inference is possible generally unless this is the case:[23] Even if Ewing is allowed the premise that all inference is deductive, his conclusion does not follow. A deductive inference from cause C to effect E is possible if an appropriate premise is added. "C is the cause of E" or "All C and D are E; and D" would do. The inference would then be deductive although there is no logical connection between the sentence describing the cause and the sentence describing the effect.

It is self-evident that each specific change has only one total cause. The regularity theory, however, is compatible with the denial of this self-evident truth:[24] It does not seem to me to be at all self-evident that each specific change has only one total cause. Cannot events be overdetermined? If John sustains a cerebral hemorrhage at the moment he is shot through the heart, one might be prepared to ascribe his death to either factor. Of course, the specific effect of each

[23] Ibid., pp. 167-68.
[24] C. D. Broad, *Examination of McTaggart's Philosophy* (Cambridge: Cambridge University Press, 1933), I, pp. 233-34.

cause was slightly different, and the use of the term "death" tends to obscure these differences. But the thesis that two qualitatively distinct events must have qualitatively distinct effects is not self-evident either. There is certainly no logical absurdity in denying it. Moreover, even if it turns out to be true, we do not have to abandon the regularity theory. Either the thesis (one effect implies one cause) is interpreted as a general empirical fact, in which case it cannot be incompatible with a statement of philosophical analysis, or it is interpreted as a principle which should be incorporated into the analysis of causal propositions. The regularity theory may not *entail* this principle; but the principle may be added independently without affecting the truth of the regularity theory.

It is self-evident that every change has a cause. The regularity theory, however, is compatible with the denial of this self-evident truth:[25] By "cause," Broad means "necessary condition." Although it may be self-evident that every change has necessary conditions, the regularity theory need not entail this principle. As a matter of fact, the principle is not entailed by anti-regularity views either. From the fact that causes necessarily produce effects, it does not follow that all changes are effects.

It is self-evident that the cause of any change contains a change. The regularity theory, however, is compatible with the denial of this self-evident truth:[26] We do not, it is true, countenance as a complete causal explanation of E the fact that some non-changing state C existed for n units of time. We believe there is an answer to the question "Why did C produce E at the time it did?" Perhaps part of the reason is that we have found answers to this question in the psychology of forgetting, the chemistry of spontaneous combustion, and so on, where no apparent change existed to provide the answer. Again, however, if we wish to stipulate that a change must be included in the cause of any change, we may

[25] Ibid., p. 232.   [26] Ibid., pp. 232-33.

add this stipulation to the regularity theory. We already have restrictions of a temporal nature on predicates admissible into laws. There would be problems for the regularity theory only if the reasons for these additions and restrictions conflicted with the regularity theory. I have no reason to think a conflict exists.

Some proponents of the identity theory of causation, however, have argued that a factor that is present in all causal relations proves the falsity of the regularity theory. We shall simply discuss Cohen's statement of this position.[27]

Cohen argues that the specification of the cause of an event provides the reason for the occurrence of the effect. Moreover, the characteristic of the causal situation which enables us to understand the cause as a reason for the effect also makes it possible for us to see that the cause produces the effect necessarily. This characteristic is the presence of an identical element in both cause and effect. An examination of the examples adduced by Cohen in support of his position indicates that the nature of the identity involved is numerical. Let us accept Cohen's claim that all causal situations involve the presence of an element common to cause and effect in order to see whether or not he is justified in inferring from this that there is a necessary connection between cause and effect.

Cohen points out that the velocity of a projectile is explained in terms of a physical constant, momentum, which is identical in both the propellant and the projectile. One can evidently generalize this example in order to embrace other mechanical explanations. Cohen is here pointing to the fact that, in physics, predictions about the values of some variable V are made on the basis of a knowledge of the values at a particular time of a set of variables which includes V. In other words, he is talking about the pervasive use of differential equations in which the successive values of a vari-

[27] Chap. IV.

able are given as a function of their immediate predecessors. But there are also cases in which the identity between cause and effect is distinct from the cause identifying expression or the effect identifying expression. For example, Cohen says that the centralization of power in Soviet Russia is causally related to the centralization of power in Tsarist Russia, because there is a large measure of identity between the two in terms of institutions and personnel. Moreover, he acknowledges the existence of emergent or organic properties. But the cause of the instantiation of an emergent property cannot, by definition, be identical with a prior instantiation of the emergent property.

Thus, Cohen's position can be stated in terms of two arguments. First, if A is the cause of B, then there is some element or property which is common to A and B; and the common possession of this element or property—which may be distinct from the properties whose instantiation is entailed by "A" and "B"—enables us to see that the cause is a reason for the effect. Second, since the first proposition is true, then, if A is the cause of B, A necessarily produces B. We have agreed to accept the first argument in order to examine the second.

It is difficult to see why we should believe that there is a necessary connection between cause and effect on the basis of the presence of some common factor P unless we also believe that there is a necessary connection between the presence of P in the cause and its continuation in the effect. For example, if the identity of government personnel is the common factor in the two Russian regimes, then, if we do not believe that there is any necessity in the fact that the government personnel of the Tsarist regime is identical with the government personnel of the Soviet regime, we cannot infer that there is any necessary connection between the centralization of power in the two regimes. Cohen might respond by committing himself to the view that the ultimate explanatory predicates of any science will be like the predicates of physics, e.g., mass, velocity, insofar as they will apply to the entities covered by the theory at all times. In this way, we know that entities must continue to have these properties at all times. This thesis is not physicalistic since these predicates need not be "physical": one may, for example, characterize all forms of social organization in terms of some value of the variable "degree of cohesiveness."

Even if Cohen's program ought to be adopted, it is difficult to see how its adoption in some domain of inquiry shows that the cause and effect are related necessarily. Suppose that there are good reasons to believe that a certain phobia P_1 is caused by a traumatic experience T_1. One must find an appropriate property represented by a variable V_1 which satisfies the requirements of Cohen's position. Suppose that V_1 represents a neurological property, and we can correlate T_1 and P_1 with different values of V_1. We then discover a law L_1 which enables us to predict subsequent values of V_1 on the basis of a knowledge of its previous values. Let us also grant that the neurological law explains the causal law of the psychologist. Since, however, L_1 is not necessary (for only the presence of *some* value of V_1 is necessary), there is no reason to suppose that the production of P_1 is necessary. In other words, a condition of the necessity of "$T_1 \supset P_1$" is the necessity of L_1; but the latter cannot be justified on the basis of Cohen's position. The fact that there must be some state of V_1 at t_1 does not tell us that P_1 will hold at t_1. Since Cohen's position does not enable us to judge that L_1 is necessary, and since the connection between T_1 and P_1 is grounded in L_1 rather than in the fact that there is some value of V_1 at any time, there is no reason provided by his position for viewing the causal relation as necessary.

Having examined and dismissed all the above objections, I conclude that the thesis of adequacy is established and, with it, the regularity theory.

VIII. DETERMINISTIC ACCOUNTS

GIVEN SOME *R*-sentence that follows from laws plus a state-description sentence, additional conditions must be imposed in order for this account to be considered deterministic. We distinguish causal laws from other kinds of laws and we might, therefore, naturally suppose that the laws in a deterministic account be or contain causal laws. But the concept of a causal law is defined in various ways.

Sometimes, a causal law is thought of as a law which enables us to compute the state variables for all future times if they are given for the present.[1] We pointed out earlier that this condition is unnecessarily restrictive since certain sciences may wish to employ laws that enable prediction of the determinates of a determinable from state-descriptions which make no reference to this determinable.[2]

A causal law has also been defined as a law which asserts a functional dependence of the time-rate of change in one magnitude upon other magnitudes.[3] Although the advantages of quantificational techniques are clear, we do not wish to restrict laws to those referring to magnitudes. It is certainly determined that a person will die before the end of a year if he does not eat during that year, even if this law is not expressed in terms of magnitudes.

Various restrictions concerning the spatial relationship between cause and effect have been suggested in defining a causal law.[4] Some considerations are technical and will be

---

[1] Philipp Frank, *Philosophy of Science: The Link Between Science and Philosophy* (Englewood Cliffs: Prentice-Hall, 1957), p. 271.
[2] Above, pp. 162-64.
[3] Nagel refers to this conception of causal law on p. 278.
[4] See Braithwaite, pp. 309-10.

ignored here. We shall impose no restrictions on the spatial relationship between cause and effect. Let it suffice as a defense that Newtonian mechanics was considered satisfactory even though gravitational attraction is not reduced to contact action in that theory. (Many did not like this facet of it; but it was not rejected because of it.) The fact that the notion of action at a distance is not current in contemporary physics does not mean that there are any *a priori* grounds for its exclusion from physical theory.[5]

Analogous restrictions concerning the temporal relationship between cause and effect have been made in the definition.

One of these restrictions insists that the cause must not succeed the effect. The intuitive plausibility of the statement that no determining factors of an event can succeed that event has already been taken into account as a temporal constraint on state descriptions.[6]

Another restriction is that the cause must not be simultaneous with or later than the effect. Although we may wish to restrict the term "causal law" to a law which satisfies this requirement, I see no reason to reject an account as nondeterministic because the only laws in it state functional relationships among magnitudes at a single moment. The Boyle-Charles law for ideal gases certainly shows that the pressure of a gas is determined even though the law relates the pressure at t to the volume and temperature at t. Moreover, a "law of succession" is derivable from this "law of coexistence."[7] That is to say, one can derive a law that describes the sequential order of changes when a particular change is introduced. Thus, even if the law in question is not a causal law, it entails a causal law. At any rate, no one

---

[5] See Patrick Suppes, *The Problem of Action at a Distance* (Ph.D. Dissertation, Columbia University, 1950).

[6] Above, p. 162.

[7] These quoted expressions are used by Carl G. Hempel, "Deductive-Nomological vs. Statistical Explanation," p. 108.

would want to say that the pressure of a gas may be undetermined in a case that is an instance of the Boyle-Charles law.

Yet another restriction requires that the cause must be both earlier than and temporally continuous with the effect. In addition to the first two restrictions cited here, this proposal excludes events which are earlier than, but are not temporally continuous with, the effect. The acceptance of this proposal would necessitate the rejection of laws that do not enable us to predict the effect simply from a knowledge of the immediately preceding state. Psychological theorists differ on this question. Lewin would accept the proposal and Freud would reject it. The acceptance of this stipulation would entail a rejection of the Freudian position; whereas the rejection of this stipulation would favor neither theorist. Since there is no *a priori* reason to expect that psychological theory, with the help of neurophysiology and allied sciences, will adopt Lewin's position, the rejection of the proposal seems called for. In other sciences, also, laws that violate continuity are employed. Although many of these laws may be replaced, there are no *a priori* reasons to suppose that they are all temporary makeshifts.

But, in fact, philosophers have advanced *a priori* arguments against the possibility of causation at a temporal distance, or what is called mnemic causation, i.e., the kind of causation embodied most clearly in the occurrence of memory-experiences in which part of the cause seems to be an occurrence that took place long before the memory-experience. Pap cites an argument once used by Russell to the effect that the idea that the cause produces the effect necessarily entails that cause and effect are temporally continuous.[8] Russell argued that a lapse of time between cause and effect allows for the occurrence of some event which prevents the effect from occurring. The only way to preserve both the idea that the cause produces its effect necessarily and the

[8] *An Introduction to the Philosophy of Science,* p. 268.

idea that there may be a temporal interval between cause and effect is to employ causal laws referring virtually to the entire state of the universe in order to guarantee that nothing will prevent the effect from occurring. But this "solution" constitutes a *reductio ad absurdum* of the attempt to preserve both ideas.

If the demand for causal laws which refer virtually to the entire state of the universe is unacceptable, however, as the above argument presupposes, it follows that causes do not produce their effects necessarily anyway. For the fear that some force may intervene to prevent the customary effect from occurring is equally justified when cause and effect are simultaneous. We know, for example, that the gravitational attraction between the sun and the earth at some instant *t* is determined by the masses of the two bodies and the distance between them *at the same instant t*. Thus, there is no temporal interval between cause and effect. But positions and velocities of the earth, as calculated from this assumption, differ significantly from the actual positions and velocities. When it is recognized that these discrepancies are accounted for by other forces acting on the earth, greater precision may be attained if these forces are taken into account. We have, therefore, a case in which cause and effect are simultaneous, yet the cause does not necessarily produce the effect. The reason is the same as the one which is given when the cause precedes the effect, viz., that other factors are present which prevent the expected effect from occurring.

Clearly, if we can produce an example like this one in which cause and effect are simultaneous, the conclusion must apply, as well, to causal relations in which cause and effect are temporally contiguous. We have taken a case of simultaneity because there are serious difficulties in the notion of temporal contiguity. For example, if states are specified at an instant, then no states can be contiguous, for the series of point instants is dense.

In effect, then, to adopt the notion that the cause produces the effect necessarily, only truly exceptionless laws may be admitted.[9] Although reference to the entire universe in the law is one completely impractical way to guarantee non-interference with the effect, there may be exceptionless laws that refer to just a few conditions. The antecedent of most laws, it is true, does not specify a genuine sufficient condition of the effect because the other conditions of the effect are tacit (e.g., x is a freely falling body, y's nervous system is normal, air pressure is negligible). Thus, given an instance of the antecedent without the consequent, the lawlike sentence is not considered disconfirmed if one of these tacit conditions is not satisfied. But there may be some genuinely exceptionless laws (E-laws), e.g., whenever there is oxygen, a combustible material, and sufficient heat, fire will occur. E-laws, of course, must satisfy the requirement of temporal continuity; but as we have just seen, laws that satisfy temporal continuity may not be E-laws.

Although we are not obviously concerned to placate someone who wants to show that causes necessitate their effects, we do want to consider whether or not a deterministic account should include only E-laws.

A prediction made with an E-law need not include disclaimers like "other things being equal" or "assuming a closed system." But very few laws if any are E-laws, and scientists are not dissatisfied with the other type of law. If the system to which the law is applied is well-defined, and if occasional discrepancies are accounted for in terms of independently verifiable external influences, then the law is acceptable even if the scientist deems it necessary to enlarge the system in order to account for an occasional discrepancy.

[9] This presupposes that the law must refer to the entire cause. I frankly see no reason for this presupposition, but make it for purposes of discussion. Without it, one could simply say that the entire cause necessitates the effect; but the law only mentions part of the cause.

If we were to require E-laws, it would probably be impossible to point to scientific progress as more than minimal evidence for determinism.

Since a deterministic account is always of a true sentence "Pa_t," then, if a non-E-law is being used, the situation must be one in which the system really is closed. The law shows that Pa_t is determined because the conditions mentioned in the law will produce Pa_t if the system is closed and it is. If, on the other hand, some external influence makes "Qa_t" true, the deterministic account of "Qa_t" must evidently refer to the external influence and employ different laws that show how the influence results in Qa_t. Again, though, there can be a deterministic account of "Qa_t" even though this account contains no E-laws.

We reject, therefore, the proposal to restrict the laws in deterministic accounts to the E variey. Hence there is no reason to reject laws merely because they allow a temporal interval between cause and effect.

Perhaps the basic a priori argument against the possibility of mnemic causation is simply that an event cannot have an effect if it goes out of existence before the effect begins. This is certainly an intuitively appealing argument.

Even an advocate of the above argument would not deny the legitimacy of employing causal laws in which the cause or part of the cause does not occur just before the effect. Argument takes place about the possibility that some of these laws are not deducible from or ultimately eliminable in favor of laws in which there is no interval between cause and effect. Thus, all *prima facie* cases of mnemic causation are claimed by some to be explicable in terms of traces (usually believed to be neurological) which are activated under the appropriate conditions. With respect to historical laws in physics, it is usually claimed that a deeper understanding of the successive microstates of the system would eliminate the necessity for such laws.

258

Defenders of the possibility of mnemic causation are usually advocates of the regularity theory.[10] Thus, critics of mnemic causation often point out the inadequacies of the regularity theory in an attempt to undermine the regularity defense of this type of causation. In other words, if causation is basically constant conjunction, there is no reason to suppose that classes of events may not be constantly conjoined even if they are not temporally contiguous. Hence, an attack on the regularity theory may be construed as an attack on mnemic causation.

We argued in the previous chapter, however, that there may be conditions for the presence of a causal relation, e.g., temporal continuity, that have nothing to do with the factors debated about by regularity advocates and their opponents. Hence a regularity theorist may concede the desirability or necessity of adding temporal continuity to the definition of the causal relation. Of course, an anti-regularity theorist might insist that the only rationale for such an addition reveals the presence of a factor eschewed by regularity theorists: for example, the cause must be continuous with the effect because the cause has to *act on* the effect. But we have reviewed and rejected the arguments for the activity and necessity theories of causation.

We shall not deny the possibility of mnemic causation. Although there is a good deal of intuitive force behind the claim of the critics of mnemic causation, it is not clear that the same kind of force did not support the criticisms of action at a distance. In other words, if the critics of mnemic causation are relying upon a model of contact action, the acceptability of physical theories allowing action at a distance is sufficient grounds for rejecting their claims about mnemic causation. Moreover, if we find that it is impossible

---

[10] See, for example, Arthur Pap, *An Introduction to the Philosophy of Science,* pp. 267-72; and Bertrand Russell, *The Analysis of Mind* (London: George Allen & Unwin, 1921), Lecture V.

(on the basis of a great deal of evidence) to replace mnemic laws by non-mnemic laws in some domain, we shall clearly retain the mnemic laws. Indeed, the existence of criteria for the establishment of mnemic laws shows that they are not arbitrarily derived. Hence, if they cannot be replaced by non-mnemic laws, it is wrong to claim that their retention is arbitrary. To put it quite simply, we know very well that a certain childhood experience caused a present phobia although we cannot offer a completely non-mnemic explanation. It is doubtful, therefore, that we shall reject this causal fact if we come to believe that no non-mnemic explanation is possible even if a good deal of surprise accompanies this discovery. We reject, therefore, the view that the cause must be earlier and temporally continuous with the effect.

Although we have so far found it unnecessary to add new restrictions, the pendulum case shows that some will be required. There is a physical law according to which the period of a simple pendulum is proportional to the square root of its length, such that a knowledge of its length (together with a knowledge of certain constants) enables us to assign a unique value to its period. The same law enables us to assign a unique value to the length of the pendulum if we know its period. We do not hesitate to say that the length, in part, determines the period; but we do not say that the length is determined by the period although calculations of unique values are possible in either direction. As a matter of fact, we can envisage a situation in which we might be willing to say that the length of the pendulum is "undetermined." It may fluctuate in an apparently capricious manner and we may conclude that "there is nothing governing the changes in length." This conclusion is not incompatible with the law for, at any particular time, a knowledge of the period of the pendulum enables us to determine its length. We have, therefore, a lawful but non-deterministic account of the length of the pendulum.

The reason why the lawful account of the length of the pendulum fails to be deterministic is that the truth of the account is compatible with the length's being undetermined. The reason is not that the state description does not refer to the "cause" or the "determining factors" of the length. Although the period is certainly not the cause of the length of the pendulum, there are accounts I would wish to call deterministic in which the state description can be thought of as describing the cause only on pain of great artificiality. For example, in a closed mechanical system, knowledge of the position and velocity of a particle at a specified time may be gained from information about its position and velocity at an earlier time plus the appropriate laws. The account would certainly be deterministic, because it would show that the position and velocity of the particle at the specified time is determined even though we might prefer to think of the cause as a force which is presumed to be acting on the system rather than the antecedent position and velocity of the particle. Or consider a body at rest from t to $t + n$. Newton's first law plus information about the body's position at t comprises a deterministic account of the body's position at $t + n$ even though it would sound odd to say that its position at $t + n$ is determined by its position at t.[11]

A stipulation that would appear to eliminate the account of the length of the pendulum in terms of the law of the pendulum requires each condition mentioned in the state description (because it is mentioned in a generalized way in the law) to be a contributory or necessary condition of the event or state the account is about. It would seem that the constant of gravity is not a condition of the length of the pendulum, although it is a condition of the period.

C is a contributory condition of e if and only if there is a disjunction "$c \lor a_1 \lor a_2 \lor \ldots a_n$" such that $c \lor a_1 \lor a_2 \lor \ldots a_n$ is a necessary condition of e and the dis-

[11] See above, p. 130.

junction contains no proper subset that is a necessary condition of e. If, therefore, $-a_1 \cdot -a_2 \cdot \ldots -a_n$, e will not occur unless c. (So no disjunct is vacuously present.)

Evidently the fact that the constant of gravity is 32 is not a necessary condition of the pendulum's being two feet long for there can be pendulums that are two feet long under different gravitational conditions. Nor does this fact appear to be a contributory condition of the pendulum's length, because the appropriate disjunction cannot, it would seem, be formulated. Any condition that is known to be connected lawfully (not necessarily causally) to length will not be a contributory condition whose associated disjunction mentions as one of the disjuncts the constant of gravity. For example, if the pendulum is made out of a material that expands when heated, the pendulum's being in a certain temperature range will be a condition of its being two feet long. If the pendulum is outside this range it does not matter that the constant of gravity is 32—the pendulum will expand anyway. And if the pendulum is within the range, it does not matter what the constant of gravity is—the pendulum will be two feet long on the moon or the earth. Of course, we may be wrong about the irrelevance to length of the constant of gravity. But I have tried to formulate the content of this belief and, should it be true, we might use the above stipulation to conclude that the law of the pendulum does not provide a deterministic account of its length.

But the constant of gravity is a contributory condition of the period of the pendulum. If conditions are constant, changes in the constant of gravity are correlated with (not a causal term) changes in the period. Under specified conditions, therefore, the period would not take the value it does were the constant of gravity different.

Consider another example: we discover that under psychological conditions P, a person becomes schizophrenic if and only if he has blood chemistry B. We can, therefore, provide a lawful account of his schizophrenia and of his blood chemistry. The account of his blood chemistry is not deterministic because P is irrelevant (neither necessary nor contributory nor, of course, sufficient) to B, and we can presumably show this in an analogous manner.

This approach is ineffective, however, for there is a trivial way to concoct an appropriate disjunction in each case from the law itself. Assume, to make matters simple, that there are only three relevant variables in each case, G (gravity), R (period), L (length) in the first, and P (psychological condition), S (schizophrenia), B (blood chemistry) in the second. To prove that G (P) is a contributory condition of L (B) we must produce a condition C such that $-C$ implies $(L \supset G)[(B \supset P)] \cdot -R$ $(-S)$ satisfies this condition. In other words, in the first case, since the constant of gravity must be 32 if the period and length of the pendulum take certain values r_1 and l_1, then should r_1 change to r_2, l_1's remaining l_1 would presumably "depend on" appropriate adjustments in G. If we reject this conclusion because we imagine changes in R that leave L and G intact, we are imagining a situation in which a new variable is relevant, e.g., M (mechanical manipulation of the period). When this variable is taken into account, the paradox reappears. C simply becomes an appropriate function of R and M. For example, if r_1 changes to r_2 and $M = 0$, L would again "depend on" the constant of gravity. In the second case P is a contributory condition of B because, should a person have schizophrenia, he will have B only if he has P.

A natural suggestion at this point is that the cause is the event that can be manipulated to produce the effect. Thus, we can manipulate the height of the pendulum in order to change the period; but we cannot manipulate the period to change the height. Nor can we manipulate gravity in order to change the height. The obvious difficulty of this proposal is that there are cases in which we cannot manipulate the cause in order to produce the effect. For example, we cannot manipulate the occurrence of sunspots although we believe that the appearance of sunspots may be the cause of widespread radio disturbance and reject the view that radio disturbance is the cause of sunspots (even if the appearance of sunspots is a necessary condition of the kind of disturbance associated with it).

Even if we had been successful in showing that the pendulum's period is not a contributory condition of its length, or that psychological condition P is not a contributory condition of blood chemistry B, we would still have to deal with cases in which a single condition, say fire, is sufficient for another condition, say oxygen. Here, we cannot cite some condition different from fire that must be mentioned in a lawful account of the presence of oxygen that fails, on analysis, to be really necessary or contributory to oxygen.

Certain temporal facts might be thought pertinent. Oxygen is present before the fire; the pendulum has its length before it has a period; schizophrenia succeeds the development of blood chemistry B. These facts do not constitute a technical violation of the requirement that antecedent conditions must not succeed the fact being accounted for, because the latter might be given as "the length (oxygen, blood chemistry) at t" where t is the time of the period (fire, schizophrenia)—and there can be simultaneous causation. But we might then stipulate that an account of "Pa_t" fails to be deterministic if it cannot account for "Pa_{t-n}" where the latter is true and a has been P at all times between $t - n$ and t. An account of the length of the pendulum at $t - n$ in terms of the period at t would obviously violate the aforementioned temporal requirement on state descriptions and could not, therefore, be used, according to the suggested stipulation, as an account of the length of the pendulum at t.

But this proposal is too strong: it would eliminate genuine deterministic accounts of certain facts about homeostatic systems. For example, suppose a particular human body during one day maintains a temperature of 98° F to 99° F. A deterministic account of this temperature in the evening would perhaps fail as an account of the same temperature at midday. Through certain physiological mechanisms, the body is able to adjust to external temperature shifts. Thus, in the evening, when it is cool outdoors, the account will vary from the account that would be given at midday, when it is warm outdoors, even though there is no change in the body temperature during the day.

Another temporal consideration is that for each lawful, nondeterministic account of "Pa_t," there is an alternative account that links Pa_t to past states and events. We can account for the length of the pendulum in terms of its creation; we can account for blood chemistry B in terms of genetic facts; and so on. But if "$P \supset (B \equiv S)$" is a law, we can apparently account for B_t in terms of S_t plus P, where P is a psychological condition, say some set of childhood experiences, that precedes B_t. It may even be that B does not come into being until after P because the development of this state of the blood requires a certain maturation level.

The solution to this problem requires the introduction of concepts used to define the concept of law earlier (see Chapter VI). A necessary condition for L's being a law, we said, is that L satisfy a comprehensiveness-requirement. Roughly, L must belong to a DS that accounts for a certain set of facts such that no other DS accounts for that set plus others of the same type. Let us call the facts in this set the DS's C-facts.

Lawful, nondeterministic accounts share an interesting feature. The length of a pendulum is not one of the C-facts of the DS that includes the law of the pendulum and enables that law to satisfy the C-requirement. The same is true for the relation between blood chemistry B and the law "$P \supset (B \equiv S)$" and the relation between the presence of oxygen and the law "Fire occurs if and only if there is oxygen, a combustible material, and sufficient heat." But, relative to the appropriate DS's, the periods of pendulums, all cases of schizophrenia, and all fires would appear as C-facts. The following proposal ("Deterministic—D—Condition") suggests itself: A lawful account of "Pa_t" is deterministic only if there is no DS that shows that the laws in the account are not part of a DS that includes Pa_t as one of its C-facts.

Apply this condition to a new case. There is a lawful connection between a tuning fork's vibrating at 440 cycles per second and its vibrating at the pitch of A (assume that the latter is defined in audial terms). But if we use this law to account for the frequency of vibrations, the D-condition is violated. There is an alternative account of the frequency that is part of a comprehensive physical theory which can account for many facts about the frequency of emitted vibrations that fail to be accounted for by the psychophysical theory connecting frequency to pitch. Facts about pitch, therefore, are the C-facts of the psychophysical theory.

Suppose we wish to know the reason why a certain planet is deviating from the orbit it should be following. Now the theory that enables us to calculate the orbit is the same theory that suggests the presence of a body which is attracting the planet in such a way as to produce the deviation. When this body is found (another planet), we may say that its presence (or position, or gravitational force) *caused* the deviation. When this knowledge becomes familiar, of course, we do not think of the planet as deviating and do not, therefore, speak of the cause of the deviation. Rather, we think of the two planets as mutually attracting. How do we account for this case on the present proposal? It does show that the selection of the cause is sometimes a contextual matter. The selection may depend on considerations such as our expectations or the state of our knowledge. We are obviously interested only in cases in which the direction of causation depends solely on objective considerations, and all the previous examples in this chapter show that such cases exist. Our proposal does explain why the idea of one-way causation is dropped in the example from astronomy whereas it is retained in other cases. Since the same theory accounts for the position of the new planet and the position of the old planet, the D-condition is satisfied. Hence, any laws of the form "$P \equiv Q$" can be used to account deterministically for P-facts and Q-facts.

A deterministic account, therefore, is a lawful account that satisfies the D-condition.

IX. DETERMINISM DEFINED

THE RESULTS OF Part II may now be summarized in a definition of determinism and a definition of a deterministic account.

We have already proposed a definition of determinism (above, p. 178):

$(x)[x$ is an R-sentence $\supset$ $(\exists y)(\exists z)(y$ is a state description-sentence $\cdot z$ is a law-sentence $\cdot \dashv (y \cdot z) \supset x)]$

An R-sentence is true, contingent, singular, and temporal. It must not contain a causal, evaluative, or basic dispositional predicate. Any logical consequence of either an R-sentence or any conjunction of R-sentences is an R-sentence. If the predicate of the R-sentence is a determinable whose determinates admit as values any or almost any real number, the laws in the deterministic account of this sentence must contain variables for that determinable that may also take values from any or almost any real number (Continuity-requirement).

A state description-sentence is a conjunction of any mathematical, logical, and linguistic truths, any true sentences of the form "$x = y$," and the state description proper. The state description proper is a subset of R-sentences except that sentences containing basic dispositional predicates are allowed, and sentences containing positional and temporal predicates are ruled out. The state description must be logically and criterially independent of the sentence the deterministic account is about; and no sentence may refer to a time period subsequent to t where t is the temporal designation in the sentence the deterministic account is about.

No other temporal restrictions on state descriptions are made.

A law (as used in the definition of determinism) is a true, logically contingent universal conditional with non-self-contradictory, open-ended, nonpositional, and qualitative predicates that meets five requirements (*DS, C, S, AE, D*). ("A law" may actually be a conjunction of laws.)

A deterministic account of some *R*-sentence is, of course, a specific state description-sentence and a specific law (or laws) that entails the *R*-sentence. Thus, any deterministic account of *x* is a deterministic account of each logical consequence of *x*. Moreover, a deterministic account of an *R*-sentence may be povided by several deterministic accounts of sentences which conjunctively entail that *R*-sentence.

PART 3

THE TRUTH OF DETERMINISM

X. THE ALLEGED TRIVIALITY OF DETERMINISM

VIEWS ON DETERMINISM'S truth-value are as varied as the possibilities. Determinism has been said to be neither true nor false; necessarily true; necessarily false; contingently true; or contingently false.

Arguments for the necessary truth of determinism are not usually impressive. Given the definition of determinism, its denial certainly seems conceivable or imaginable. But indeterminism has been deemed inconceivable on the grounds that it violates the principle of sufficient reason or a similar principle. If indeterminism could be true, then in two different cases under identical circumstances, two different events might occur. Thus, there is no sufficient reason for whichever event does occur. I agree that the principle of sufficient reason is violated; but I see no *a priori* reason to accept that principle.

In a famous paper, Russell argued for the necessary truth of determinism by arguing for its trival truth.[1] He contended that it is always possible to construct a deterministic theory for any set of observational data without expanding the system. For example, a system consisting of a single material particle is deterministic, he maintained, because there must be a function which relates the coordinates of state to the time such that, if the function were known, the path of the particle could be plotted.

Russell's charge is important in the context of the debate

---

[1] "On the Notion of Cause," *Mysticism and Logic* (New York: W. W. Norton and Co., 1940).

between determinists and libertarians. A libertarian would hardly be impressed by analogues to Russell's example in psychology. To use the fact that a person's decisions and actions must be a function of the time of occurrence, even if the function is unknown, as evidence that the decisions and actions are not performed freely can only be interpreted as a poor joke.

Given any moving particle, one can construct a graph whose axes represent position (z) and time (t). Regardless of the complexity of the curve which is constructed from the points representing particular values of z and t, an equation can be formulated in which z is a function of t. Russell argues, therefore, that, in a trivial sense, the position of *any* particle can be said to be determined. One reply to this claim is that such "laws" are illegitimate since they contain the time variable explicitly. But this reply is met in the following way: Suppose the curve is a parabola whose equation is $z = t^2 + 6t + 9$. Now one can easily eliminate the time variable by differentiating this equation twice with respect to the time. The result is: $d^2z/dt^2 = 2$. (T occurs, of course, in the definition of the derivative.) Moreover, some recommend that the term "law" be restricted to the differential form in which t is absent (or eliminable through further differentiations).[2] If no restrictions are placed on the order of differential equations, determinism seems to become a trivial thesis, for its truth is guaranteed regardless of what occurs in the world.

Physicists are, however, reluctant to accept laws involving derivatives of arbitrarily high order.[3] Hence, tacit restrictions are invoked; but due to the vagueness of these restrictions, determinism itself becomes vague. Moreover, if Margenau is correct in maintaining that "high-order equations would

[2] Henry Margenau, *The Nature of Physical Reality: A Philosophy of Modern Physics* (New York: McGraw-Hill Book Co., 1950), p. 181.

[3] See Nagel, p. 321; and Margenau, p. 409.

274

become acceptable causal laws"[4] if the search for more simple ones were in vain, the vagueness of determinism is transformed into triviality again.

But equations, whether or not they are in an integrated form, are not identical with laws. We have construed laws as true propositions, and equations are neither true nor false. Consider, for example, the differential equation $d^2z/dt^2 = g$. The specification of the constant in this equation is not sufficient to convert it into a law. The equation $d^2z/dt^2 = 32$ is neither true nor false, since no specification of the bodies whose motion satisfies this equation has been made. The equation is satisfied by a body falling solely under the force of gravitation, but is not necessarily satisfied by a moving automobile. Equations, therefore, can be satisfied, and until the range of application of some equation is known questions of truth or falsity cannot be decided. Thus, equations may be construed as the consequents of laws whose antecedents specify the properties a system must possess if its behavior is correctly described by the equations. Some of the characteristics referred to in the antecedent are what some philosophers of science have called boundary conditions. We shall use the expression "system-defining property" to refer to any property which limits the range of application of an equation.

System-defining properties should be distinguished from properties which define the state of the system. If we wish to know the position of a particle whose system-defining property is "falling to the earth solely under the force of gravitation," we must integrate the equation $d^2z/dt^2 = 32$. Integration ultimately yields $z = 16t^2 + v_1t + z_1$ (where z represents position and v velocity). Relative to the determinable position, therefore, the state of the system is specified in terms of the position (z_1) and velocity (v_1) at a single instant (t_1), for a knowledge of these values enables us to

[4] Margenau, p. 409.

275

calculate the position of the particle at any time. System-defining properties tell us to what entities the equations apply, and state properties tell us what information is required to calculate the values of a particular variable at any time. Since system-defining properties can be incorporated into the antecedent of a law, it was not considered necessary to single them out in the definition of determinism. But they are important here because of their role in our reply to Russell.

Suppose $z = t^2$ expresses the various positions of a moving particle as a function of the time of occurrence. A second-order differential equation is derived in which t does not occur explicitly. But since the statement of a law is incomplete unless the system-defining properties are given, it is legitimate to request the specification of the law of which $z = t^2$ is a part. Since laws may not contain positional predicates, system-defining predicates may not mention absolute date. System-defining properties may recur, therefore. And we may, therefore, discover that another particle, belonging to a system defined in the same way as the particle that satisfies $z = t^2$, fails to satisfy this equation.

We may try to make some revisions. For example, we may redefine the state, or change the system-defining properties. But one possibility is that the various positions of these particles are undetermined. Russell is, therefore, mistaken in concluding that the existence of an equation, with t explicit or not, that applies to a particle shows that the behavior of the particle is determined.

Temporal predicates may appear in a system-defining predicate just so long as the temporal designation is not absolute. For example, temporal intervals are legitimate. The logical possibility of reinstantiation of a system requires, in addition, the rejection of predicates that are not qualitative. This requirement was instituted earlier.[5]

Suppose, however, that the equation of motion of another

[5] Above, pp. 194-97.

particle belonging to a system defined in the same way as the first two is $z = t^2 + 6t + 9$. Although both particles satisfy the equation $d^2z/dt^2 = 2$, determinism has been disproved (on the assumption that the system may not be expanded and that no redefinition of state is allowed) because the system is not deterministic relative to the determinable "position," even if it is deterministic relative to the determinable "instantaneous acceleration." Thus, the equation which contains t explicitly, if it is part of a law, is stronger evidence for determinism than the equation which does not. (This is a consequence of the fact that integration yields unique equations whereas different equations may result in the same differential equation.)

The above conclusions apply to "Russell's particle" as well. As Russell stated the example, the particle was assigned no system. We are supposed to take any particle and plot its coordinates of state as a function of time. Proceeding thus may give us an equation; but in order to derive a law, system-defining properties must be introduced, and they must allow for the resumption of the same state either by this particle or by another which constitutes an identical system.

Sometimes this particle is supposed to constitute the entire world. Since there is no second system to confirm some law that might apply to this particle, determinism can be verified only by seeing what happens when the state of this system recurs. We know that the history of a closed deterministic system from t to $t + n$ is identical with its history from $t + m$ to $t + m + n$ if the state of the system at t is identical with its state at $t + m$. Assuming, for simplicity's sake, only one coordinate of state z (a coordinate of position), determinism holds in this world if the particle's history of movement is identical whenever it returns to a previous position. In other words, the graph of motion would contain a repeating curve. Determinism can, therefore, be easily falsified if the particle returns to a prior position.

277

Suppose the particle does not return to an earlier position, but travels through eternity in a straight line. Since the particle is doing what it is supposed to be doing according to Newton's first law, why may we not say that determinism is true in this world?

We have reason to think that Newton's first axiom is a law because we have confirmed the theory in which it appears in *our* world. Hence, I would be prepared to say that the behavior of our particle is deterministic if the destruction of our world left this single particle as the only remnant. But Newton's axiom has no special status if we are considering a purely hypothetical world.

The only reason we might have for construing the behavior of this particle as deterministic is that its behavior is simple. But there are other simple forms of motion. The concept of simplicity is so vague that any definition of determinism in terms of simplicity of behavior would be hopelessly arbitrary.

Strictly, determinism cannot be defined in this world. Since the particle is the only entity, z represents absolute position. The variable can only be interpreted as relative position if there is something else in the world relative to which the particle's position can be described. Hence, no state description of this particle can be given, for it would have to employ a positional predicate.[6]

In our discussion of positional predicates we concentrated upon temporal positionality. But the appearance of a spatially positional predicate in a law or a state description is intuitively just as objectionable. Most philosophers and scientists who impose a requirement of temporal invariability on laws also insist on an analogous requirement for space.[7]

Suppose we bypass this difficulty by introducing a second particle into our world and specifying the position of the first

[6] See the discussion of positionality above, pp. 186-94.

[7] See, for example, James Clark Maxwell, *Matter and Motion* (London: Society for Promoting Christian Knowledge, 1920), p. 13.

(P_1) in terms of its distance from the second. Two attitudes are possible.

If the state of P_1 is given as some value of z, we can define circumstances under which P_1's behavior is indeterministic, viz., it returns to an earlier state, but does not repeat the behavior it displayed subsequent to the first time it was in this state. If the history is always identical, determinism is (nontrivially) true. If, on the other hand, P_1 never returns to an earlier state, I would prefer to say that its behavior is neither deterministic nor indeterministic. "If P_1 were to return to an earlier state, its subsequent behavior would be identical to its behavior subsequent to the earlier state" is, I would say, neither true nor false.[8] Since it is certainly not necessarily true, Russell cannot say that determinism is trivially true in such a world.

The attitude I prefer refuses to allow z to be considered a state variable. Normally a variable is chosen as a state variable because it is believed to be causally relevant to the property whose presence is predicted from a knowledge of the state of the system. Causal relevance cannot, however, be defined for a world with one system. In such a world, states follow, but are not causally related to, each other.[9] Hence, the selection of z because it is the only candidate is purely arbitrary. We must bear in mind, too, that the fact that position is a deterministic function of earlier states of position (and velocity) in our world is irrelevant to the facts regarding our hypothetical world. In that world, the choice of position as the state is justified only because there is no other candidate. Strictly, the notion of a state is not definable for this particle. Determinism, therefore, does not apply to this world.

According to either attitude, determinism is not a trivial thesis. If it applies, it can be false.

[8] The reasons are given above, pp. 210-13.
[9] See Chap. IV.

What is the relevance of these conclusions to systems that do not appear to be instantiated more than once? Do not cosmologists study the origin of the universe and biologists the evolutionary history of species? Yes, but the laws that are invoked to explain the sequences refer to systems that are capable of reinstantiation. For example, the law "All inheritable variations are due to mutations" has many instances although it can be invoked to explain, as part of a theory, *the* evolutionary process.

Temporal invariability is sometimes discussed in connection with the requirement that laws of nature may not change. Disagreement on the latter often takes the form of disagreement about the possibility that the essential constants in laws of nature change. Plainly, if the constants are changing, the laws are changing as well, for a particular law is falsified if the constant must be revised. Now, such talk makes no sense on the supposition that laws are true, for if a law is a true proposition that contains a constant $k = 2$, it is self-contradictory to suppose that there is a time at which $k = 3$. In order to discuss this suggestion, we must suppose that laws are only "true at a certain time." Ordinarily, when we say that a statement is true "at a certain time," that expression can be eliminated by a more careful specification of certain expressions in the statement, e.g., by the replacement of indexical expressions. But the view that laws of nature change asserts that the reference to time is essential, because the variations of the constants are not due to changing conditions such that a more careful specification of the system would convert some disconfirmed lawlike sentence into a timelessly true law. The variations are due to the changes of time itself. Thus, a law that holds for one epoch may not hold for another, simply because it is a different epoch and not because conditions vary.

If this possibility is taken seriously, one might wish to know the manner in which a constant varies in time. Should the values of the constant depend simply on the time, however, there are no restrictions on the equation expressing the changing values of the constant as a function of time. It must be ascertained empirically, and any equation should do. To restrict the function in any way is to assume that factors other than time are relevant. Thus, one may "usher in a new epoch" by the disconfirmation of some lawlike proposition. I am not denying that scientists may adopt this suggestion if the function is a relatively simple one. But if they do, determinists cannot appeal to the progress of science as evidence for their thesis. Determinism would then be a trivial thesis. Thus, determinism requires that the laws of nature do not change in time, and this requirement is embodied in the conception of laws as true *simpliciter*.

Finally, it is noteworthy that we have not had to restrict deterministic laws or theories to "simple" laws or theories. Scientists may wish to impose restrictions on complexity. We saw earlier that there may be conditions of lawlikeness imposed on individual sciences for reasons peculiar to those sciences.[10] In this philosophical discussion we cannot deal with these matters. But we can say that any restrictions on the complexity of a theory have nothing to do with the deterministic or indeterministic nature of the theory.

[10] Above, pp. 184-85.

XI. DETERMINISM AND FALSIFICATION

THE CHARGE THAT determinism is neither true nor false is based on the premise that it is not falsifiable. (The debatable assumption that only sentences capable of falsification possess truth-values will not be discussed here; I believe it can be shown that determinism is falsifiable in *some* important sense.) Proponents of this view often make the further claim that determinism ought, therefore, to be construed as a methodological postulate or rule of procedure.

If determinism is falsifiable, alleged deterministic accounts must be falsifiable. Let us use the term "theory" for the lawlike sentence or sentences that can appear in many alleged deterministic accounts. (There are a number of requirements a set of lawlike sentences must satisfy to be a theory that are not and need not be discussed in this book.) Suppose some theory T has appeared in several alleged deterministic accounts each one of which satisfies all conditions on deterministic accounts except, *perhaps,* the requirement that T be true. In a new use of T, however, the R-sentence entailed by T plus the state description is false—and, therefore, not really an R-sentence. The actual value of the variable in question differs significantly from the predicted value, so that an account of the discrepancy in terms of random error is not feasible.

Several paths are open to the scientist. He may retain T intact and account for the discrepancy in terms of the introduction of extraneous factors into the system. Hence, T is not falsified, although a deterministic account of the (true)

R-sentence will have to include laws that link the R-sentence to these external influences.

Or he may retain T intact and account for the discrepancy in terms of a mistake in the specification of the initial conditions or state description. That scientists do this occasionally is undeniable, especially when T is well-confirmed and comprehensive. It may be impossible to test his explanation in a particular case; but it is clear that there must be criteria in terms of which such explanations may be rejected. The fact that theories are revised or rejected indicates that there are criteria. For example, if discrepancies occur frequently under carefully controlled conditions, the repeated use of this explanation becomes dubious. Now, a necessary condition of the existence of such criteria is the independent specifiability of the state description, a condition we have made[1] In other words, the discrepancy cannot be the criterion in terms of which values are assigned to the state variables. Again, however, it is undeniable that scientists do this occasionally. For example, the apparent disconfirmation of a well-confirmed lawlike sentence "$A \supset B$" may be taken as evidence that A was not really present even though A is specifiable independently of B. Since "$A \supset B$" is so well-confirmed, the absence of B is taken as a sufficient criterion of the absence of A even though other criteria of A exist.

Although it may be necessary to revise or reject T, most generalizations in T, perhaps all but one, may be retained. If T contains well-entrenched, higher-order generalizations, a scientist will be disposed to retain these at the expense of other parts of T, a fact that has led some philosophers to construe certain generalizations as definitional truths or rules of procedure.[2]

Although a particular contrary instance may, however, be

---

[1] See above, p. 161.
[2] Henri Poincaré, *Science and Hypothesis* (New York: Dover Publications, 1952), chap. VIII.

accounted for by revision in parts of T other than G, where G is a well-entrenched, higher-order generalization, conditions under which the retention of G would not be feasible can be described. To quote Pap:

> The statement "In an isolated system the sum of all the different forms of energy (mechanical, heat, electrical) is constant in time" is not "merely" analytic, for the assumptions made in order to reconcile it with the observations must be independently confirmed. Thus some mechanical energy is obviously lost in a changing isolated system owing to friction. To say that this lost mechanical energy is regained by the system in the form of heat energy is to say that there is a strict proportionality between the work involved in the frictional dissipation of mechanical energy and the independently measurable heat that the system gains at the same time.[3]

It may be fruitful, therefore, to speak in terms of rejectability rather than falsifiability. In other words, there are propositions which are fairly immune to falsification although one can describe conditions under which their rejection is warranted. This sentence is vague; but it does seem to be a correct description of certain scientific propositions. I am not denying that scientific theories are capable of falsification; I am rather referring to certain generalizations which are parts of theories.

Another alternative open to the scientist is to revise T by expanding the state. Sometimes this counts as an expansion of the system and sometimes it does not. For example, if the new state property is a property of the same entities, it may be said that the system is intact. If the new state property is a property of an entity outside the original system, the system may be considered expanded. The new property might be relational, and the terms of the relation may em-

---

[3] *An Introduction to the Philosophy of Science,* p. 311.

brace entities both within the system and outside the system. The distinction between mere state expansion and system expansion may be vague; but the vagueness is unimportant for our purposes.

Again, however, it must be possible to provide an independent specification of the new state property. Some have contended that this maxim is violated in the case of certain physical theories when disconfirmation is viewed as evidence for the existence of hitherto unknown particles, the sole evidence for their existence being the disconfirmation. If this contention is justified, then Frank's assertion that state specifications are made to satisfy the deterministic thesis appears warranted.[4] It will be recalled that we did not rule out the possibility that scientists may accept the possibility that laws of nature change. We concluded, however, that in such an eventuality, scientific progress may no longer be considered as evidence for determinism.

A similar conclusion must be drawn here. The significance of determinism requires that some kind of independent specifiability requirement be stipulated even if scientists in practice occasionally bypass this requirement. For example, at a certain stage in the development of some theory, it may not be clear whether or not scientists accept a requirement of this kind. For a determinist, this means that it is not clear whether or not the theory satisfies all the conditions that are requisite for labeling it "deterministic." This vagueness in the formulations or practices of scientists does not, of course, entail a vagueness in the definition of determinism.

Evidently, more radical paths are open to the scientist (e.g., he may reject the theory altogether and search for a whole new set of state variables); but the rejectability of any new theory will be guaranteed by the same considerations that guaranteed the rejectability of the old theory.

[4] *Modern Science and its Philosophy* (Cambridge: Harvard University Press, 1950) pp. 56-57.

Although deterministic theories can be rejected or falsified, can determinism itself be falsified or rationally rejected? Evidently the mere failure to find a deterministic theory for some determinable need never be construed as sufficient grounds for rejection, since the failure to find something does not prove its nonexistence. But what is true of determinism is true of any proposition containing an existential quantifier. If "There are centaurs on the earth" is irrational to believe, why might there not be conditions under which "There is a deterministic theory for determinable D" is irrational to believe? In other words, even if one grants that all propositions containing an existential quantifier are incapable of falsification, it does not follow that the belief in each is warranted. It will be recalled that the conditions of falsification of certain higher-order generalizations are difficult to state even though there are conditions under which continued belief in these propositions is unwarranted. Is there any merit in the position that the status of determinism is similar?

An argument against this suggestion is that "There are centaurs on the earth" is not rejected simply because no centaurs have been found. This proposition is also incompatible with certain facts and theories for which there is a good deal of evidence.

But is not determinism incompatible with quantum mechanics, for which there is a great deal of evidence? And if the claim of incompatibility is debatable, can we not construct a hypothetical theory that contradicts determinism, thereby overthrowing the view that determinism *cannot* be falsified? It will be helpful first to specify four relations any theory T has to any R-sentence R_1 (or class of R-sentences):

T *is deterministic relative to* R_1: There is a state description such that T conjoined with the state description consitutes a deterministic account of R_1.

T *is indeterministic relative to* R_1: T is not deterministic relative to R_1; but it is deterministic relative to some probability assignment to R_1.

T *is essentially indeterministic relative to* R_1: T, perhaps together with certain facts, entails that there is no deterministic account of R_1.

T *is nondeterministic relative to* R_1: None of the above applies.

A theory is strictly incompatible with determinism only when it is essentially indeterministic relative to some *R*-sentence. A case might be made for the inconsistency of determinism with quantum theory on the basis of the latter's relation to sentences ascribing a specific momentum to some particle whose position has been measured with great precision. But we shall not base the view that determinism is capable of rational rejection on this possibility, because there is reason to believe that the sentences ascribing specific momenta under these conditions are not *R*-sentences. If they were *R*-sentences, they would be true; and if they were true, particles would have precise simultaneous positions and momenta, whether or not we can measure them precisely. But some (not all) commentators believe that quantum theory itself implies that " 'the precise simultaneous values of the position and momentum of an electron' has no defined sense."[5]

Many theories, including quantum theory, are indeterministic relative to genuine *R*-sentences. In only a few cases, however, does the feeling arise that the theory implies or even suggests the nonexistence of any deterministic account of these *R*-sentences. Statistical mechanics, for example, is indeterministic relative to sentences describing the mechanical state of an individual gas molecule. But no one believes that statistical mechanics shows or suggests that the mole-

[5] Nagel, p. 305.

cule's mechanical state is undetermined. It is assumed, rather, that the individual molecules obey Newton's deterministic laws of motion. Similarly, if a sociologist can calculate from a knowledge of relevant sociological factors the probability that Jones will commit suicide, we do not feel that a deterministic psychological analysis is precluded. But if we have reached a level of analysis that is believed to be basic, e.g., the constituents cannot be construed as composites of more fundamental objects whose behavior might be deterministic, or the behavior of the more fundamental objects does not deterministically account for the behavior of the constituents, the presence of a theory that is indeterministic relative to some R-sentence (even if it is deterministic relative to many other R-sentences) should concern a determinist.

Hence, quantum mechanics is again our example. For example, this theory is indeterministic relative to "Atom a passes from energy level$_1$ to energy level$_2$." Since atoms are composites of other particles, one might think that a subatomic theory could conceivably provide a deterministic account of this sentence in perhaps a general reduction of quantum theory to the subatomic one. Heisenberg and other interpreters of quantum theory rejected this possibility on the grounds that a precise knowledge of certain magnitudes is required to provide a deterministic account of the behavior of a quantum system and that the indeterminacy principle sets limits on the precision with which these magnitudes can be measured at *any* level of analysis. Although this argument is debatable, von Neumann proved that its conclusion is inescapable. According to his theorem, "current quantum theory cannot be supplemented by introducing additional 'hidden parameters' for defining the state of a system, so as to convert the theory into a non-statistical one, without obtaining consequences from the embedded theory incompatible with the vast quantities of experimental data that

288

confirm so impressively the current theory.'⁶ " . . . von Neumann's theorem implies that . . . a deeper level of precise causal law could not even exist. Thus, one is led to the conclusion that the precise manner of occurrence of these irregular fluctuations cannot be traced by means of experiments to any kind of causes at all, and that, indeed, it does not even have any causes."⁷

Thus, quantum mechanics is essentially indeterministic relative to some R-sentences. If the theory is true, determinism is false. All the evidence for quantum theory, therefore, is evidence against determinism. Thus, if the belief that centaurs exist is irrational because it is incompatible with certain facts and theories for which there is a good deal of evidence, so is the belief in determinism.

Furthermore, we are really concerned with the theoretical question of whether or not conditions of the rational rejection of determinism can be stated. Since quantum mechanics is essentially indeterministic relative to some R-sentences, we need only suppose that the theory becomes firmly entrenched by confirming new predictions, providing explanations for phenomena hitherto unexplained, and resolving any difficulties in the internal structure of the theory.

Under these conditions a person can still accept determinism and reject quantum mechanics. But a person today can in the same sense accept the Ptolemaic theory of the solar system and the existence of centaurs. If these beliefs are not strictly falsifiable, they are surely irrational just as the belief in determinism is irrational under the cited hypothetical conditions.

Determinism, like certain higher-order scientific generalizations, e.g., G, is difficult to falsify. But G, unlike determinism, is part of a theory that is more easily falsified. I

---

⁶ Ibid., p. 311.
⁷ David Bohm, *Causality and Chance in Modern Physics* (New York: Harper & Bros., 1957), p. 87.

do not, however, see the importance of this difference in the current context. The disconfirmation or falsification of many propositions may lead us to reject G, just as the continued confirmation of some indeterministic theory may lead us to reject determinism. In each case a point can be reached where rejection is rationally demanded.

We conclude, therefore, that determinism is true or false, a conclusion that is not incompatible with the view that determinism is a rule of procedure or a maxim of inquiry. Many sentences can be interpreted in both ways. A well-confirmed lawlike sentence functions as a rule, for example, when apparent disconfirmation leads to the search for factors which will indicate that the specification of initial conditions was mistaken.

XII. DETERMINISTIC THEORIES
AND THE OBSERVABLE WORLD

THE POSSIBLE truth-statuses for determinism have been reduced to three: contingent truth, contingent falsity, and necessary falsity. An interesting argument for determinism's falsity arises from a consideration of the relationship between theories or sets of laws that appear in deterministic accounts and the observational data that confirm or disconfirm these theories.

Since a deterministic account may contain only true sentences, the theories and laws in deterministic accounts must be true. Indeed, according to our view, a sentence is not a law if it is not true. But sentences are considered laws and theories are considered acceptable even if there is a discrepancy between the empirical data and either the laws or the theories. In fact, if the laws are embodied in a theoretical framework, they may contain variables ranging over theoretical states of the entities involved, and these cannot be measured directly. For example, classical mechanics is formulated in terms of magnitudes capable of mathematically continuous variation, whereas the values obtained by experimental measurement never form such a series. Quite simply, one cannot measure instantaneous velocity and must be satisfied with average values of this variable during some interval of time. Hence, one can arrive only at approximations to the theoretical state of the mechanical system.

Since we have rejected the view that there *must* be deterministic theories for *R*-sentences, the sole evidence for determinism is constituted by whatever evidence exists for particular deterministic accounts. Some of this evidence will be evidence for the truth of the general statements in the account. It now appears that this latter evidence is often not and sometimes cannot be sufficient to justify ascriptions of truth to laws and theories. And the insufficiency in question is not the existence of unexamined cases; it is rather a lack in the relation between the generalizations and the supporting data.

Sometimes, a law is only approximate because certain initial conditions, whose relevance is stipulated by the very theory in which the law is embedded, are ignored. Convenience or difficulty of computation may dictate the ignoring of the conditions. To use an earlier example, calculations of the positions and velocities of the earth, if only the sun is considered, will be in error to a certain degree. The error is substantially reduced when the gravitational attraction of the other planets is taken into account. Here, a determinist might want to say that we have grounds for believing that the theory is strictly true even if the evidence does not precisely confirm the theory. But this type of response has limited applicability and is of no use in dealing with the indeterminist's point that many theories have variables for instantaneous magnitudes.

Where the relation between theory and observation is inexact, philosophers would appreciate the presence of criteria to decide whether or not the approximations are sufficient to retain the theory. The criteria, however, are not clear-cut, and it does not seem possible to formulate general criteria since contextual considerations such as the advanced or preliminary state of the science are, as a matter of fact, taken into account.[1] Nonetheless, scientists are dissatisfied with cer-

---

[1] For a discussion of this point, see Michael Scriven, "The Key Property of Physical Laws—Inaccuracy: A Symposium," *Current Issues in the Philosophy of Science,* Proceedings of Section L of the American Association for the Advancement of Science, ed. Herbert Feigl and Grover Maxwell (New York: Holt, Rinehart, and Winston, 1961), pp. 91-101.

tain generalizations when discrepancy with data is too great. Laws that can replace cruder formulations will then be sought. Often, the search has proven successful, as in the case of the law governing the conductivity of electrolytes.[2] Thus, scientific progress is in the direction of greater accuracy. This fact also substantiates the presence of a criterion, granted vague, which scientists use to decide whether or not a lawlike sentence corresponds sufficiently to the data.

Nonetheless, we do face a choice. If we insist on the truth of deterministic accounts, an indeterminist will be in a better position than a determinist to appeal to science, the only possible source of evidence for determinism. If we relax the requirement on deterministic accounts, allowing "approximate truth," an indeterminist can justifiably charge determinism with serious vagueness.

There is a third alternative that is more appealing. Suppose a scientist is trying to ascertain the "true value" of some magnitude—of a certain object A. Six measurements produce six different results, $m_1 \ldots m_6$ that are, however, sufficiently similar and sufficiently random to warrant the belief that no systematic mistake is being made. There are statistical techniques the scientist may now employ to calculate the "true value" of m and the probability that the "true value" is accurate. Although several techniques with slightly different results are used for making the latter calculation, let us say that one of these yields the result that the "true value" of m, m_t, has a measure of uncertainty or a tolerance of u.

We now have a simple device for deciding whether or not some purported deterministic account of "A is m_n at t" is confirmed as true. The account is true only if m_n is within the range $m_t \pm u$. The fact that some young sciences may not wish to submit themselves to this rigor means simply that they are not yet prepared to offer genuinely deterministic ac-

[2] Ibid., p. 101.

counts of the phenomena they study and are not prepared to adhere to strict standards of confirmation; this policy may be justified.

"But," an indeterminist might say, "you are conceding that deterministic accounts do not apply to this world because the great majority of sentences accounted for will really be false. Why not be honest and concede that determinism is strictly false, although, in a sense perhaps, approximately true?"

This question can be partially answered by changing the form of "A is m_n at t" to "M_n of A at t is within a range that intersects range r" (S) where r is calculated from the tolerance assigned to the measurements of the state description variables.[3] S may be true even though there are several conflicting measurements of m.

The indeterminist may reject this proposal as a devious evasion. We have saved truth at the expense of specificity. But there are really two issues that have to be distinguished. In the first place, the fact that S is inspecific creates no problem. Many perfectly good R-sentences, e.g., "This apple is red," can be more specific. Second, although we may be able to provide a deterministic account of S, determinism demands accounts for all the true sentences more specific than S. In the original example there are six R-sentences more specific than S corresponding to each measurement. Moreover, some of these measurements may even be outside the range that intersects r. That is, S does not even entail that every specific measurement is included in the confirming range.

The entire value of this third alternative, therefore, is that it reduces this specific problem for a determinist to a general problem he must face anyway. For example, a psychological theory of aggression may allow for deterministic accounts of

[3] Margenau's discussion of this issue in *The Nature of Physical Reality*, pp. 107-121, is particularly helpful.

aggression, but not for deterministic accounts of "*P* is verbally aggressive." And if the theory is expanded to provide deterministic accounts of verbal aggression, it may not be able to tell us the specific form the verbal aggression might take. Similar examples from other sciences could be chosen. Analogously, a deterministic account of *S* is not a deterministic account of any specific measurement. We are, thus, forced to recognize the great discrepancy between the number of kinds of *R*-sentences for which there are deterministic accounts and the number for which there are not.

It would be simpler, therefore, to adopt the third alternative and retain the requirement that deterministic accounts be true and strictly entail the (true) sentence being accounted for.

The indeterminist may feel vindicated because we have had to acknowledge the limits of an appeal to scientific progress as evidence for determinism. The only way a determinist can respond is by stipulating a level of specificity below which deterministic accounts are not required for the truth of determinism, thereby making further restrictions on *R*-sentences.

Whether or not a determinist can define this level, the concept of a deterministic account remains unaffected because that concept is defined relative to some given *R*-sentence. Thus, we understand perfectly well the meaning of "Smith's decision to study medicine is determined" (*M*) even if we remain uncommitted regarding a level of specificity for the thesis of determinism. We can, therefore, consider the relation between *M* and sentences like "Smith could have decided otherwise." Thus, crucial issues in the determinist-libertarian debate can be discussed without a general definition of determinism.

If a determinist sets out to define this level of specificity, he will undoubtedly distinguish post-theoretically important factors from pre-theoretically important ones. For example, prior to Freudian theory, a determinist might have considered the failure to provide a deterministic account of slips of the tongue as unimportant. But now, if Freudian theory is correct, slips of the tongue are important as indices of other important psychological traits. Thus, we shall want a deterministic account of any R-sentence that is causally connected to R-sentences that are independently recognized to be important.

But I cannot conceive of any feasible way to decide whether or not some R-sentence concerns a factor that is pre-theoretically important. Intuitively, some facts are important, others are unimportant, and there is a vast area where intuitions are unclear.

I propose, therefore, that no restrictions on R-sentences be made. Thus, determinism really is a universal theory, requiring "predictability down to the last detail—lock, stock, and barrel, and even down to the last scratch on the barrel."[4] Those who accept determinism on an *a priori basis* (we do not) will only be satisfied by a definition, like ours, that makes determinism an unrestricted thesis.

In many contexts we may wish to restrict our interests to a small subset of R-sentences, e.g., psychological sentences on an arbitrary level of specificity. We can ask whether or not there are deterministic theories relative to this subset and inquire into the implications of the answer to this question without bringing the thesis of determinism into the picture at all.

Thus, the indeterminist point that scientific progress is not strong evidence for determinism is accepted. Scientific progress is, however, very often evidence for the truth of particular deterministic theories and these theories may involve factors we intuitively acknowledge as important.

[4] William Barrett, "Determinism and Novelty," *Determinism and Freedom in the Age of Modern Science,* ed. Sidney Hook (New York: Collier Books, 1961), p. 47.

In an earlier discussion, we described a hypothetical situation in which theoretical states are introduced into a theory, only to show that they are undetermined.[5] We pointed out that this possibility does not establish indeterminism because the introduction of theoretical terms must satisfy certain criteria. (A complete discussion of these criteria would constitute a treatise in itself.) We argued that, given the satisfaction of these criteria, a determinist might not have to be concerned if the undetermined state is not important, e.g., all observational states are determined. We see now, however, that the truth of determinism requires the existence of deterministic accounts for sentences about all theoretical states.

[5] See above, pp. 146-49.

XIII. PSYCHOLOGICAL
DETERMINISM

ARE DETERMINISTIC theories in psychology possible? If not, why not? If so, can we state the general form they will take? Or perhaps there can be deterministic accounts for some, but not all, psychological R-sentences?

Most arguments for the necessary falsity of determinism conclude that determinism must fail in psychology.[1] If these arguments fail, then the fact that the unrestricted character of determinism described in the preceding chapter implies its probable falsity is not that important. For if there can be deterministic theories for all "important" psychological R-sentences, the implications for human freedom must be dealt with.

Actions and decisions are alleged to be the aspects of human beings that do not admit of determination as defined here. The movements that may be involved in the performance of some action or decision may be determined; but the deterministic account of the movement (in perhaps neurophysiological terms) cannot be the deterministic account of the action or decision. Consider the following action descriptions:

1) Smith murdered Jones.
2) Smith discovered a cure for cancer.
3) Smith placed Jones in check.
4) Smith told Jones that he, Jones, was a liar.

[1] A preferable, but less dramatic, way of making this point is to say that certain psychological sentences cannot be R-sentences. If the claim is put this way, the possibility that determinism is true remains open.

298

5) Smith is trying to protect his roses.
6) Smith built a house.
7) Smith raised his arm.

In each case a deterministic account of the movement(s) involved in the action does not entail the sentence describing the action. Smith may have killed Jones; but (1) implies an evaluation of Smith's conduct. For that reason, though, (1) is not an *R*-sentence and the evaluative component in action-referring sentences may henceforth be ignored;[2] (2) may fail if a cure for cancer already exists; (3) implies the existence of another entity, Jones, and a rule-governed activity, chess, and that Smith's movement was performed in accordance with the rules of chess; (4) implies that Smith's utterance was intentional, e.g., he was not muttering in his sleep; (5) implies that Smith's movements are purposive; (6) implies that Smith's movements had as a consequence the creation of a house. Even (7) says more than "Smith's arm rose," although each type of additional component just enumerated may not be present. The action may not even have been intentional because it may have been done unthinkingly or out of habit. The additional component in (7) is not the truth of something like "Smith would have prevented his arm from rising if he had chosen to" for Smith may discover that his arm rises "of its own accord" every so often although a slight effort on his part can prevent this occurrence. In chapter IV we rejected the appeal to agent causality as an explication of the difference. Whatever this component might be, let us label it simply the "action component."

The question before us then is whether or not it is possible to supplement or replace the deterministic account of movement with state descriptions and laws that will entail sentences like (2) to (7). The discovery factor of (2) poses

[2] See above, pp. 137-39.

no problem because we may derive (2) from the deterministic account of "Smith arrived at a cure for cancer" plus the additional state description-sentence "Smith = the individual before whom no one had discovered a cure for cancer," an addition allowed by our rules. These rules also allow references to persons, conventions, institutions, and any other required contextual features, in the state description.[3] Since (6) might be construed as a partly causal sentence, we may have to be content with a deterministic account of Smith's actions and a deterministic account of the creation of the house in terms of Smith's actions.

We have reduced the number of potentially troublesome components to four: acting, acting intentionally, acting purposively, and following a rule. Consider purposive action: most philosophers who propose analyses of purposive concepts concede that there are at least two explicanda involved, the concept of a teleological or self-regulating mechanism, and the concept of a being who intentionally selects an action in order to achieve some goal. Since the first applies to machines, human purposiveness, if it is distinctive, requires a separate analysis.

But, as Scheffler points out, there may be several analyses, each of which captures the pre-analytic notion of self-regulation or directedness for *some* cases.[4] Our concern with each proposal is to see whether or not an explanation along its lines precludes a deterministic account, and we shall not, therefore, attempt a general critique.

Behavior controlled by negative feedback is teleological:[5] The typical example is a torpedo that adjusts its direction

[3] Although primary *R*-sentences are singular and not, therefore, existential, the logical consequence of an *R*-sentence is an *R*-sentence, too. Existential sentences like "The institution of matrimony exists at *t*" can, therefore, be *R*-sentences and may, then, appear in state descriptions.

[4] *The Anatomy of Inquiry*, pp. 110-23.

[5] See Arturo Rosenblueth, Norbert Wiener, and Julian Bigelow, "Behavior, Purpose and Teleology," *Philosophy of Science*, X (1943).

in the light of signals emitted by the potential goal. A detailed teleological account would not only be compatible with a deterministic account, it would actually provide the outlines of that deterministic account, for the movement at any time is determined by its antecedent movement, the structure of its target-seeking mechanism, and the signals it has received from the target.

Braithwaite claims that *the concept of plasticity captures the idea of goal-directed behavior*:[6] Roughly speaking, a system is plastic relative to a goal if the system can achieve the goal under several (more than one) sets of environmental circumstances. A prediction that the system will attain its goal on the basis of its plasticity may be made on the basis of past observations, in ignorance of the laws governing the system's behavior. But the existence of deterministic laws, Braithwaite makes clear, is not precluded.

Scheffler suggests that *some cases of non-purposive teleological behavior can be understood in terms of learning*:[7] In saying that an infant is crying for its mother, we are explaining the crying in terms of earlier sequences of crying followed by motherly solace. Hence, the original cause of crying, some internal condition, is inoperative in the present case.

Although the earlier sequences were causal (the mother was *responding* to the child's cries), we may and should refer in the explanation simply to the temporal relation between crying and motherly solace. If we insist that the explanation be given in terms of a causal relation, we are supposing, contrary to fact, that the infant would not now be crying for its mother if the earlier sequences had been accidental. If this supposition were not contrary to fact, the only explanation I can conceive is that the infant cries only if it *believes* on the basis of past experience that crying will produce its mother. Hence, if he believes that the earlier sequences were

[6] *Scientific Explanation*, pp. 329-36.
[7] Pp. 115-16, 121-22.

accidental, he will not bother to cry. But Scheffler does not want to bring in the infant's beliefs, if it has any, because he is offering an analysis of *non-purposive* teleological behavior, the sort that both machines and humans can exhibit.

Even if the infant's belief is relevant and, therefore, its behavior is fully purposive, no mention need be made of the earlier causal sequences in the explanation of the infant's crying. If we want to explain the infant's *belief,* we will have to refer to the sequences; and here again I would insist that the temporal relation (plus other facts perhaps) is sufficient. This point was made earlier when we ruled out causal sentences from the class of *R*-sentences and the class of state description-sentences.[8]

C. Taylor, on the other hand, requires a *teleological explanation of* e *to exehibit* e *as a function of the causal fact that* e *is required for some end:*[9] He makes the important point that the reduction of this type of account to an ordinary deterministic one, although possible, is not guaranteed *a priori*. That is, the question as to the existence of an intrinsic condition of the system that can replace the condition of *e*'s being required for some end is an empirical one. This conclusion does not disturb us because we view determinism as an empirical hypothesis.

Taylor also offers an analysis of purposive behavior, where the *behavior is a function not of its being required for some end, but of its being* seen *or* believed *to be required for that end:* Thus, a condition of the behavior is the man's purpose or intention. Behavior that satisfies this description is, by definition, action (in a strong sense). Purposive behavior or action, therefore, cannot be explained by a deterministic account that makes no reference to purpose or intention. For an account of this sort would imply the irrelevance of pur-

[8] See above, pp. 157-60.
[9] Charles Taylor, *The Explanation of Behavior* (London: Routledge & Kegan Paul, 1964), chap. I.

pose or intention, i.e., the behavior would ensue regardless of the man's intentions.

We must suppose, then, that a deterministic account of an action in terms of what Taylor calls a programming condition is also a deterministic account of the intention with which the action was performed. Since, however, a deterministic account of a behavior-explaining intention cannot be given according to Taylor, actions cannot be determined. We face the first *prima facie* conflict between determinism and purposiveness.

No deterministic account of a behavior-explaining intention (or desire) exists, because such an account would mistakenly render the relation between intention and behavior contingent. The relation between intention and behavior is not contingent, however, because "If I intend x I will do x, other things being equal" is analytic.

Since the relation between intention and behavior is non-contingent, the intention cannot be identified with the programming condition itself because the latter's relation to behavior is contingent. For the same reason, the intention cannot be identified with the mental state (thoughts and feelings) of the agent. The latter identification is independently unacceptable because it would render impossible self-deception with regard to intentions.

Even assuming that the relation between intention and behavior is non-contingent, the argument fails. Taylor does not show that the programming condition P does not determine action or purposive behavior. P determines neither intention nor behavior; it determines behavior that is intentional, i.e., action. In other words, the law is "$P \supset A$" where A is action or intentional behavior.

An analogy may help here: Suppose "If a man is intelligent, he will pass this I.Q. test, other things being equal" is analytic; but the test can be passed by an unintelligent man who is very lucky. If we call the first pass a "non-fortuitous pass," a deterministic account of it in terms of the causes of intelligence plus facts about the particular test might be provided. The account would not mention intelligence, just as the account of action would not mention intention. But, and this is crucial, the behavior would not have ensued had the intention been different, just as the man would have failed had he not been intelligent. So the defining characteristic of action is present because P determines *intentional* behavior.

"$P \supset A$" would not, as Taylor suggests, explain the connection between intention and behavior (no explanation is necessary because the connection is non-contingent); but it does not follow that "$P \supset A$" could not provide a deterministic account of A. It should be pointed out that this tack would allow for a nondeterministic conception of explanation (since the reference to intention in the account of the behavior is explanatory); but we have taken great pains to divorce the concepts of determinism and explanation.

Taylor does not rule out "$P \supset$ Behavior" laws *a priori;* but their discovery, he says, would necessitate changes in our action concepts. If P is the condition that explains behavior we still wish to view as action, we would always have to infer, from behavior and mental events, that we are acting, i.e., that P is present. Under our present conceptual schema, observing behavior and/or mental events is sometimes observing the intention itself and this fact is bound up with the non-contingent connection between intention and behavior on the present schema.

But "$P \supset A$" laws do not require this conceptual revision. Actions may sometimes be identified directly and there is, of course, the retention of the non-contingent link between intention and behavior.

The difficulty with "$P \supset A$" laws is that the ordinary explanations of behavior in terms of intention, desire, purpose, motive, and reason are entirely replaced by non-intentional

304

concepts like programming conditions. For the arguments that are advanced in defense of the non-contingent relation between intention and behavior can and are advanced in defense of a non-contingent relation between these other states and behavior. But I see no *a priori* reason to suppose that a gap of this sort between ordinary and scientific explanation will not arise.

On the other hand, it is certainly important to see if deterministic accounts that make use of intentional notions are genuinely impossible, since these accounts would be an extension of ordinary explanations of action. Although the literature on this subject is vast, much of it is comprised of weak arguments for the impossibility position that have been exposed.[10]

A number of arguments for the impossibility view assume the generality theory of causation in some form and then argue that explanations in terms of desire (the intentional concept usually chosen to make the point) are sometimes known directly or incorrigibly, in which case they cannot be causal. These arguments have already been dealt with.[11]

Other arguments for the view that the relation between desire and action cannot be causal are based, like Taylor's, on the premise that the relation is really non-contingent or logical. We, too, require logical and criterial independence between state description and sentence being accounted for.[12] But I think it can be shown that the relation between desire and action is such that reference to desires can appear in the state description of a deterministic account of an action.

[10] See, for example, William P. Alston, "Wants, Actions, and Causal Explanation," *Introductory Philosophy,* eds. Frank Tillman, Bernard Berofsky, and John O'Connor (New York: Harper & Row, 1967) pp. 197-209; Donald Davidson, "Actions, Reasons, and Causes," *The Journal of Philosophy, LX* (November 7, 1963), 685-700; and Bernard Berofsky, "Determinism and the Concept of a Person," *The Journal of Philosophy, LXI* (September 3, 1964), 461-75.
[11] See above, pp. 89-100.
[12] See above, p. 161.

First of all, a man may want something and fail to do anything about it, or a man may do something he does not want to do. So desires and actions are logically independent of one another in the ordinary sense. Of course, an action may be described in terms of the desire that explains it, e.g., "He is satisfying his sexual desire." But effects are often described in terms of their causes. For example, a skin opening may be called a cut once we know it was produced by a razor blade. There are descriptions, e.g., "movement of a razor blade across a face with pressure p" and "skin opening" that render cause and effect logically and criterially independent of each other; so we must see whether or not the same relation holds between desire and action.

As Alston points out, there is not even the hint of a conceptual connection between desire and action in the many cases in which action A is done out of a desire to do B, where A is thought to enable one or put one in a better position to do B, e.g., "He stretched his arm out in order to grab the ring."[13] (Alston can make a more general point because B need not be an action at all, e.g. "He ran very hard in order to receive a gold medal.") His comment is addressed to the claim that reference to a desire is really a further description of an action rather than a causal explanation. In these examples, the reference to the desire is obviously not a more detailed characterization of the action.

He also makes the point that wanting to do A can be causally related to doing B even where A and B are in a sense the same action ("I raised my arm in order to swat a fly"; "I am giving you this money in order to pay for the ice cream") because causal explanation is intensional.[14] That is, if "A" and "B" denote the same events, but are logically

---

[13] P. 202.

[14] David Pears, too, has argued along lines similar to Alston's. See "Are Reasons for Actions Causes?" *Epistemology: New Essays in the Theory of Knowledge,* ed. Avrum Stroll (New York: Harper & Row, 1967), pp. 204-28.

independent (e.g., "raising my arm" and "swatting a fly"), reference to A may appear in an explanation of B because an explanation of B is not an explanation of A. A physical law can explain "The object is falling"; but the explanation will not explain "Jones is attempting suicide" even if the two sentences refer to the same event.

Our conception of a deterministic account embodies this intensional feature. An R-sentence must follow logically from laws and the state description. Hence, the deterministic account of some R-sentence R_1 will not be the deterministic account of R_2 where, on some criterion of identity, R_1 refers to the same event as R_2, if R_1 does not entail R_2. There is it is true, a trivial way to convert a deterministic account of "The object o is falling at t_1" into a deterministic account of "Jones, who is attempting suicide by falling from the roof at t_1, is falling at t_1" by adding "The object o is identical with Jones, who is attempting suicide by falling from the roof at t_1" to the state description. But this is simply a way of embodying our knowledge of identity in the reference to the subject. The deterministic account is not yet an account of a suicide attempt. The predicate, not the subject, indicates the kind of fact being accounted for.

What disturbs advocates of the impossibility view is that desires are identified and distinguished in terms of their objects, and are then supposed to cause those objects as well. The term "object," however, is ambiguous. A man may desire an apple, in which case the object of his desire may be conceived to be any one of a number of objects, or he may desire a specific apple, in which case the object may be conceived to be that specific apple. But the man need not examine, identify, or even be sure of the existence of the object of his desire in this sense in order to identify and distinguish his desire. He can do the latter even if there is no object in this sense, e.g., "He wants the Holy Grail."

The other sense of "object of desire" is one that will pro-

307

vide an object for all desires, even the desire for the Holy Grail. A central problem of intentionality is the problem of defining this sense; no one, to the best of my knowledge, has formulated a fully adequate definition. This problem is one for *both* sides of the dispute we are here discussing. The only consideration relevant to that dispute is that the identification of the object of desire in this sense has nothing to do with the identification of any action that may be explained by this desire because, again, a man may know what he wants even if he performs no action explained by that want.

The identification of the object of desire in this second sense is independent not only of the identification of the object in the first sense or the action that may be explained by the desire (the action may be the object in the first sense or it may be the means to that object), but also of the identification of the desire as "the desire that explains (causes) the action." It is evident that a man knows what he wants to do independently of his knowledge that his action is caused by that desire. I may know that I want an apple that is in the refrigerator and also know that I opened the refrigerator in order to get some milk.

"But," replies the impossibility theorist, "there is a logical connection between the desire and the performance of the action under *normal* or at least under *some* specifiable conditions." Alston has shown, I think, that this claim is very difficult to justify. His argument is worth summarizing.[15]

The attempt to formulate a logical truth that will connect desire to action results in a very complex proposition: "Whenever A wants to do x, doesn't want to do anything incompatible with doing x more than he wants to do x, believes that doing y will put him in the best position for doing x, has both the capacity and opportunity for doing y, doesn't feel obliged to do anything incompatible with doing x or y, has no scruples against doing x or y, hasn't forgotten about

[15] Pp. 203-209.

308

doing x, is not too emotionally upset to do x, then he will do y"[16] (D).

It is still difficult to tell if D is a logical truth, if, that is, we have exhausted the required antecedents. Appeals to the "oddity" of a denial are not convincing, especially since the oddity may be due to facts other than D's presumed logical truth, e.g., its obviousness. If we have some doubt about the logical truth of D, we shall have the same doubt about the claim that D is analytic of the term "want," a claim whose truth would, of course, establish the logical truth of D. Other definitions of "A wants to do x," e.g., "If A believes that doing y will put him in position to do x, he will be more likely to do y than he would have been without this belief"[17] (B), although possibly acceptable, will plainly not suffice to ground the logical truth of D.

Finally, Alston finds the attempt to link desire analytically with action somewhat arbitrary because desires find expression in avowals, thoughts, and feelings as well as actions. Although behavior may be a superior or more reliable indicator of desire than these other indicators, the elevation of the relation of desire to behavior to analyticity, with other indicators having a mere synthetic connection to desire, is not justified as an account of the ordinary concept. I concur.

Perhaps advocates of the impossibility view wish only to advance a definition like B, where the analytical link is between desire and the probability of acting. A closely related point made by Melden is that the proposition that no one ever acts out of a desire is conceptually impossible.[18] Surely, they would add, ordinary causal relations are not as intimate as this.

Perhaps this minimal claim goes through. But the claim

[16] Ibid., p. 205.
[17] Ibid., p. 208.
[18] A. I. Melden, "Desires as Causes of Actions," *Current Philosophical Issues*, ed. Frederick C. Dommeyer (Springfield: Charles C. Thomas, 1966), p. 133.

has less to do with the intentionality of sentences about desires than with the entrenchment of explanations of action in terms of desire. Just as it is virtually a truism to point out that well-entrenched scientific generalizations sometimes become quasi-definitional, so ought it to be obvious that explanatory principles like "Some actions are explained by reference to desires" can become quasi-analytic, especially when we have no active scientific competitor *as yet*. Perhaps final purposes, spirits, and mechanical states are examples of concepts people have mistakenly believed to be analytically necessary for the explanation of certain classes of phenomena. Beliefs of this sort tend to infect the language in terms of which phenomena are purportedly pre-theoretically described, thereby creating the impression that scientific progress cannot overthrow certain cherished ways of looking at the world. Taylor, although he endorses a version of the impossibility position, recognizes that our conceptual structure makes certain presuppositions that are not immune to scientific revision.

Even if this minimal claim is acceptable, any actual deterministic account of an action in terms of a desire will have to include a great deal of *specific* information about the man's desires, beliefs, opportunity, capacity, etc., such that the account or the laws in the account will be far from conceptually necessary. Even the fact that the man did what he wanted is not empty since we allow other explanations of action, e.g., a sense of obligation. So even if the principle "Some actions are explained by desires" is necessary, any deterministic account of an action that includes reference to a desire will be contingent.

The fact that action-concepts appear in a description of the desire ("He desires to *do* that") should raise no problem—the concept of position appears both in the state description and the *R*-sentence being accounted for in the paradigm of a deterministic account, an account in terms of the laws of classical mechanics.

I conclude that intentional concepts may appear in a deterministic account, but do not conclude that science will necessarily choose intentional concepts to explain action. Three kinds of developments are possible. First, ordinary explanations in terms of desires, beliefs, etc., are supplemented, crystallized, and quantified. In addition, scientific explanations are sought for these states themselves. Second, if the identity theory (the view that psychological states and processes, e.g., sensations, desires, thoughts, feelings, are in fact identical with physiological, e.g., neurological, states and processes) turns out to be plausible, explanations in terms of desire and related concepts may be replaced by explanations in terms of physiological states. These explanations will have to be supplemented to deal with cases like "Smith placed Jones in check" since the truth of this sentence requires far more than whatever can be produced by a physiological state in Smith. But, of course, the same additions must be made to explanations in terms of desire. Third, scientific accounts turn out to conflict with ordinary explanations of behavior, because the distinctions made in the former do not coincide with the distinctions embodied in everyday explanations. The scientific categories may be physiological or theoretical psychological categories.

In any case, purposive behavior might be determined. No *a priori* arguments to the contrary are cogent.

Having an intention is different from wanting or feeling obliged to do something. The latter concepts explain why a man might do something, whereas the former is the report of a resolve or commitment or decision to do something. A man may have conflicting motives, but it sounds odd to say that a man has conflicting intentions because it sounds odd to say that a man has resolved to do inconsistent things.

311

Once a man has acted, it matters little whether we say "His intention in doing A is B" or "His reason for doing A is B" since B is the reason that triumphed over possibly competing desires, in which case the desire that explains the action and his intention have identical contents, and there may not have been any identifiable act or state antecedent to action that can be called "formulating an intention" or even "having an intention." A man may want something and proceed forthwith to procure it.

But if a man formulates or has an intention to act, we may wish to know whether or not a deterministic account of the formulation or the possession of the intention is possible. This problem is evidently no different from the problem of whether or not there are deterministic accounts of decisions and choices.

Since explanations of intentions and decisions refer to the same kinds of factors that are referred to by explanations of intentional behavior or purposive action, e.g., desires and beliefs, no barrier to deterministic accounts, as far as I can see, exists. Also, just as an account of an action in terms of a desire may be supplemented by reference to events that "activate" the desire, e.g., the appearance of a juicy apple, and thoughts, e.g., "How nice it would be to eat!," so an account of a decision in terms of a desire may be supplemented by similar references, e.g., to what goes on in the deliberative process.

A man may have an intention without having formulated one. If this is a certain kind of dispositional state, it need only be pointed out that dispositions generally can be determined.

With respect to intentional behavior, a man may logically do something intentionally without having had an antecedent intention, e.g., I may simply raise my arm intentionally (A). Now since deterministic accounts of action in terms of desire are conceptually possible, there may be a deterministic account of *A* in terms of some desire. With regard to the intentionality of *A,* there are three possibilities: Either the content of the desire is identical with the content of the intention with which *A* was done; or the content of the desire is identical with the purpose that explains why *A* was done with a certain intention: "Because he wanted to get to the airport quickly, he (intentionally) asked the driver to hurry"; or, finally, the desire causes him to do *A* where *A* is unintentional: "The desire to poison his uncle caused him to unintentionally poison Mr. Jones, whom he wrongly took to be his uncle." To sort this matter out and see where there might be problems for a determinist, we must examine more closely the notions of intention and purpose.

Although the typical explanation of the act of doing *A* in order that *x* refers to a desire or reason (the second possibility above), I do not believe that the analysis of "*P* does *A* in order that (for the purpose of, with the intention that) *x*" entails reference to a desire or reason of *P*. There is no logical absurdity in supposing that a man does something in order for some end to come about without having *any reason.*

Some act descriptions, of course, logically imply the existence and explanatory efficacy of a reason, e.g., "He is satisfying his sexual desire." But even if we suppose that this act cannot be redescribed without any implications regarding its explanation, as some theorists believe, I am simply saying that *some* purposive actions require no reason.

What I think has happened is this: When a man does something for some purpose, the explanation we seek is in terms of that man's desires or reasons. And we suppose that if we dig deeply enough, some reason will appear. Now this suspicion may be correct. But we ought to distinguish the *nature* of purposive action from the normal *explanation* of purposive action. I shall, therefore, drop the concept of desire from my version. Let me present an analysis that has some initial plausibility even if it turns out to be ultimately unsuccessful, and then explain some key terms in it:

$$P \text{ does } A \text{ at } t \left\{ \begin{array}{l} \text{in order that} \\ \text{for purpose} \\ \text{with the intention that} \end{array} \right\} x$$

$$\underset{\text{Df}}{=} \left\{ \begin{array}{l} (1) \ \ P \text{ does } A \text{ at } t. \\ (2) \ \ P \text{ believes at } t \text{ that } A \text{ has} \\ \quad \quad \text{some chance of bringing } x \\ \quad \quad \text{about.} \\ (3) \ \ (2) \text{ is a necessary condi-} \\ \quad \quad \text{tion } in \ esse \text{ of } (1). \end{array} \right.$$

"Bring about" (2) can mean "lead to" or "satisfy." In other words, the definition is supposed to cover cases in which a man does something so that it will lead in the future to some consequence, e.g., I invest in the stock market to get rich, and cases in which the purpose is the act itself under a different description, e.g., I give you this money in order to pay back a debt.

(2) is often expressed more strongly, e.g., P believes that A will probably bring about x. But it is clear that a man might act purposively where he has only a slim chance of success. A man might undergo an operation to save his life even if he has, say, a five percent chance of success if his chances of survival are zero without the operation.

C is a necessary condition *in esse* of e if and only if c is a necessary condition of e and c exists at every moment e exists. Thus, at any moment during e's existence, e would cease if c were to cease. Being born is a necessary condition of a person's being five years old, but not *in esse*. Oxygen is a necessary condition *in esse* of fire because fire would cease whenever oxygen was removed. Oxygen, in other words, sustains fire, while being born does not sustain being five years old.

C is a necessary condition of e in a situation S if and only if S is an instance of a general (non-logical) law that entails the occurrence of c given e and a set of conditions f in S. Since action-types can be performed for an indefinitely large number of purposes, the belief-*token* described *in* (2) is necessary to the action-*token* described in (1). Hence, the applicable general law takes the form "(1) and *f* imply (2)" (where "f" is instantiated in the situation) rather than "(1) implies (2)."

We may also stipulate that where the analysis fails for some belief b_1, but succeeds for a disjunction of beliefs of the form of (2) that includes b_1 (where each belief in the disjunction is non-vacuous in the sense that its omission from the disjunction makes the disjunction fail the analysis), then the action is multipurposed. Thus, if I invite friends to dinner in order to satisfy an obligation and in order to have a pleasant evening, it may be that neither purpose is necessary to the act of inviting them in that situation, but the disjunction of purposes is.

If this analysis succeeds, a statement reporting the purpose with which an action is done is a rudimentary deterministic account: it mentions a condition of the action. It is important to notice, however, that the statement is compatible with the action's not being determined, since no sufficient condition may exist.

The reason why the belief is a condition *in esse* will become clear during an examination we shall now undertake of two objections to the extensional adequacy of the analysis.[19]

R. Taylor[20]*:* A man in an audience wants to attract the speaker. This state makes him fidgety and he thereby attracts the speaker. But he did not fidget *in order* to attract the speaker. Moreover, he may believe (correctly) that his fidgeting would attract the speaker.

---

[19] For a detailed examination of many other objections to the analysis, and a defense of the analysis against these objections, see the author's "Purposive Action," *American Philosophical Quarterly,* vii (October, 1970).

[20] *Action and Purpose* (Englewood Cliffs, N.J.: Prentice-Hall, 1966), p. 249.

My analysis deals successfully with this case. It is true that the man did not fidget in order to attract the speaker because, although he believed that fidgeting would attract the speaker, this belief was not a condition of the fidgeting. If his desire to attract the speaker made him fidgety, the belief that he would attract the speaker was irrelevant and, if anything, might have inhibited the behavior. But if it is true that he would have ceased fidgeting upon coming to believe that the speaker is not being attracted by it, then he really is fidgeting in order to attract the speaker.

But, it may be objected, there are cases in which a man who wants very much not to attract the attention of the speaker fidgets ("involuntarily") *because* he believes that fidgeting would attract the attention of the speaker. The belief, in other words, makes him nervous and causes the fidgeting; but he is surely not fidgeting in order to attract the speaker.

It seems clear that this man did not fidget in order to attract the speaker because he did not fidget intentionally. A similar case would be that of a pianist who believes that he will play badly if he looks at the music and looks at the music (unintentionally) just because he has this belief.[21] Since a man does not do A in order that x unless he does A intentionally, we ought to modify (1) in the analysis to read "P does A intentionally at t."

We now face the dual task of analyzing the appropriate sense of intentionality and replying to the following charge of circularity.[22] Even if an analysis like ours, viz., a causal analysis, is extensionally adequate, it will not succeed in reducing purposiveness to a causal relation between states and behavior because the states, viz., beliefs or beliefs and desires, must be construed as causes of actions, and the concept of action here is intrinsically purposive or intentional.

---

[21] I am grateful to R. Shope for this example.

[22] The charge was made by A. Collins in conversation.

There are, it seems to me, at least two concepts of action, one purposive, the other non-purposive. I may wish to distinguish the fact that I raised my arm, where this act may have been performed unintentionally, unthinkingly, out of force of habit, etc., from the fact that my arm simply rose. That is, we may wish to distinguish doing from undergoing in a sense whose elucidation requires no appeal to the concept of purpose. We may call this sense of action which just involves the action component "action₁." Since it involves no covert reference to purpose, its use in this context is not circular.

We may now use the causal analysis to define the purposive sense of action. "I raise my arm intentionally (on purpose)" means "I raise my arm (action₁ sense) and this action has as a necessary condition *in esse* the belief that I raise my arm." In other words, to do P intentionally is, roughly, to do P "because" you believe you are doing P.

But there is a difference between doing P intentionally and having P as one's intention. It is not my intention to wear down the carpet when I walk to the other side of the room to get a book. But I know that I am wearing down the carpet and I could have walked around it. I can be held responsible by a neurotically fussy housekeeper. Hence, there is a sense in which I wore the carpet down intentionally, although wearing the carpet down was not my intention. Since I would have worn the carpet down even if I had come to believe that I was not wearing it down (I am misinformed about the carpet's properties), this case fails my analysis. Hence my analysis analyzes the stronger claim that such-and-such is the man's intention. In other words, "Jones raises his arm and this action has as a necessary condition *in esse* Jones's belief that he raises his arm" analyzes "In raising his arm, it is Jones's intention to raise his arm."

That is all well and good because the stronger claim is the one implicit in purposive action. If my belief that I was

317

wearing down the carpet was causally irrelevant to the act, I could not have been wearing down the carpet in order, say, to anger the housekeeper.[23] Hence, the concept of action implicit in purposive contexts can be analyzed in terms of a causal relation between two beliefs, a belief about what one is doing and a belief about the outcome of what one is doing, and the action itself, the latter being understood in a non-purposive sense.

The weak sense of intention whereby I wore the carpet down intentionally may be understood simply in terms of the presence of the belief (knowledge) that I was wearing down the carpet plus, perhaps, the fact that I could have acted otherwise. It is well known that the expression "could have done otherwise" requires clarification; but we may need it here if doing something intentionally (even in the weak sense) implies responsibility.

This analysis of intentionality enables us to say that the man who fidgeted involuntarily did not act intentionally, because the belief that he was fidgeting was not a condition of the fidgeting. But it is not clear that all such cases are so easily handled. May it not be the case that the pianist would not look at the music he is playing unless he believed he was looking at the music he is playing? Or can a neurotic husband claim that he does not intentionally insult his wife although he would not do it unless he took himself to be insulting his wife?

These two cases differ in important respects. The neurotic husband's claim is plausible because, as we suggested earlier, intentionality suggests the power to act otherwise, and the neurotic husband presumably lacks that power. Even so, he may be insulting his wife in order to rile her, and we said earlier that a man does not do A in order that x unless he does A intentionally, in which case it follows that the hus-

---

[23] If the modification that will be mentioned under Chisholm's objection is adopted, this statement will have to be amended accordingly.

band's insults are intentional. This result would not really be counterintuitive were it not for the suggestion of the freedom to act otherwise. (A psychoanalyst would certainly say, and the husband might come to agree, that his insulting is intentional.) Since purposiveness is our primary concern, and since his behavior is clearly purposive, we shall say that his insults are intentional (for this result is not, as we have seen, fundamentally counterintuitive).

The other case includes an interesting feature that seems to account for our regarding the act of looking at the music as non-intentional. The act takes place only because the person wants it not to (although he is not acting out of a general resolution to do what he does not desire to do). Although I have argued that a man may do A intentionally even though he does not want to do A, he does not do A intentionally if he does A out of the very fear of doing A—unless another condition of A is his general resolve to do what he fears (or the specific resolve to do what he fears in this case).

Thus, there are connections of a sort between desire and intentionality—I only object to the claim that intentionality or purpose implies desire.

R. Chisholm[24]: A young man wants the money he is to inherit when his uncle dies and believes he would get the money sooner if he were to kill his uncle. This desire and belief agitate him so severely that he gets into his car, drives recklessly, and accidentally kills a man he later learns is his uncle. So the desire for money plus the belief that killing his uncle would satisfy the desire causes the young man to kill his uncle. But obviously he did not kill his uncle *in order to* get the money. This interesting case causes us no difficulty because the man did not kill his uncle intentionally. Moreover, the second condition above (see p. 314) requires that there be some belief *at the time the act is performed* of the

---

[24] *Freedom and Determinism*, pp. 29-30.

form "this act has some chance of getting me my uncle's money." If the act is described as "running over a man," the nephew does not believe that this act will make him rich because he does not know that the man is his uncle. If the act is described as "running over his uncle," then at the time of the action, the man does not believe that the act of running over his uncle will make him rich because he does not know that he is running over his uncle. He has the general belief that if he ever kills his uncle he will be rich. But my analysis requires that he have a specific belief about the act he is performing, and a man cannot believe that his specific action A will lead to B if he does not believe he is doing A.

I am not maintaining the patently false position that a man who is doing A must believe he is doing A. I may sit down on a wet seat without realizing it is wet. But I cannot sit down on a wet seat in order to have a good excuse for changing my slacks if I do not believe I am sitting down on a wet seat.

But what about a man who turns on his radio in order to hear music, oblivious of the fact that the radio contains tubes that must warm up if the radio is to work? We may say that he is heating up tubes without realizing it when he turns on the radio. May we also say that he is heating up tubes in order to hear music? If so, a man may do A in order that x without believing he is doing A.

If we accept this counterexample, we can revise the analysis by converting the second condition (p. 314) into a disjunction of itself and: There is an A' such that P does A', A' is causally relevant (necessary or sufficient) to A or in fact identical with A, and P believes at the time he does A' that A' has some chance of bringing x about. We shall then have to revise the third condition (p. 314) by adding the disjunct: P's belief at the time he does A' that A' has some chance of bringing x about is a necessary condition *in esse* of (1).

This revision allows us to say that a man heats up tubes in order to hear music, but does not require us to say that the nephew killed his uncle in order to inherit the money. If A is "running over a man," the nephew neither believes that running over a man has some chance of getting him his uncle's money nor does he believe at the time that he is doing something (although he is, in fact) related in the specified way to A that may result in the desired consequence. If A is "running over his uncle," since he does not believe he is doing this, he does not believe that running over his uncle has some chance of getting him the money. Nor is there an appropriately related act that he believes will have this result (although there is).

Shall we accept this revision? Since I am really concerned with the possibility of deterministic accounts of purposive and intentional actions, this question does not interest me. The revision would, if adopted, neither preclude a deterministic account of some purposive action nor require us to suppose that the nature of the determination is special. There may be analogous occasions where *prima facie* counterexamples to my definition of purposive action can be "emasculated" by showing that they do not upset determinism in these ways.

(If we accept this revision, we shall have to allow that a man can do A in order to x where he does not do A intentionally, although there always will be an action A' related in the specified way to A that he does intentionally.)

Even if we waive the above considerations and allow that some appropriate belief was a condition of the man's act, the case fails the third condition because the man's belief that killing his uncle would make him rich was not a condition *in esse*. Beliefs and desires do not only initiate action; they sustain action, and it is in their sustaining role that they are purposive. If I have a sudden urge to do something and do it an hour later I will not be doing it in order to satisfy the urge if I no longer have the desire at the time the action takes place. I have tried to incorporate this sustaining role of beliefs in the analysis by requiring that the belief be necessary at the time of the act, i.e., the act would cease whenever the belief ceases.

Thus, I see no insuperable problems for a determinist in the sphere of intentional and purposive actions. Since beliefs are so crucial to my analysis, we shall turn now to the determination of beliefs.

Beliefs are usually, or must of necessity, be held by language users. A determinist is committed to the view that the acquisition of a language is determined by innate mechanisms plus environmental learning. The details are extraordinarily complicated and, for the most part, unknown.

Deterministic accounts of perceptual beliefs in terms of sense data might be attempted; but if people can have beliefs about the sense data, these beliefs will have to be determined by patterns of stimulation on sense organs plus, perhaps, states of the central nervous system and, perhaps, past learning situations (or the brain traces left by those situations). I thus disagree with Hamlyn who argues that laws of normal perception are not possible.[25]

Hamlyn makes the point that explanation is sought for deviations from normality or the expected, i.e., perceptual illusions. This is obviously wrong; we have laws which explain how an automobile engine works as well as laws which explain its breakdowns.

Another of his arguments cuts more deeply because it suggests not only that there are no laws of normal perception, but also that there is something unusual even about the laws of illusions. Hamlyn points out that terms like "normal" and "illusory" and terms like "naïve" and "sophisticated," the latter pair being required in the explana-

[25] D. W. Hamlyn, *The Psychology of Perception* (London: Routledge & Kegan Paul, 1957), chap II.

tion of perceptual phenomena, are not purely descriptive: they involve the application of standards. Hamlyn fails to see that every science has this problem. I may seek to learn the laws governing automobile engines in order to learn why mine is a "lemon"; but these laws do not contain the term "lemon." I may ask a psychologist why Jones is a louse; but no psychological law contains the term "louse." Scientific theories can help us even if they don't mirror our evaluative categories. A term like "sophisticated," therefore, might be replaced by a set of terms each of which refers to learning experiences or resultant brain states.

Finally, Hamlyn argues that the laws of normal perception will not look like "Red objects look red under normal conditions" because, as he says, this sentence is a logical truth. Either "normal conditions" are spelled out to give the sentence content or, as we suggested earlier, "red object" is replaced by terms denoting a distinctive pattern of stimulation on the retina. Hamlyn is right in pointing out that this pattern is not a sufficient condition of a perception; but it may be part of a sufficient condition.

Non-perceptual beliefs have many possible conditions: language, perceptual beliefs, desires, emotional states, intelligence, training, character traits, physiological states, actions. Many of these factors might enter into the deterministic account of a belief that one is doing A.

Since a man can act unintentionally, a deterministic account that contains no reference to beliefs may be an account of an action or simply an account of a bodily movement. Since there is a clear difference between "I raise my arm" and "My arm rises," must a determinist suppose that all action is intentional, in which case the distinguishing feature of deterministic accounts of action is the reference to beliefs?

Since many unintentional actions are performed because they are parts of or identical with actions done intentionally, e.g., the act of wearing out the carpet, deterministic accounts of intentional actions can be supplemented in order to create deterministic accounts of these unintentional actions. For the others, e.g., habitual and unthinking behavior, we do suppose that deterministic accounts of the movements involved have to be supplemented. For example, "Jones puts on his right shoe first this morning" is logically independent of any sentence that describes his movements only. He may habitually put on his right shoe first every morning and yet make slightly different movements each morning. He is habituated not to make certain movements, but to perform this act. Hence, the deterministic account of the *act* will refer to the original learning situations (or again the present brain traces), while the account of the movement *per se* will not.

Finally, if I unthinkingly, unintentionally, but not habitually, raise my arm, the only conceivable deterministic account is one that refers to aspects of the central nervous system that are not required for the movement *per se*. In this way, these minimal actions will have a kinship with more sophisticated actions. If these accounts do not exist, determinism is false.

"Following a rule" can be explicated in terms of the action's having as a condition the belief that it is in accordance with some rule.

I conclude that determinism in psychology is not conceptually impossible.

INDEX

325